Prison Epistles: Colossians, Philemon, Ephesians, and Philippians

by LeRoy Bartel

An Independent-Study Textbook

Third Edition

**Berean School of the Bible,
a Global University School**

1211 South Glenstone Avenue
Springfield, MO 65804 USA

1-800-443-1083
Fax: (417) 862-0863
E-mail: berean@globaluniversity.edu
Web: www.globaluniversity.edu

LeRoy Bartel received his bachelor's degree from Trinity Bible College, Ellendale, North Dakota, and a master of divinity degree and doctorate from the Assemblies of God Theological Seminary, Springfield, Missouri. Dr. Bartel pastored various churches for over twenty years in North Dakota, South Dakota, Minnesota, and Washington. He also served the Assemblies of God as a denominational officer for five years as national director for the Division of Christian Education and Commissioner on Discipleship. Dr. Bartel currently serves Southwestern Assemblies of God University, Waxahachie, Texas, as dean of the College of Bible and Church Ministries. In the past, he served for over twelve years at the University in a variety of roles, including professor, vice president for Student Life, and chairperson for the Division of Bible, Theology, and Church Ministries Department.

Global University
Springfield, Missouri, USA

PN 03.15.02

ISBN 978-0-7617-1457-6

Printed in the United States of America

Table of Contents

Digital Course Options

This printed independent-study textbook (IST) represents only one of the ways you can study through Global University's Berean School of the Bible (BSB). Global University offers electronic delivery formats that allow you to complete courses without using printed material.

You may choose one or more of these course delivery options with or without the printed IST.

Digital Courses

- <u>Online Courses</u>. Complete your entire ministry training program online with fully interactive learning options.

  You can complete your chapter reviews, unit progress evaluations, and final exam online and receive instant results, even if you use print or other digital study versions.

- <u>Logos Bible Software</u>. Purchase an entire digital library of Bibles and Bible reference titles and the Berean courses specifically created to function inside these digital library environments.

- <u>Electronic courses</u>. Check Global University's website for additional electronic course versions (for e-readers and other devices) and their availability.

Enrollment Policies and Procedures

Enrollment policies and procedures are provided in the most current Berean School of the Bible Academic Catalog. An electronic version of the catalog is available at the Global University website.

Contact Global University for Enrollment Information

Phone: 1-800-443-1083 (9 a.m. to 6 p.m., CST, Monday–Friday)

    Spanish language representatives are available to discuss enrollment in Spanish courses.

E-mail: berean@globaluniversity.edu

Web: www.globaluniversity.edu

Fax: 417-862-0863

Mail: 1211 S. Glenstone Ave., Springfield, MO 65804

How to Use Berean Courses

Independent study is one of the most dynamic and rapidly growing educational methods. Although different from traditional classroom study, the goal is the same—to guide you, the student, through a systematic program of study and help you gain new knowledge and skills. Berean courses are independent-study courses. Some students may participate in a Berean study group, where a facilitator enhances the learning experience for a group of Berean students. Other options include studying the courses online and/or purchasing digital study tools made possible through Berean's partnership with Logos Bible Software.

All Berean courses are printed in a comprehensive independent-study textbook (IST). The IST is your teacher, textbook, and study guide in one package. Once you have familiarized yourself with the course components, explained below, you are ready to begin studying. Whether you are studying for personal growth or working toward a diploma, the Berean faculty, advisers, and student service representatives are available to help you get the most out of your Berean program.

General Course Design

- Each course is based on course objectives.
- Each course is composed of several units.
- Each unit is composed of several chapters.
- Each chapter is composed of two or more lessons.
- Each lesson contains one or more lesson objectives.
- Each lesson objective corresponds to specific lesson content.

Course Objectives

Course objectives represent the concepts—or knowledge areas—and perspectives the course will teach you. Review these objectives before you begin studying to have an idea of what to focus on as you study. The course objectives are listed on the course introduction page.

Unit Overview

A unit overview previews each unit's content and outlines the unit development.

Chapter, Lesson Content, Lesson Objectives, and Numbering System

Each *chapter* begins with an introduction and outline. The outline presents the chapter's lesson titles and objectives. Chapters consist of short lessons to allow you to complete one lesson at a time (at one sitting), instead of the entire chapter at one time.

The *lesson content* is based on lesson objectives.

Lesson objectives present the important concepts and perspectives to be studied in the course.

Each chapter, lesson, and objective is uniquely numbered. This numbering system is designed to help you relate the lesson objective to its corresponding lesson content. Chapters are numbered consecutively throughout the course. Lessons are numbered within each chapter with a two-digit decimal number. For example, Lesson 2 in Chapter 3 is numbered 3.2. The first number is the chapter (3), the second number is the lesson (2) within the chapter.

Lesson objectives are tagged with a three-digit decimal number. For example, Chapter 1, Lesson 1, Objective 1 is identified as Objective 1.1.1. Chapter 1, Lesson 2, Objective 3 is Objective 1.2.3. The first number is the chapter, the second is the lesson, and the third is the objective. The numbering system is to assist you in identifying, locating, and organizing each chapter, lesson, and objective.

took the place of Hebrew as the langu
Pharisees, Sadducees, and **Scribes**—
(small places of worship, study, and so
Jews were ruled by the powerful and h
years under the cultural influence of th
completely (Scroggins 2003, 328).

The Greek Period

The Persian Empire was in power a
and Nehemiah rebuilt Jerusalem's wal

 Test Yourself

Circle the letter of the ***best*** answer.

1. Why are only two chapters of the entire Bibl
devoted to the never-ending eternity?
a) Eternity will be a constant repeat of regular
activity, so no more space is needed.
b) The eternal fate of the wicked should not be
given any more attention
c) Greater details of New Jerusalem would be
meaningless.
d) The purpose of Scripture is to encourage ho
living now

2. What happens to the present heaven and eart
make way for new heaven and earth?
a) They are gradually cleansed and changed in

What to Look for in the Margins

Left margins contain numbers for units, chapters, and lessons. In addition, margins contain two learning tools—*lesson objectives with their respective numbers* and *interactive questions* that focus on key principles. Read, understand, and use these two learning tools to study the lesson text.

Interactive questions relate to specific lesson content and specific lesson objectives. Interactive questions, along with lesson objectives, will help you learn the concepts and perspectives that are tested in exam questions. Interactive questions are numbered consecutively within each chapter. Once you understand what the interactive question is asking, search for the answer as you study the lesson's related content section. You can compare your responses to our suggested ones at the back of each chapter.

Lesson objectives present the key concepts. These tips on using lesson objectives will help you master the course content and be prepared for exams:

- Identify the key concept(s) and concept perspectives in the objective.
- Identify and understand what the objective is asking you to do with the key concept(s).
- Think of the objective as an essay test question.
- Read and study the lesson content related to the objective and search for the answer to the "essay test question"—the objective.

Lesson Titles and Subheads

Lesson titles and subheads identify and organize specific lesson content.

Key Words

Key words are presented in **boldface** print and defined in the glossary of this IST; they are words that are used with a specific meaning in the lesson.

Reference Citations

Outside sources are documented using in-text citations in parentheses. These sources are compiled in more detail in the Reference List at the end of the IST.

Test Yourself

The Test Yourself section concludes the chapter with multiple-choice questions based on the lesson objectives, interactive questions, and their supporting lesson content. Test Yourself answer keys are in the Essential Course Materials at the back of this IST.

Glossary and Reference List

A *glossary* (which defines key words) and *reference list* (works cited in each chapter) follow the last chapter of the IST.

Recommended Reading Textbook

An optional textbook is recommended for use with each course. The textbook recommended to accompany this course is listed on the course introduction page. Some courses may provide additional suggested reading lists following the *reference list*.

Essential Course Materials in the back of this IST contain the following:

- Service Learning Requirement (SLR) Assignment and SLR Report Form
- Unit Progress Evaluation (UPE) Instructions and UPEs
- Answer Keys for Test Yourself quizzes and UPEs
- Forms: Round-Tripper (as needed) and Request for a Printed Final Examination (if needed)

Two Requirements to Receive a Course Grade:
To receive a grade for this course, you must:

1. Submit your SLR Report Form. The instructions for the SLR assignment are in the Essential Course Materials at the back of this IST. The report is required, but not graded.

2. You must also take a closed-book final examination. Your course grade is based on the final exam. The Berean School of the Bible grading scale is 90–100 percent, A; 80–89 percent, B; 70–79 percent, C; and 0–69 percent, F.

Checklist of Study Methods

STUDY METHODS	√	If you carefully follow the study methods listed below, you should be able to complete this course successfully. As you complete each chapter, mark a √ in the column for that chapter beside each instruction you followed. Then continue to study the remaining chapters in the same way.																
1. Read the introduction in the Independent-Study Textbook (IST) to learn how to use the IST.																			
2. Study the Table of Contents to familiarize yourself with the course structure and content.																			
CHAPTERS	1	2	3	4	5	6	7	8	9	10	11	12	13	14	15	16	17	18
3. Pace yourself so you will study at least two or three times each week. Plan carefully so you can complete the course within the allowed enrollment period. Complete at least one lesson each study session.																			
4. Read Scripture references in more than one translation of the Bible for better understanding.																			
5. Underline, mark, and write notes in your IST.																			
6. Use a notebook to write additional notes and comments.																			
7. As you work through each chapter, make good use of reference tools, such as a study Bible, a comprehensive concordance, a Bible dictionary, and an English dictionary.																			
8. Complete all interactive questions and learning activities as you go.																			
9. In preparation for the Test Yourself, review the objectives for each lesson in the chapter and your notes and highlights to reinforce the key principles learned in the chapter.																			
10. Discuss with others what you are learning.																			
11. Apply what you have learned in your spiritual life and ministry.																			
UNIT EVALUATIONS																			
Review for each Unit Progress Evaluation by rereading the																			
a. lesson objectives to be sure you can achieve what they state.																			
b. questions you answered incorrectly in Test Yourself.																			
c. lesson material for topics you need to review.																			

Student Planner and Record

*This chart is for you to record your personal progress in this course. Be sure to keep it **up to date** for quick reference.*

In the boxes below, record the unit number, the date you expect to complete each chapter, the date you *do* complete the chapter, and the date of review.

Unit Number	Chapter Number	Expected Completion Date	Actual Completion Date	Date Reviewed
	1			
	2			
	3			
	4			
	5			
	6			
	7			
	8			
	9			
	10			
	11			
	12			
	13			
	14			
	15			
	16			
	17			
	18			

UNIT EVALUATIONS	Date Completed
Unit Evaluation 1	
Unit Evaluation 2	
Unit Evaluation 3	
Unit Evaluation 4	
Unit Evaluation 5	
Unit Evaluation 6	

WRITTEN ASSIGNMENTS & FINAL EXAM	Date Completed
Service Learning Requirement (SLR) Report	
Final Examination	
SLR report & closed-book final exam materials submitted (The SLR report does not apply to the internship courses.)	

Sincerely, Apostle Paul

The Prison Epistles are the correspondence of Paul, the consummate apostle, traditionally assigned to his period of house arrest in Rome about AD 60–61. Unable to visit the churches personally, Paul wrote these apostolic letters: Colossians, Philemon, Ephesians, and Philippians. They reflect and express his personal friendship, apostolic passion, and pastoral concern. In these letters Paul articulates his apostolic message, his theological reflection, and his characteristic emphasis upon practical Christian living. Three of these characteristics deserve special attention.

Apostolic passion. Paul in these letters speaks with apostolic authority. Whether writing to a church he had not directly founded or visited (Colossians) or writing to a congregation he had intimate relationship with (Philippians), or a group of congregations (Ephesians), his apostolic passion shines through. His concern for the truth of the gospel, its progress and extension, and the cause of Christ are hallmarks of these epistles.

Pastoral concern. The spiritual health and welfare of congregations was clearly the driving force behind these letters. Paul's pastoral concern, however, extends beyond congregations to individuals. His letter to Philemon on behalf of Onesimus is a primary example. Paul's heart throbs for the welfare of each church and its individual members.

Practical emphasis. Paul insists that Christians must live out what it means to be "in Christ." His message is "Be what you are!" His instruction encompasses life within the community of faith, relationships within marriage and family, and behavior out in the marketplace life. The ultimate example for the daily lifestyle of Christians is the servant leadership of Christ. The Prison Epistles are not the ethereal musings of an out-of-touch-with-life theologian but the practical instruction of one who lived out his Christianity while "in chains for Christ" (Philippians 1:13).

This text is designed as a *preacher-friendly* commentary. In each lesson a transcultural truth, transcending time, ethnicity, and social background, is identified. Sermonic points are then stated as principles. Within each point the following expository preaching pattern is presented:

Exposition—explanation of the biblical text in terms of the original situation and audience

Application—consideration of the principle in the biblical text in terms of contemporary situation analogous to the one in the biblical text

Illustration—the attempt to identify an apt illustration that elucidates the point within the text

It is my prayer that my imperfect, but sincere effort of love will provoke much good preaching and teaching within the local church. Even more important however, is the goal Paul expressed in Philippians: "I want to know Christ and the power of His resurrection and the fellowship of sharing in his sufferings . . ." (3:10).

Course Description   BIB117 Prison Epistles: Colossians, Philemon, Ephesians, and Philippians (5 CEUs)

A practical study of the principles Paul wrote to the churches during his imprisonment. The concepts are presented in language that is easy to understand with explanations, illustrations, and applications that make the concepts helpful to students in both their personal lives and ministries.

In addition to using your Bible, we also recommend that you use *The Letter of Paul to the Ephesians* by Francis Foulkes to enhance your learning experience.

Course Objectives

Upon completion of this course, you should be able to

1. Summarize background information related to the Prison Epistles.
2. Identify key facts related to authorship, dating, and the recipients of these letters.
3. Identify the major themes of each letter, and explain how these themes can apply to modern believers.
4. Describe the organizational structure of each epistle, identifying major divisions.
5. Recount key issues addressed in the Prison Epistles, such as conflicts, false teaching, and church successes.
6. Identify key Christian doctrines addressed by Paul, and describe how Paul develops these teachings.

BEFORE YOU BEGIN

Successfully completing this course requires that you apply content you study in a ministry activity. The instructions for this Service Learning Requirement (SLR) are found in the Essential Course Materials in the back of this IST. Please take time now to become familiar with these instructions so that you can be planning your SLR activity throughout your study of this course.

Colossians and Philemon

Have you ever experienced the frustration of having to deal with problems and situations long distance? Can you imagine how complicated things would be if you could not use your cell phone or e-mail? What if the only way to travel to deal with a situation was walking or, at best, on horseback or a long trip on a slow ship? What if you had to cope with the added difficulties brought about by imprisonment, which would mean there would be no traveling to anywhere at all? The only recourse left to you would be snail-mail, better known as a personal letter, but it would be one of such a sensitive nature it would have to be hand-delivered by a trusted friend.

That was precisely the challenge the great apostle Paul faced as he wrote the epistles or letters to the Colossians and to Philemon. Paul was in prison in Rome for the sake of the gospel. His apostolic letter to the Colossians was written to an individual congregation located in a small city in ancient Asia, about one hundred miles east of Ephesus. The letter to Philemon, on the other hand, was a very personal letter written to a wealthy church leader by the name of Philemon, on behalf of a slave, Onesimus, who had run away. The blessing was that Onesimus had been converted through Paul's ministry.

Colossians was written to deal with the problems Paul had heard the church in Colosse was facing. The letter begins with a customary greeting, a prayer of thanksgiving for their Christian character and vitality, and an apostolic prayer. Paul was deeply concerned about an unhealthy emphasis and false teaching that had found a footing in the congregation at Colosse. The dangerous doctrines that had infiltrated the church played to human pride, emphasized esoteric ideas and unusual experiences, and de-emphasized the sufficiency of Christ. Therefore, Paul extolled the supremacy, centrality, and sufficiency of Christ. In order to avoid the esoteric emphasis of this false teaching, Paul emphasized how being "in Christ" and putting Him first in one's life made all the difference in the world in daily living and interpersonal relationships. Being in Christ was to be lived out in the marriage and at home, as well as in the work-a-day world. Although he could not visit them personally because of his situation, the apostle was sending a delegation of trusted friends and colleagues with his apostolic letter to help them through this crisis.

On the other hand, the letter to Philemon was written to a respected member of the church in Colosse. Philemon was a wealthy landowner and businessman. Onesimus, one of his valued servants, had run away and escaped to Rome. Somehow he had come in contact with Paul in Rome, heard the gospel, and experienced the life-transforming power of Christ. Now Paul was sending him back to Philemon. This was a risky venture, for legally Philemon could have Onesimus severely punished or even killed. Yet Paul writes an amazing appeal on behalf of Onesimus. The letter is filled with Christian character and values. It asks Philemon to demonstrate Christian forgiveness, full **restoration**, and even hints at freedom for Onesimus. The social and spiritual dynamics of this letter have been revolutionary through the ages, undermining racism, assisting in the abolition of slavery, and affirming the inclusion of all people on equal footing in the gospel and within the church.

Chapter 1   **Introducing Colossians (1:1–14)**

Lessons
1.1   Introducing Paul's Letter to the Colossians (1:1–14)
1.2   Paul's Reasons for Giving Thanks (1:1–8)
1.3   Paul's Prayer of Intercession (1:9–14)

Chapter 2   **Who Christ Is and What He Has Accomplished (Colossians 1:15–2:23)**

Lessons
2.1   Jesus Christ: Supreme Creator, Sustainer, and Reconciler (1:15–23)
2.2   Paul's Ministry and Message (1:24–2:5)
2.3   A Warning about False Teaching (2:6–23)

Chapter 3   **How Christians Should Live (Colossians 3:1–4:18)**

Lessons
3.1   Living the Christ-Life in Your Interpersonal Relationships (3:1–17)
3.2   Living the Christ-Life at Home (3:18–4:1)
3.3   Closing Challenges, Observations, and Greetings (4:2–18)

Chapter 4   **Introducing Philemon (Philemon vv. 1–25)**

Lessons
4.1   Understanding Philemon (vv. 1–25)
4.2   Paul's Appreciation of Philemon (vv. 1–7)
4.3   Paul's Appeal on Behalf of Onesimus (vv. 8–25)

Introducing Colossians (1:1–14)

An important key to effectiveness and success in life is expressed by the saying, "Keep first things first." The truth of this saying is also applicable to Christians. We can easily lose sight of godly priorities. We can forget what is most significant in our lives—Jesus first, last, and everything in between. The believers in the ancient city of Colosse (also commonly spelled Colossae) were in danger of this error. Paul wrote the letter to the Colossians to emphasize this single principle: the absolute **supremacy** and **sufficiency** of Jesus Christ in the Christian life. And the ultimate objective is "so that in everything He might have the supremacy" (1:18). Paul was saying, keep first things first! Believer, keep Jesus first.

> • *Read Colossians 1:1–14 before you begin study in this chapter.*

Lesson 1.1   **Introducing Paul's Letter to the Colossians (1:1–14)**

Objectives
1.1.1   Summarize the background of Paul's letter to the Colossians.
1.1.2   Describe what is known about the church at Colosse.
1.1.3   Explain the similarities between Paul's letters to the Colossians and the Ephesians.

1.1.4 List and explain ten characteristics of false teaching identified in Paul's letter to the Colossians.

1.1.5 Identify the purpose and theme of Paul's letter to the Colossians.

Lesson 1.2   Paul's Reason for Giving Thanks (1:1–8)

Objectives

1.2.1 Summarize Paul's greeting to the Colossian church.

1.2.2 Explain why Paul expressed thankfulness at the beginning of his letter.

1.2.3 Explain how the gospel changes the lives of those who believe its message.

1.2.4 Summarize the gospel's effect on society, in spite of persecution.

1.2.5 Describe how God used Epaphras to start the church at Colosse.

Lesson 1.3   Paul's Prayer of Intercession (1:9–14)

Objectives

1.3.1 Name and describe three characteristics of Paul's prayer for the Colossians that can guide how we pray for others.

1.3.2 Identify the two things Paul asked God to do for the Colossians.

1.3.3 List and explain four ways Paul wanted the Colossians to please the Lord.

LESSON 1.1

1.1.1 OBJECTIVE

Summarize the background of Paul's letter to the Colossians.

1   Which letters are the prison epistles, and why do they have this title?

Introducing Paul's Letter to the Colossians (1:1–14)

The Prison Epistles

Colossians, Ephesians, Philippians, and Philemon are a group of New Testament letters usually referred to as the prison or captivity letters. They are referred to in this way because Paul was in prison when he wrote them. They each make reference to Paul's imprisonment or bonds (Colossians 1:24; Ephesians 3:1; 4:1; 6:20; Philippians 1:12–13; Philemon 1).

The issue of who wrote the four letters has been argued from various perspectives based upon the style, language, and content of the letters. Evidence within each letter credits Paul with the authorship of all four (Ephesians 1:1; Philippians 1:1; Colossians 1:1; Philemon 1), and this is the most commonly held view. Until convincing evidence is brought forth, both from within the letters themselves (internal evidence) and from reliable historical sources (external evidence), the clear statements within the letters regarding authorship should stand.

The traditional view has been that these letters were written from Rome. However, Caesarea and Ephesus have also been advanced as possible locations. It is known that Paul was imprisoned twice. His first imprisonment was in Caesarea, under the governorships of Felix and Festus (Acts 23:23–26:32). The second was in Rome, while he awaited trial before Caesar (Acts 28:30–31). Some suggest Paul was also imprisoned in Ephesus. This belief is based upon Paul's statements in 2 Corinthians 11:23 about "frequent" imprisonments (Gundry 1994, 390). Since the letters do not clearly state where Paul was when he wrote them, it is best to avoid being dogmatic. A Roman imprisonment, however, is in keeping with allusions to the praetorian guard (Philippians 1:13) and to Caesar's household (Philippians 4:22). The traditional view that these letters were written from prison in Rome is preferred for this commentary.

Based upon the available historical evidence and the known facts about Paul's imprisonment in Rome, the writing of the four prison epistles is placed between AD 60 and 61. This period of Paul's ministry, although confining, was not unfruitful. Though chained to two centurions in rotating shifts, he lived in his own hired house where he carried on an effective ministry (Acts 28:30–31). Paul had the liberty of receiving visitors, hearing reports from the churches, and writing letters to encourage, solve problems, teach, and direct them. His ministry of intercessory prayer and personal evangelism were significant in spite of his incarceration (Ephesians 1:15–23; Philippians 1:3–6, 12–18; Colossians 1:3–14; Philemon 4–6).

The Church at Colosse

1.1.2
OBJECTIVE
Describe what is known about the church at Colosse.

Colosse was a small city in the ancient Roman province of Asia (the area now known as Turkey) on the banks of the Lycus River. It was located about one hundred miles east of Ephesus. Neighboring cities were Laodicea and Hierapolis. At one time, Colosse had been a city of considerable importance. However, changes in commercial patterns and needs brought about its decline (Vaughan 1978, 163). It has been said that the Colossian church was "the least important to which any epistle of Paul was addressed" (Lightfoot 1879, 16). However, a forceful argument could be made that any church receiving a letter from Paul that was eventually included in the New Testament canon cannot be considered insignificant.

2   Who started the church at Colosse? When?

The New Testament provides no direct account of how the church in Colosse was planted. Colosse receives no mention in Luke's account in Acts. All we know about this church and its origins are found in allusions within the letter and its companion letter Philemon (Vaughan 1978, 163). Most likely, the church was planted during Paul's ministry in Ephesus as recorded in Acts 18–19. The work of the Holy Spirit in Ephesus impacted all of Asia. Epaphras, a native of Colosse, was likely converted to Christ at that time and returned to his hometown to plant the church (1:5–7). It is also possible that he started the churches in neighboring Laodecia and Hieropolis.

Information in Colossians leads one to the conclusion that this church existed in a small city in which differing cultural and religious elements intermingled. The church was largely Gentile in nature and existed within a pagan culture, but there was also a significant Jewish influence (O'Brien 1982, 142–143). Those converted in Colosse had been "alienated from God" and were standing as His "enemies" (1:21). Immorality of all kinds characterized their lives (3:5–9). Before these people found Christ, they had been victimized by satanic power and were spiritually dead in their sins (2:13–15). When they believed on Christ, they were liberated and transformed by His power. They were now being discipled to follow Christ (2:6–7).

The church in Colosse was facing some significant challenges to be sure. But the congregation was made up of good people who loved God, upon the word of Epaphras, who had described them to Paul as people whose lives were characterized by faith, love, and hope. They had a good reputation, were evangelistic in their orientation, firm in their faith, and orderly in their church life (1:1–8; 2:5). Although warning was appropriate, there was much for which the Colossian believers could be commended.

1.1.3
OBJECTIVE
Explain the similarities between Paul's letters to the Colossians and the Ephesians.

The Relationship of Colossians to Ephesians

One of the issues that has troubled Bible scholars over the years is the similarities between Colossians and Ephesians. It is my opinion that Paul, after hearing the report from Epaphras about the unhealthy situation in Colosse, wrote Colossians to deal with the dangerous issues raised by the Colossian error. Shortly

3   What errors had crept into the Colossian church?

after writing Colossians, Paul became aware, through reports he was receiving, that the problem was more widespread than first imagined. The error had influenced churches throughout the Lycus Valley, including Ephesus. Consequently, Paul probably wrote the letter we call Ephesians later, as a circular or type of open letter, to deal with many of the same issues on a broader, more systematic scale.

The Occasion

1.1.4
OBJECTIVE
List and explain ten characteristics of false teaching identified in Paul's letter to the Colossians.

Paul had not personally planted this church although it could be considered the extended fruit of his ministry in Ephesus through Epaphras. We have no record of Paul ever visiting this congregation. Paul's letter was prompted by a visit from Epaphras, who shared a generally good report of the congregation at Colosse (1:8). However, he also shared the spiritual challenges and doctrinal errors the church was facing.

The Colossian letter provides no systematic description of the doctrinal errors and imbalanced teaching in the church. What we do know about this strange teaching or heresy is drawn from clues within the letter, especially those found in chapter 2. Based upon these clues the following observation can be drawn: influential teachers within the church were attempting to deceive the believers with persuasive arguments (2:4). Consequently, some of the Christians were accepting deceptive philosophy based on human reasoning and perhaps even demonic suggestion (2:8). Others were judgmental regarding ceremonial religious practices (2:16). Some Christians felt unworthy of God's best because they had not experienced the highly mystical experiences of others (2:18). Clearly some members of the congregation were deceived by this unhealthy emphasis (2:20–23).

At least ten characteristics (listed below) of the false teaching can be identified from clues within Paul's letter (Guthrie 1990, 565–571; Gundry 1994, 394–395; O'Brien 1982, 148–149).

Philosophic

Paul warns the Colossian believers not to be deceived "by fine-sounding arguments" or taken "captive through hollow and deceptive philosophy" (2:4–8). It appears the false teaching came through ideas and philosophies. The Christians were being persuaded that in order to be truly godly, they must have an esoteric or uniquely exclusive knowledge. Some of the error may have come from the beginnings of gnosticism, the belief that matter—anything physical—was evil. Thus salvation and a real religious experience supposedly had to come through knowledge.

Syncretistic

Syncretism is the combining of ideas and beliefs of other religions with Christianity. It results in a belief system that is neither Christian nor fully pagan. It is possible that the Colossian error was not a single, clearly defined belief system, but a mixture of beliefs and practices from paganism, Judaism, and Christianity. In addressing the error at Colosse, Paul clarifies the place and/or significance of circumcision, baptism, and food regulations, as well as various religious festivals and holy days (2:11–12, 16).

Demonic

It appears the Colossian believers had not been fully liberated from their pre-Christian past. An elaborate system may have been developed to protect them from evil forces they believed dominated the expanse between the underworld, the material world, and the heavenlies. Thus it appears that some of the believers in Colosse continued to feel tyrannized by the demonic forces that had once held them captive. Paul felt it necessary to declare the complete victory of Christ over "powers and authorities" (2:15). He urged believers to recognize that they had already "died to the basic principles of the world" (2:20). Complete victory was theirs in Christ.

Ritualistic

Another error Paul addressed was the belief that authentic Christians must follow an elaborate system of rituals and ceremonies. Paul urged these believers, "Do not let anyone judge you" in these matters (2:16). Authentic Christianity was to be characterized by a Christ-centered life and faith, not a human-made system of religious rituals.

Asceticism (Mystical)

Evidence seems to point to an influential teacher or teachers within the Colossian community who were stressing certain practices of self-denial (possibly ritual fasting and other rigorous treatment of the body). Supposedly, these practices helped restrain sensual desires and induce mystical experiences in which it was possible to be elevated into the heavenlies and worship angels, or God with the angels (O'Brien 1982, 142–143). Paul argues such practices were unspiritual, prompted by pride, and completely counterproductive and ineffective (2:18–23).

Legalistic

A strong element of **legalism** characterized the Colossian error (2:20–23). False teachers emphasized **submission** to a list of rules: "Do not handle. Do not taste. Do not touch." These rules did not line up with the law of love (James 2:8), the law of Christ (Galatians 6:2), or the law of liberty (James 2:12). Paul claimed they were merely "human commands and teaching." Rules made by humans have plagued the body of Christ throughout the centuries and the group of believers in Colosse was no different.

Elitist in Focus

A critical problem caused by the false teaching was its elitist tendencies. It fed pride, encouraged arrogance, and resulted in a group within the congregation whose "unspiritual minds puffed [them] up with idle notions" (2:18). In that sense the teaching caused divisions. It created a group of supposed *super saints* within the body who intimidated, judged, and belittled the other Christians. They claimed to have deeper knowledge, higher experiences, and greater spirituality. Paul vigorously denied the truth of each of their claims.

Human-Based

Paul argued there was nothing godly about these dangerous teachings. He pointed to the source of such ideas. He said they were "based on human commands and teaching" (2:22).

Appearance-Oriented

Paul claimed that the ideas and principles that characterized the Colossian error had the appearance of wisdom and religious devotion. They seemed to be able to lead one to a higher level of knowledge and a deeper dimension of spirituality. They seemed to offer a good solution to wrong desires and passions. But Paul declared they were without value and ineffective. It was all a façade, merely appearance (2:23). Reality could be found only in Christ (2:17).

Christ-less

The most insidious and dangerous aspect of the Colossian error, in Paul's mind, was its Christology. It de-emphasized Christ and elevated human effort. It elevated the importance of intermediary spiritual beings (2:18) and probably placed Christ in a position somewhere greater than humans but less than fully God. It stressed mystical experiences and **esoteric knowledge** but marginalized the centrality and **sufficiency** (no deficiency) of the Lord Jesus Christ.

The Purpose and Theme

1.1.5
OBJECTIVE
Identify the purpose and theme of Paul's letter to the Colossians.

In light of the scope of this false teaching, Paul clearly proclaims the absolute **supremacy** and complete sufficiency of Christ. The message of Colossians is that everything that is needed in the Christian experience is to be found in Christ. Legalistic requirements or ritualistic practices add nothing to Christ's work on our behalf. Neither do rigorous self-denial or mystical experiences. Focusing on anything but His supremacy leads to error. Christ is enough. Christ is the answer. Christ is sufficient. Christ is supreme. Paul's message to the Colossians and to us is that anyone who believes on Christ as Savior has found all that is needed.

4   What does Paul emphasize to correct the Colossian heresy?

He is the image of the invisible God, the firstborn over all creation. For by him all things were created: things in heaven and on earth, visible and invisible, whether thrones or powers or rulers or authorities; all things were created by him and for him. He is before all things, and in him all things hold together. And he is the head of the body, the church; he is the beginning and the firstborn from among the dead, so that in everything he might have the supremacy. (Colossians 1:15–18)

The supremacy and sufficiency of Christ was Paul's answer to the false teaching and error of the Colossian church in the first century. It must also be the church's message today. Just as the fixed stars in the heavens guide ships to safe harbor, and the gravitational pull of the earth establishes true north for the traveler, Jesus Christ is and must remain as supreme focus of the ministry of the church and the life of every believer. That supremacy must neither be compromised nor lost sight of. He keeps us on track. He is our antidote to error, the hope of the world, and our key to effectiveness.

The Outline of Colossians

   I.   Introduction
      A. Greeting (1:1–2)
      B. Thanksgiving (1:3–8)
      C. Prayer for the Colossian Believers (1:9–14)
  II.   Powerful Doctrine: Our Supreme Savior (1:15 to 2:23)
      A. The Supremacy of Christ (1:15–23)
      B. Paul's Work for the Church (1:24 to 2:7)
      C. Warnings Against False Teachers (2:8–23)
 III.   Practical Teaching: Guidelines for Holy Living (3:1 to 4:6)
      A. The Old Self and the New Self (3:1–17)
      B. Rules for the Family of God (3:18 to 4:1)
      C. More Teaching (4:2–6)
 IV.   Conclusion (4:7–18)

Paul's Reason for Giving Thanks (1:1–8)

Few things are more satisfying in difficult and trying circumstances than good news. A positive report about people we care about can lift our spirits. Paul, the great apostle to the Gentiles, was in prison for the sake of Christ and the gospel. In the opening remarks of his letter to the congregation in Colosse, Paul expresses his thanksgiving for the good report he received about the church from Epaphras, their founding pastor. News of how many people are coming to faith in Christ, strong response to the gospel, and the growth of believers in Christian life and character are always reasons for thanksgiving.

The Greeting (1:1–2)

1.2.1
OBJECTIVE

Summarize Paul's greeting to the Colossian church.

Paul opens his letter to the believers in Colosse with a greeting that he characteristically adapts to the needs and situations of the various congregations to whom he writes. He indicates who the letter was from, naming himself, and refers to his apostleship. He mentions Timothy as a fellow "brother" in Christ, probably as a courtesy and to honor to this faithful servant of the Lord (1:1).

Paul then indicates to whom he is writing the letter, using highly affirming language (1:2). He draws attention to the exalted position of these believers by referring to them as holy and the quality of their character by indicating they were faithful.

5   In what two places do Christians live simultaneously?

With the words in Christ and at Colosse, Paul draws attention to the dual citizenship of these believers. "At Colosse" reveals their geographical location. "In Christ" identifies their spiritual location, for in both spheres these believers were called upon to live out the Christian life simultaneously. They lived it out, first in a Gentile city. But they also drew upon the life and power of Christ, their spiritual location (Barton et al. 1995, 145).

Finally, Paul writes a standard, but Christianized greeting: "Grace and peace to you from God our Father" (v. 2). This final phrase should probably be understood as a prayer or blessing. The Greek word normally used in letters of that time would have meant "greetings to you." However, Paul deliberately chooses a word with distinct Christian significance, "grace." His additional choice of "peace" draws on the rich Jewish dimension of faith characterized by the Hebrew greeting, Shalom. This later term meant a comprehensive and valued gift from God, that is, completeness, soundness and wholeness (Youngblood 1986, 732–733). By the use of these two words Paul summarizes the dynamics and blessings of the Christian life.

Reasons for Thanksgiving (1:3–8)

1.2.2
OBJECTIVE

Explain why Paul expressed thankfulness at the beginning of his letter.

Paul then expressed his reason for thanking God for this congregation. He was thankful for how the gospel was transforming their lives in terms of character (1:4–6). He also thanked God for the impact of the gospel in Colosse and its spread over the world (1:6). Finally, Paul expressed appreciation for Epaphras, the faithful servant of God who had taken the message of the gospel to them (1:7–8).

The Gospel Transforms Lives (1:4–6)

In thanking God for the growth of their Christian character, Paul draws upon a well-known trilogy of Christian virtues. He speaks of their "faith," "hope," and "love" (cf. Romans 5:1–5; 1 Corinthians 13:13; Galatians 5:5–6; Ephesians 1:15–18; 4:2–5; 1 Thessalonians 1:3; 5:8; Hebrews 6:8–12; 10:22–24; 1 Peter 1:3–8, 21, 22).

Paul's first expression of thanks was for the fact that their faith was in Christ Jesus. Biblical faith always involves commitment to and trust in God. Their faith was anchored in Jesus Christ. Their faith was Christ-centered.

6 How is saving faith different from the faith found in non-Christian religions?

Faith is not what we know. A person can know a lot and not have saving faith. James 2:19 explains that even demons believe there is one God and tremble. Demons actually have an impressive understanding of theological truth, but they are not saved. A factual knowledge of theological truth is not enough. A sentimental, general faith is not enough, either. To be saved, an individual must have "faith in Christ Jesus" (1:4). That is the kind of faith Colossian believers had embraced, and it had transformed their lives.

Second, Paul gave thanks for their "love for all the saints." Love is the central and supreme Christian virtue (1 Corinthians 13). In verse 8, he expands on the source of this love by stating it was "love in the Spirit." The Holy Spirit was the source of their love (Galatians 5:22–23). Very likely, Paul was contrasting the elitist attitudes of those swept in by the Colossian error with the all-encompassing love of true believers in Christ.

7 Is it possible to follow Jesus and not love fellow believers? Explain.

One of the most visible proofs that a person's life has been transformed by the gospel is the evidence of love. This is foundational, non-negotiable evidence of a changed life. Jesus said, "'By this all men will know that you are my disciples, if you love one another'" (John 13:35). When people accept the gospel message, their lives are marked by God's love in all kinds of circumstances through the power of the Holy Spirit (Romans 5:5).

8 How is a believer's hope different from that of someone who wishes something will happen?

Finally, Paul offers thanks for their hope. He believes their hope is foundational to their faith and love. Hope, in Scripture, is not simply a wish—it is a confident expectation founded upon God's promise, provision, and character. God guarantees a wonderful eternity in His presence. Paul declares their inheritance is "stored up" for them "in heaven" (v. 5). This was proclaimed to them as an integral part of the gospel message (1 Corinthians 15:12–22; 1 Peter 1:3–5) (Barton et al. 1995, 149).

1.2.3
OBJECTIVE

Explain how the gospel changes the lives of those who believe its message.

The gospel gives believers hope beyond this life. Believers have the hope of a future in heaven. Why do people accept the gospel? Why do they sacrifice for the gospel? Why do people live for the sake of the gospel? Because of the hope they have. Unbelievers today often want to buy something now and pay for it later. Christians are willing to pay now and receive later. Paul said, "I consider that our present sufferings are not worth comparing with the glory that will be revealed in us" (Romans 8:18). Jim Elliot, a modern-day martyr, put it this way, "He is no fool who gives what he cannot keep to gain what he cannot lose" (Elliot 1958, 172). Paul recognized the power of hope to inspire faith and love. The gospel's foundational message is hope.

9 Give an example of someone you know whose life has been dramatically changed by the gospel.

Do you know someone whose life and character has been dramatically transformed by the gospel? I think of Tom, a foul-mouthed, brawling alcoholic who never passed up a chance to fight. Tom experienced one defeat after another, a great loss in his finances—until he finally reached the end of himself. Someone shared the message of the gospel with him—a message of forgiveness and hope through Christ. A marvelous transformation began in his life. As his pastor, I saw Tom become a kind, tender, compassionate husband and father. He developed a deep love for Jesus and a passion to reach the lost. When I think of Tom's story it causes my heart to swell with thanksgiving for the life-transforming power of the gospel.

The Gospel Changes the World (1:6)

1.2.4
OBJECTIVE

Summarize the gospel's effect on society, in spite of persecution.

The second major thing that prompted Paul's thanksgiving was the report he received regarding the spread of the gospel in Colosse and in the world (1:5–6). Paul viewed the gospel as a living thing. It was like a plant that took root and grew wherever it was planted. For Paul, the Colossian church was living proof of the power of the gospel. They had heard it and understood its message of God's saving grace by faith (cf. Ephesians 2:8–9). The result was phenomenal growth, both in Colosse and wherever it was preached.

The gospel is not a stagnant system of ethics, but a living, growing reality. It produces personal growth (1 Peter 2:2) and it increases the **corporate** body while growing all into spiritual unity. The gospel is a message with divine energy. Paul gave thanks over the growth and fruitfulness of the gospel everywhere.

Paul believed the roots of the gospel were in God's grace. It was a message of God's grace—His marvelous, undeserved provision through Christ. Grace, not works, brought salvation (Ephesians 2:8–9). Salvation and transformation began "the day you heard it and understood God's grace in all its truth" (1:6).

10 What is the gospel's effect on society, in spite of the persecution of Christians?

The reality of the power of the gospel is exciting! The gospel spreads; it cannot be confined or stopped. Paul was in prison, but the gospel was active all over the world (cf. 2 Timothy 2:9). Jesus said, "'This gospel of the kingdom will be preached'" (Matthew 24:14). Take John Bunyan and put him in the Bedford jail for preaching the gospel. What happens? He preaches at the top of his lungs, and crowds gather outside the prison walls to listen. Throw him into an inner cell to silence him, and he writes *Pilgrim's Progress*, a book that has influenced millions with the gospel. Take China and impose upon it a repressive, anti-God agenda—and the gospel still goes forth, bringing life literally to millions. The gospel cannot be stilled or stopped—it reaches throughout the world.

The Gospel Is Communicated by Faithful People (1:7, 8)

12.5
OBJECTIVE

Describe how God used Epaphras to start the church at Colosse.

Finally, Paul expresses appreciation for Epaphras (1:7, 8), the one who first took the gospel to Colosse. Everything known about Epaphras is found in Colossians 4:12–13 and Philemon 23. He may have been converted during Paul's ministry in Ephesus (Acts 19). It appears he was a native of Colosse, had probably planted the church there (as well as in Laodicea and Hierapolis), and had been a fellow-prisoner with Paul. Paul uses several terms of endearment and honor when referring to Epaphras, such as a "dear fellow servant" and "faithful minister of Christ."

11 In what way is Epaphras an encouraging example to all believers?

The point is, God uses people to spread the message of the gospel. Epaphras, a hometown boy, was the one God used in Colosse. As wonderful as the message of the gospel is, angels are not the ones who spread the message. A voice does not thunder from the clouds to communicate it to the nations. The gospel is proclaimed by ordinary people with all their fears, faults, and failings. Incredible as it may seem, God even uses imperfect churches, often torn by division and plagued by imbalanced doctrine, to be His agents of proclamation within a community or to the uttermost places in the world. The New Testament is filled with examples, such as Colosse, Corinth, and Galatia. May we, like Epaphras, faithfully proclaim the gospel.

12 What principle does the story about Edward Kimball illustrate?

Edward Kimball, a faithful Sunday school teacher in Chicago, Illinois, driven by a heavy burden, finally decided to share the gospel with a young shoe salesman by the name of Dwight Moody. Moody prayed to receive Christ as his Savior that day and later became one of the most passionate preachers of his generation. Some time later a well-known author by the name of F. B. Meyer was so moved by the might and power in the message of Moody that he embarked on the evangelistic trail with the message of the gospel. Of the many who came to a saving knowledge through Meyer's ministry was a young college student by the name of Wilbur Chapman, and Chapman went out to proclaim the message of Jesus.

During one of the evangelistic tent meetings held by Chapman, a young ball player hired to help erect the tents was ignited by the gospel message and influenced to step out with all his life's energy to take that gospel to all. That sportsman was the famous Billy Sunday. Sunday's zeal for the gospel took him at one point to Charlotte, North Carolina, where a small prayer group was formed after one of Sunday's meetings. Mordecai Hamm, a member of that men's prayer group, was moved to become an answer to his own prayer for laborers by holding crusades throughout the city of Charlotte. At one crusade where few converts were won, the message did transform the life of one tall lanky boy who became one of the world's greatest gospel preachers to this day—Billy Graham (Wilson 1984).

From person to person this wonderful message of the gospel spreads and grows. Thank God for those who faithfully share it with others.

Are you grateful for the gospel? Do you give thanks for what it is accomplishing around the world? Are you helping spread its message within your community and to the ends of the earth?

LESSON 1.3

1.3.1
OBJECTIVE
Name and describe three characteristics of Paul's prayer for the Colossians that can guide how we pray for others.

13 For what reason did Paul keep praying for the Colossians?

14 What three notable things about Paul's opening prayer should guide our praying?

Paul's Prayer of Intercession (1:9–14)

Ancient letters in the Greco-Roman world often opened with thanksgiving and prayer. Paul follows this cultural pattern. Verses 3–8 are a thanksgiving for the positive elements of the report Paul received about the church in Colosse. The words *for this reason* in verse 9 link verses 3–8 and verses 9–14. Paul continues his prayer, addressing issues of concern for the church in Colosse. These concerns will surface again later in the letter.

Godly leaders, with great hearts, have a passionate concern for the spiritual welfare of Christians everywhere. They long for Christians to understand God's will for their lives and to live in a way that honors and pleases the Lord. This principle, one that should be expressed in every Christian's life, was clearly evident in Paul's prayer for the believers in Colosse.

How should we pray for Christians we have never met? How should we pray for missionaries working in situations unfamiliar to us? Paul shows us how in these opening verses of Colossians. We can listen in on a prayer of Paul for a church he neither founded nor visited.

Effective Intercessory Prayer Is Corporate, Continual, and Filled with Concern (1:3, 9)

Three things are to be noted about Paul's opening prayer. First, it is a corporate prayer: "We always thank God, the Father of our Lord Jesus Christ, when we pray for you" (1:3). Since Paul has just included Timothy in his introductory greeting (1:1), this might be expected. However, it is also likely that Paul is drawing attention to regular gatherings of prayer he led with colleagues in ministry as well as those who visited him in prison (O'Brien 1982, 9). They joined in thanksgiving and intercession for the needs of the churches.

The second feature of their prayer is that it was frequent and continual: "We always thank God . . . when we pray for you" (1:3) and "We have not stopped praying for you" (1:9). Intercessory prayer, bathed with thanksgiving, was the regular practice of this great Christian statesman and his friends (cf. Philippians 4:6–7).

Finally, this was informed praying, not just general, ambiguous prayer. It was prayer based on reports Paul had received about the Colossian congregation's welfare. Reports came from Epaphras (one of their own and perhaps the founding pastor of their congregation) and perhaps others as well (cf. 1:4, 7, 9). Interestingly,

Paul had not been involved in the planting of this church, nor had he ever visited it. Yet his passion and concern for its welfare is expressed in continual intercession. This is truly a distinguishing mark of authentic spiritual leadership. Paul was reporting to the Colossian congregation that their specific needs were continually brought before the Lord during his imprisonment.

The story of the salvation of Christie Borthwick's father illustrates the power of continual, corporate prayer. This father seldom expressed interest in spiritual things. In fact, for twenty-nine years he aggressively resisted any conversations about his spiritual welfare or attempts to lead him to Christ. Christie kept praying for him. She called friends and asked them to join her in prayer. She marshaled the prayers of more than five hundred friends and associates, using e-mail. Finally, her father's heart miraculously softened. He indicated an interest in a relationship with God. After twenty-nine years of resisting God and concerted prayer on his behalf, he prayed a simple prayer to receive Christ. Two weeks later he died (Borthwick 2001).

Effective Intercessory Prayer Expresses Concern that Others Fully Comprehend God's Will for Their Lives (1:9)

1.3.2
OBJECTIVE
Identify the two things Paul asked God to do for the Colossians.

Two requests dominated Paul's intercession for the believers in Colosse. Paul's first request was that God might "fill" the Colossian believers "with the knowledge of his will" (1:9). The goal of the false teachers in Colosse, by contrast, appears to have been the seeking of a deeper, esoteric level of knowledge. The Greek word that Paul used for "knowledge" bears the idea of a thorough and accurate understanding of moral or religious truth (Vaughan 1978, 177). The knowledge Paul prayed for was fundamentally spiritual in nature and centered itself in a revelation of God in Christ (cf. 1 Corinthians 2:6–16). It is also clear from verse 10 that its goal was a Christian lifestyle, not simply an esoteric knowledge that tended only to produce pride and arrogance.

15 With what knowledge did Paul pray the Colossian believers would be filled?

Sincere Christians sometimes become preoccupied, almost immobilized, trying to determine God's will for their lives. God's will is not so profound or deep as to be nearly unattainable. It is not so mystical that it lacks practical significance for our daily lives. The will of God is found in knowing and following Christ personally. It involves living by His power and following His teaching and example every day. Therefore, for Paul, the ultimate aim of knowing God's will was pleasing God in daily life.

One of my Bible college professors and his wife made a powerful impact on me with their prayer example. Several of us rented sleeping quarters in their basement. Every morning, without fail, we would wake up to the sounds of the Kesslers interceding so students would know and fulfill God's will for their lives. They not only talked prayer—they consistently practiced it.

Effective Intercessory Prayer Expresses Concern that the Lifestyle of Fellow Christians Be Pleasing to the Lord (1:10–14)

This leads to Paul's second general request, which was that through this knowledge, the lives of the Colossian believers might honor and please the Lord in everything. His emphasis in verses 10–14 is therefore upon the expression of Christian belief through God-honoring behavior or lifestyle. The word Paul uses is *peripatesai*, translated "live a life," but which literally means "to walk about." This word group is a favorite of Paul's and is often used to characterize the daily life and behavior of the Christian (Romans 6:4; 8:4; 14:15; 2 Corinthians 4:2; Galatians 5:16; Ephesians 2:10; 4:1; 5:2,15; Philippians 3:17; Colossians 2:6; 3:7; 4:4) (Vaughan 1978, 178).

1.3.3
OBJECTIVE

List and explain four ways Paul wanted the Colossians to please the Lord.

16 In what four specific ways did Paul pray the Colossian Christians would please the Lord?

Genuine Christians want to honor and please God in every aspect of their lives, regardless of challenges or temptations. Paul said, "Whether you eat or drink or whatever you do, do it all for the glory of God" (1 Corinthians 10:31). He wanted Christ to be exalted in his body "whether by life or by death" (Philippians 1:20). Remember to pray that fellow Christians who are facing all kinds of pressure and temptation will be able to glorify God in everything.

Paul prayed that the Colossian believers would honor and please the Lord in four specific ways. First, he prayed that they would honor the Lord by good works, that is, "bearing fruit in every good work" (1:10). The participle translated "bearing fruit" is in the present tense, emphasizing both the present and continual nature of fruit-bearing (cf. Galatians 5:22–23). The fact that the Christian life is to be characterized by good works is emphasized by Paul elsewhere (Galatians 5:5; Ephesians 2:10; Titus 1:16; 2:7, 14; 3:8, 15).

Fruitfulness in the Christian life is the result of the Holy Spirit's working within us (Galatians 5:22–23). Fruit trees produce fruit in keeping with the kind of tree they are. Authentic Christians produce authentic Christianity. In our world we encounter many barriers to spiritual fruitfulness. Pray that Christians around the world will respond positively to the heavenly gardener as He seeks to produce much fruit or more fruit from their lives (John 15:1–5).

Second, Paul prayed that the Colossian believers would please the Lord through a growing relationship with Christ, that is, "growing in the knowledge of God." Paul was not satisfied with new birth alone. He believed the Christian life should be characterized by evidence of growth and maturity in Christ. Again, the participle used here is in the present tense and emphasizes the daily, growing knowledge of God that ought to characterize the Christian life.

Effective Christian life and ministry flow out of a consistent and continual increase in the knowledge of God. This is not simply theoretical or factual knowledge, but personal knowledge. We should be growing in our relationship with the Lord every day. Those who stagnate or stop growing are in a dangerous position. Pray that the Christian life will become an ongoing discovery and adventure for fellow believers.

Paul's third request was that God would empower the Colossian Christians with great endurance and patience (1:11). It is clear from Colossians 2 that these believers were under attack from criticism and intimidation. They were also in conflict with the powers of their pre-Christian past (1:13; 2:8–23; cf. Ephesians 6:10–18). God's power was the only thing that would enable them to stand with "great endurance and patience." Continual empowerment was what they needed, what Paul prayed for, and what God would provide (cf. Paul's personal testimony in Philippians 4:13).

Christians and church leaders in other parts of the world are facing incredible pressure and persecution. Temptations, tests, and trials come from a variety of sources, all orchestrated by the great adversary, the devil, as he mobilizes all his forces and resources to discourage devoted disciples, neutralize their influence, defeat Christian leaders, and destroy the work of God. Let us pray that fellow Christians everywhere be "strengthened with all power . . . that [they] may have great endurance and patience" (1:11).

Paul's final request for these believers was that they would express joyful gratitude to their Heavenly Father for His gift of salvation (1:12–14). In response to those in the church who were trying to "judge them" and "disqualify them" (2:16–19), his prayer was for them to remember that the Father had "qualified" them, "rescued" them, and "brought" them into the kingdom, where they found themselves now able to "share in the inheritance of the saints." They now could live in the kingdom of light instead of the kingdom of darkness. The Son of God had brought redemption to them! These were indeed reasons for rejoicing.

17   For what should we pray for other believers?

Few things are more attractive, influential, and powerful than an authentic, overflowing spirit of gratitude and joy for what the Lord has done. A negative, complaining, argumentative spirit will dilute or destroy our testimony (Philippians 2:14–16). Follow Paul's example and pray that God will fill the lives of fellow Christians everywhere with an indomitable and attractive spirit of thanksgiving and joy in the Lord.

This passage establishes a pattern for how to intercede for those we have never met—missionaries, evangelists, and fellow Christians in other parts of the world. There are sincere, faithful servants of the Lord around the world who are facing challenges beyond our imagination or understanding. Paul's prayer provides a healthy pattern for Spirit-prompted and Spirit-led intercession. Using Paul's intercession as a guide, we should pray that:

1. They fully understand God's will for their lives (1:9).
2. They honor and please the Lord in every way (1:10).
3. They continually bear good fruit (1:10).
4. They come to know God better every day (1:10).
5. The Lord empowers them to stand firm under pressure (1:11).
6. Their lives overflow with thanksgiving and joy (1:12–14).

I would like to offer a tribute to my parents who are now with the Lord— two of the most effective intercessors I ever knew. Mom and Dad believed that battles were won and spiritual progress was made around the prayer altars of our church. They would pray daily and fervently until the battle was won. I remember vividly a particular prayer project they tackled. Satan was trying to destroy a marriage. I remember my Mom clinching her delicate feminine fists, setting her jaw, and saying, "Satan will not get this one." And he did not.

Until they died, they would still receive telephone calls requesting prayer. Mornings in their modest home were dedicated entirely to prayer ministry. Name after name, prayer project after prayer project, missionary after missionary, minister after minister, and nation after nation were part of their prayers on any given day.

My parents' impact upon the world was not their skill as preachers or theologians. However, their impact as people of prayer would be difficult to calculate. They served as a model for the prayer ministry of hundreds of Christians, including their sons.

I remember standing several years ago in a chapel service at the Bible college where I taught, listening to a challenging message on the subject of intercessory prayer. As I listened, I was suddenly struck forcibly by speaker's questions, "Who will take the place of intercessors like my parents?" and "Who will serve as the models of prayer for the coming generation?"

That day, with tears running down my face, I decided to continue the legacy of prayer I had received. I determined to be a model of prayer for my generation. Will you?

Imagine how many people in your life could be touched and influenced positively by your intercessory prayer. Think about the powerful influence worldwide you could have by adopting Paul's pattern of intercession for fellow Christians and Christian leaders around the world. Let us pray.

Test Yourself

Circle the letter of the *best* answer.

1. The traditional view is that the prison epistles were written from
a) Caesarea.
b) Jerusalem.
c) Ephesus.
d) Rome.

2. Colosse was located on the banks of the
a) Lycus River.
b) Hermus River.
c) Danube River.
d) Moeander River.

3. Colosse was in what Roman province?
a) Achaia
b) Asia
c) Cilicia
d) Macedonia

4. Colosse is located in modern-day
a) Greece.
b) Turkey.
c) Syria.
d) Bulgaria.

5. Paul describes the false teaching at Colosse as
a) syncretistic, demonic, and blasphemous.
b) philosophic, legalistic, and Christ-less.
c) mystical, atheistic, and syncretistic.
d) demonic, blasphemous, and human-based.

6. In Paul's introductory remarks to the believers at Colosse, he is thankful for their
a) faith, hope, and love.
b) humility and love for all the saints.
c) patience that has endured under severe persecution.
d) generous financial support.

7. The most visible proof of a life transformed by the gospel is the evidence of
a) love.
b) patience.
c) peace.
d) self-control.

8. It is believed that the native from Colosse who started the church there was
a) Paul.
b) Apollos.
c) Timothy.
d) Epaphras.

9. According to Colossians 1, effective intercessory prayer is
a) private, continual, and filled with concern for others.
b) corporate, continual, and filled with concern for others.
c) private, intense, and continual.
d) continual, intense, and filled with concern for others.

10. A guide for intercessory prayer can be found in
a) Colossians 3:1–11.
b) Philippians 1:12–18.
c) Ephesians 3:1–6.
d) Colossians 1:9–14.

Responses to Interactive Questions
CHAPTER 1

Some of these responses may include information that is supplemental to the IST. These questions are intended to produce reflective thinking beyond the course content and your responses may vary from these examples.

1 Which letters are the Prison Epistles, and why do they have this title?

Colossians, Philemon, Ephesians, and Philippians are a group of New Testament letters usually referred to as the prison or captivity letters. They are referred to in this way because Paul was in prison when he wrote them.

2 Who started the church at Colosse? When?

The New Testament provides no direct account of how the church in Colosse was planted. The church and its origins are alluded to by the letter and its companion letter Philemon. Most likely, the church was planted during Paul's ministry in Ephesus. Epaphras, a native of Colosse, was likely converted to Christ at that time and returned to his hometown to plant the church.

3 What errors had crept into the Colossian church?

Influential teachers within the church were deceiving its members with false philosophy based on human reasoning and perhaps even demonic suggestion. Others were judgmental regarding ceremonial religious practices. Some Christians felt inferior because they had not experienced the highly mystical experiences of others.

4 What does Paul emphasize to correct the Colossian heresy?

Paul clearly proclaims the absolute supremacy and complete sufficiency of Christ. Everything needed for salvation and for serving God is found in Christ, not legalistic requirements or ritualistic practices.

5 In what two places do Christians live simultaneously?

The Colossian believers lived in the physical world at Colosse. Their spiritual location was in Christ.

6 How is saving faith different from the faith found in non-Christian religions?

Faith is not merely knowing something to be true. Demons know who God is and tremble, but they are not saved. To be saved, an individual must have faith in Christ Jesus. This kind of faith results in transformed lives.

7 Is it possible to follow Jesus and not love fellow believers? Explain.

No. The life of a person following Jesus is characterized by love. Jesus said, "By this all men will know that you are my disciples, if you love one another" (John 13:34–35). When people accept the gospel message, their lives are marked by God's love in all kinds of circumstances through the power of the Holy Spirit (Romans 5:5).

8 How is a believer's hope different from that of someone who wishes something will happen?

Hope, in Scripture, is not simply a wish. It is a confident expectation based on God's promise, provision, and character. God guarantees a wonderful eternity in His presence.

9 Give an example of someone you know whose life has been dramatically changed by the gospel.

Answers will vary.

10 What is the gospel's effect on society, in spite of the persecution of Christians?

The gospel spreads; it cannot be confined or stopped. The gospel reaches the world.

11 In what way is Epaphras an encouraging example to all believers?

Epaphras was the one who first took the gospel to Colosse. Epaphras, a hometown boy, was the one God used in Colosse. The gospel is proclaimed by ordinary people with all their fears, faults, and failings. Incredible as it may seem, God even uses imperfect churches, often torn by division and plagued by imbalanced doctrine, to be His agents of proclamation within a community.

12 What principle does the story about Edward Kimball illustrate?

From person to person, this wonderful message of the gospel spreads and grows. Thank God for those who faithfully share it with others.

13 For what reason did Paul keep praying for the Colossians?

Paul had a passionate concern for the spiritual welfare of Christians in Colosse. He longed for them to understand God's will for their lives and to live in a way that honored and pleased the Lord.

14 What three notable things about Paul's opening prayer should guide our praying?

First, it was a corporate prayer. Paul prayed with other believers.

Second, they prayed often and continually.

Third, Paul's prayers were specific. They were based on reports Paul had received about the Colossian congregation's welfare.

15 With what knowledge did Paul pray the Colossian believers would be filled?

Paul prayed that God might fill the Colossian believers "with the knowledge of His will."

16 In what four specific ways did Paul pray the Colossian Christians would please the Lord?

He prayed that they would honor the Lord by good works, a growing relationship with Christ, that God would empower them with great endurance and patience, and that they would express joyful gratitude to their Heavenly Father for His gift of salvation.

17 For what should we pray for other believers?

1. They fully understand God's will for their lives (1:9).
2. They honor and please the Lord in every way (1:10).
3. They continually bear good fruit (1:10).
4. They come to know God better every day (1:10).
5. The Lord empowers them to stand firm under pressure (1:11).
6. Their lives overflow with thanksgiving and joy (1:12–14).

Who Christ Is and What He Has Accomplished (Colossians 1:15–2:23)

In this section of his letter to the Colossian congregation, Paul deals in a straightforward way with the Colossian error. He identifies its dangerous character and prescribes the antidote—Jesus Christ, supreme Savior and Lord. He begins this section of the epistle with a hymn extolling Jesus Christ as the supreme creator, sustainer, and reconciler (1:15–23). Then, in order to insure that these believers understand his motives, he shares with them the values, character, and goals of his ministry on their behalf (1:24–2:5). Finally, he exposes the character of the error the church is facing and again proclaims the supremacy and sufficiency of Christ (2:6–23).

> • *Read Colossians 1:15–2:23 before you begin study in this chapter.*

Lesson 2.1   Jesus Christ: Supreme Creator, Sustainer, and Reconciler (1:15–23)

Objectives
2.1.1   Describe how Jesus reveals God to people.
2.1.2   Explain Christ's relationship to creation.
2.1.3   Explain why Christ must be supreme in everything.
2.1.4   List and explain five aspects of Christ's work in reconciling people to God.

Lesson 2.2   Paul's Ministry and Message (1:24–2:5)

Objectives
2.2.1   Explain the relationship between ministry and joyful suffering.
2.2.2   Define the term mystery *as Paul used it in Colossians.*
2.2.3   List and explain five aspects of Christian maturity.
2.2.4   Clarify why effective ministry is dependent upon the empowerment of the Holy Spirit.

Lesson 2.3   A Warning about False Teaching (2:6–23)

Objectives
2.3.1   List and explain three analogies Paul uses to illustrate what the Christian life should involve.
2.3.2   Explain Paul's warning about philosophy.
2.3.3   List the four ways Jesus provides all we need for salvation.
2.3.4   Define legalism, asceticism, *and* mysticism, *and explain how they are a danger to today's church.*

Jesus Christ: Supreme Creator, Sustainer, and Reconciler (1:15–23)

In ancient times, those who navigated the seas understood the importance of fixed points of reference. They determined their location by taking sightings of the heavenly bodies. By holding to a course aligned with those fixed reference points, they were able to reach their desired destination.

In Colossians 1:15–23 Paul proclaims Jesus Christ as the believer's fixed point of reference. He was concerned because the Colossian believers were in danger of being led into error by teachers whose doctrine detracted from the supremacy of Christ. Thus, Paul exalts Christ and asserts His supremacy in at least four aspects or dimensions (O'Brien 1982, 32, 42).

Jesus Christ and Revelation: He Reveals the Invisible God (1:15)

First, Paul presents Christ as the supreme revelation of the invisible God. No object we could make or imagine could adequately represent the Living God. God is beyond human comprehension. However, Jesus Christ, the "Son" the Heavenly Father loves (1:13), is God's revelation of himself. Jesus is "the visible image of the invisible God." The Greek word translated "image" expresses the idea of something (or in this case, someone) that bears an exact likeness to or appearance of another (Vaughan 1978, 181–82). In other words, Jesus makes the invisible God visible (O'Brien 1982, 43). Jesus Christ perfectly and accurately shows us who God is and what He is like (John 1:18; 2 Corinthians 4:4–6; Hebrews 1:3).

1 What did Paul mean when he said Jesus Christ was the image of God?

Before the birth of my grandson, my daughter and son-in-law sent me a vague, black and white photograph of him created with the use of ultra-sound technology. It was the best picture available human technology could provide of my grandson before his birth. Jesus, by stark contrast, is heaven's perfect and complete revelation of what the invisible God is like.

Jesus Christ and Creation: He Is the Creator and Sustainer of Everything (1:15–17)

Second, Paul argues that Christ is the "firstborn over all creation." By this he meant that Jesus existed before the world was created and is supreme over creation (Vaughan 1978, 182). All things were brought into existence by the creative act of God in Christ—everything in heaven and on earth, both the visible and invisible, including spiritual or angelic beings existing in the universe. In verse 16, with three different Greek prepositional phrases, Paul states:

1. Christ is the sphere of creation—"*by Him* all things were created" (emphasis added).
2. Christ is the divine agent of creation—"all things were created *through Him*" (emphasis added).
3. Christ is the goal of creation—"all things were created . . . *for Him*" (KJV, emphasis added; O'Brien 1982, 61–2).

In addition to all of this, Paul contends that Christ is the One who sustains all of creation, for "in him all things hold together" (1:17, cf. Hebrews 1:3).

The created world, as we know it, and humankind are not cosmic accidents–Jesus Christ is the creative force, sustainer, and unifying principle behind all things. Think of what this means. Every galaxy, solar system, star, planet, and moon in the universe was created by God. It means God created every person, bird, fish, or creature, from the most complex to the simplest. It means He created every particle, be it a molecule or a subatomic particle. Every biological, chemical, or natural process came from God. He not only created it, He has and will continue to sustain it. What an incredible God!

Jesus Christ and the Church: He Is to Be Supreme in Everything (1:18)

2.1.3
OBJECTIVE
Explain why Christ must be supreme in everything.

Third, Paul declared that Christ was supreme as head of His church (1:18, cf. Ephesians 4:15, 16). Christ's headship could point to His authority over all that took place in the church or emphasize the honor due Him (Keener 1993, 572). Just as the Colossians understood that parts of the body function properly under the direction and control of the brain, Paul emphasized that a healthy and effective church must operate under the control and authority of Christ (Barton 1995, 164).

In the last part of verse 18, Paul summarizes his argument. For these Colossian believers, Christ needed to be supreme in everything. He was not only "firstborn over creation," He was also the "firstborn from among the dead" through His resurrection. He was supreme in everything (O'Brien 1982, 51).

2 Why must believers keep Jesus as supreme in their lives?

Here Paul's argument has reached its climax. Jesus Christ must be kept supreme in everything. Jesus was the fixed point of reference God appointed to guide the believers' personal lives, as well as the **corporate** life of the church, and to protect them from spiritual shipwreck.

Jesus Christ and Salvation: He Reconciles All Things to God (1:19–23)

2.1.4
OBJECTIVE
List and explain five aspects of Christ's work in reconciling people to God.

Finally, Paul presents Jesus Christ as the supreme reconciler. In verse 19, Paul says Jesus is the One in whom all God's fullness dwells. It appears that the concept of *fullness* was popular among the false teachers in Colosse. They may have used this term to refer to the totality of spiritual beings they believed controlled the space between earth and heaven as well as the lives of humankind. The false teachers perhaps claimed that Jesus was simply one of these beings—less than fully God, but more than merely human (Vaughan 1978, 185). They claimed that spiritual success came through knowing about this hierarchy of beings and placating them.

Paul declared that no placating was necessary. Jesus Christ had reconciled "all things" to himself through His death on the Cross (1:20). Jesus Christ was supreme—He was God. Jesus is the supreme expression of God's fullness. Everything available or needed in the Christian life is found in Jesus.

In verses 20–23, Paul explains five aspects of Christ's reconciling work in the lives of the Colossian Christians:

3 What five aspects of Christ's reconciling work does Paul present and what does each include?

1. The Problem Requiring Reconciliation

Before they were reconciled to God through Christ, these believers were completely alienated from God in their thinking and lifestyle. They desperately needed **reconciliation** to God.

Their predicament was no different from ours. Colossians 1:21 declares that because of sin, all people are alienated from God. All of humanity desperately needs reconciliation to God.

2. The Plan of Reconciliation

Paul indicates that God's ultimate plan is to **reconcile** "all things" to himself through Christ. Just as the fall of humanity into sin had a universal impact, Paul asserts that Jesus' work on the Cross has the power to reconcile all people to God (cf. Romans 5:12–21; 8:18–23).

The language used here has caused some concern and given rise to some troubling questions. Will everyone eventually be saved? Will the devil ultimately be saved? Yet it would be a mistake to interpret verse 20 in such a way that the clear teaching of Scripture in other places—indicating many will be lost and Satan will spend eternity in Hell—is contradicted (cf. Revelation 20:7–15). The Bible clearly teaches that without voluntary, personal trust in Jesus Christ, salvation is impossible (John 3:16; Acts 4:12; 2 Peter 3:9) (Vaughan 1978, 186).

3. The Price of Reconciliation

Humanity's alienation from God was total. Paul makes it clear that the price of reconciling people to God was the greatest possible—Jesus' life for theirs (1:20, 22). When one sinned under the Old Testament system, a sacrifice had to be offered to **atone** for the sin (Leviticus 5:5–10; Hebrews 9:22). Jesus became the supreme sacrifice for the sins of all humankind. He offered himself on the Cross on our behalf (Romans 8:3; Hebrews 10:1–10).

4. The Purpose of Reconciliation

Paul then describes the purpose and outcome of the reconciliation God provides in Christ (1:22–23). Many of the believers in Colosse had felt the sting of criticism and rejection (2:16–19). Paul, however, proclaimed good news. "He has reconciled you . . . to present you holy in His sight, without blemish and free from accusation" at the final judgment (1:22 cf. Romans 8:31–34; Jude 24).

5. The Proof of Reconciliation

All of this was not without qualification. Paul cautions the believers against complacency. You will be presented holy to God only "if you continue in your faith, established and firm, not moved from the hope held out in the gospel" (1:23). However, Paul does not make this conditional statement because he doubts the believers will keep their faith. His expression in the Greek is stated in such a way as to communicate his confidence in God and in these believers (Vaughan 1978, 188). The proof of our reconciliation is for us to actively practice what we are by position "in Christ," that is, to live a faithful, holy life as those who have been reconciled to God "in Christ."

The story is told of two warring tribes in Alaska in the late 1800s—the Sitka and the Thlinkit. The tribes had engaged in a bitter war all summer. As a result, the Sitkas were afraid to go to the salmon streams and berry fields to gather winter supplies. One day, the Sitka chief appeared before the chief of the other tribe to appeal for his people. He said, "If this war goes on much longer, most of my people will die of hunger. We have fought long enough; let us make peace." The Thlinkit chief argued, "You may well say let us stop fighting, when you have had the best of it. You have killed ten more of my tribe than we have killed of yours. Give us ten men to balance our blood-account; then we will make peace and go home." The Sitka chief replied, "You know my rank. You know I am worth ten common men and more. Take me, and make peace." The offer was accepted and the arrows flew. The chief was shot down in the sight of the fighting bands. The chief sacrificed himself for his people and peace was established. Therefore, when missionaries brought the message of atonement and reconciliation through Christ to the Sitka and Thlinkit tribes, it was readily accepted (Muir 1915, 197).

The key principle in the Colossians 1:19–23 passage is the absolute supremacy, sufficiency, and centrality of Christ (1:19). Jesus must be supreme in our finding salvation and in our successful navigation through life to heaven. We must stay focused upon Him; otherwise our chances of being led astray are very real.

4   What does effective ministry entail?

5   What explanation exists for Paul's statement, "I fill up in my flesh what is still lacking in regard to Christ's affliction" (Colossians 1:24)?

6   In what sense may ministry mean suffering for believers?

Paul's Ministry and Message (1:24–2:5)

Observing the passion of a true spiritual leader is inspiring. Godly leaders combine the strength and resolve of a father with the tenderness and concern of a mother. They long for, work for, and are willing to sacrifice for the spiritual welfare of those they serve.

In these verses, Paul makes clear that effective ministry entails the following:
1. selfless service to Christ and His church as its motive
2. the Word of God as its message
3. growth in Christ as its goal
4. the empowerment of the Holy Spirit.

The Motive of Ministry: To Serve Christ and His Church (1:24)

Paul declares that everything he is going through is on behalf of the church. In this regard, Paul patterns his ministry after Jesus who "loved the church and gave himself up for her" (Ephesians 5:25). In verse 24, Paul says he was willing to suffer—even rejoice in suffering—for the sake of Christ and His church.`

As challenging as the ministry was for Paul, he always rejoiced. In fact, he wrote verse 24, as well as the letter to the Philippians, from prison. Both overflow with rejoicing (cf. Philippians 1:4,18; 2:2,17; 3:1; 4:4). Rejoicing should be every Christian's attitude toward ministry. Some people minister grudgingly, with pained faces and complaining voices. Others follow Paul's example. A ministry that makes maximum impact is carried out with joy. That is the true spirit of ministry exemplified by our Savior (cf. Hebrews 12:2–3).

In the last part of this verse Paul makes a puzzling statement: "I fill up in my flesh what is still lacking in regard to Christ's affliction." What does Paul mean by this? It is clear from the previous context (1:13–23), as well as other Bible passages, that he cannot mean Christ's suffering was somehow insufficient (Romans 6:9–10; Hebrews 7:26–28; 9:11–14, 24–28; 10:1–14; 1: Peter 3:18). Christ's declaration from the Cross, "It is finished," tells us that Jesus provides our complete redemption (John 19:28–30). Likely, Paul saw himself as somehow entering into a "fellowship of Christ's suffering" (Philippians 3:10, 11). It is also possible that Paul is using a rabbinical concept of suffering—the birth pangs ancient Jews believed they were to suffer leading up to the last days. Paul saw Christ's sufferings as beginning a process that led to his own suffering as well as to the suffering of fellow Christians for the sake of Christ. His and their suffering was simply a prelude to the glory to be revealed at Christ's coming (2 Corinthians 4:16–18) (Bruce 1984, 81–84).

Those who desire to represent Jesus Christ and minister for Him must be willing to suffer. Ministry involves suffering. It may involve doing without. It may involve being mistreated. If we are unwilling to suffer for the gospel, it is doubtful our ministry will make much impact. The early church considered it a privilege to suffer for Christ (Acts. 5:41). Paul stated the principle clearly, "It has been granted to you on behalf of Christ not only to believe on Him, but also to suffer for Him" (Philippians 1:29).

Karen Watson, missionary to the Middle East who was killed March 15, 2004, wrote these words in a final letter to her pastors at home: "When God calls, there are no regrets. I tried to share my heart with you as much as possible, my heart for the nations. I wasn't called to a place. I was called to Him. To obey was my objective, to suffer was expected, His glory my reward" (Watson 2004). Every minister must begin with a genuine call from God. This is the foundation for ministry that multiplies faithfulness in the midst of suffering.

The Message of Ministry: The Word of God (1:25–27)

Paul saw himself not only as serving Christ and His church, he saw himself as a minister of the gospel. God had personally confronted him and commissioned him to share His Word with the world (Acts 9:15–16; Ephesians 3:7–9). Paul saw himself as under divine obligation, both to God and to the people of the world, to share the gospel (Romans 1:14–16; 1 Corinthians 9:16–17).

Paul refers to the gospel as "the mystery"—a term used here and in other epistles (cf. Romans 16:25–27; Ephesians 3:2–9). Most people think of a mystery as something beyond understanding, something to be discovered only by diligent investigation. In the ancient world, this word was used by pagan religions to refer to religious insights available only to a select few (esoteric). In fact, the false teachers in Colosse may have been using the term in this way. Paul's use of the term, however, is very different. He uses the word *mystery* to describe something God has now revealed "to the saints" and wants to make known "among the Gentiles," that is, all of the people of the world (cf. 1:23) (Ladd 1974, 93–94). The mystery revealed is that Jesus imparts the hope of a future in heaven to all who believe (John 3:16; 1 Corinthians 2:1–9).

Paul knew his job was to preach the Word of God. He said, "Woe to me if I do not preach the gospel" (1 Corinthians 9:16–17). A powerful moment for most candidate ministers is when they hear Paul's words to Timothy spoken to them at their ordination service, "Preach the Word!" (2 Timothy 4:1–5). If our ministry does not involve clearly proclaiming and promoting the gospel, it is not a ministry.

The Goal of Effective Ministry: Maturity in Christ (1:28; 2:1–5)

Paul's proclamation of the gospel was fundamentally a proclamation of Jesus Christ (cf. 1 Corinthians 2:1–2). It involved admonishing (warning) and teaching, and was carried out "with all wisdom" (1:28). The goal of his ministry was that those who heard and responded to the message would be presented "perfect in Christ." The word *perfect* here does not mean perfection in the sense of being without sin or flaw. Instead, it refers to maturity in Christ (Barton 1995, 181). Paul indicated that this perfecting was a process taking place at the present time, but one which would only be ultimately fulfilled in heaven when they stood before Christ (cf. 1 Thessalonians 5:23–24; Jude 23–24; 1 John 3:2–3).

Paul identified five aspects of the maturity of believers toward which he worked (2:2–5).

1. That they might be encouraged (or strengthened) in their hearts (2:2).
2. That they might be united in their love (2:2).
3. That they would understand the mystery he had spoken about earlier (2:2–3; cf. 1:26–27).
4. That they would be prepared to recognize and resist deception (2:4).
5. That their faith would be stable in Christ (2:5).

What is the goal of our ministry? It is not merely to win people to Christ or see them raise a hand, walk an aisle, or pray a prayer. We do want people to commit to Christ and express their love toward Him, but we must want more. Our goal must be to bring them to maturity. We do not just want decisions—we want disciples. We want to see them become more and more like Christ. That is what true perfection is all about (cf. Galatians 4:19; Ephesians 4:11–16).

Few things are more delightful to a parent or grandparent than to watch the healthy development of the children they love. The first step—an attempted word, a

---

2.2.2
OBJECTIVE

Define the term mystery *as Paul used it in Colossians.*

7 How is the gospel a "mystery" in the biblical sense?

8 What did Paul have in mind when he said he wanted to present every believer "perfect in Christ" (Colossians 1:28)?

2.2.3
OBJECTIVE

List and explain five aspects of Christian maturity.

9 In what five aspects did Paul want believers to mature?

mimicked action or a personal achievement thrill us more than words can express. True spiritual leaders, like loving parents, long to see Christ's likeness formed in those they serve. They thrill at every indication of progress toward that goal.

The Power of Ministry: The Holy Spirit (1:29)

What a noble task. Paul saw the ministry of preaching Christ and maturing believers in His image as a calling worthy of receiving the full energy and commitment of his life. He engaged in ministry on behalf of all believers—not just those to whom he had personally ministered (2:1). In verse 29, where he describes the extent of his commitment to ministry, he first uses a word that means hard, hard work. Then he describes ministry as a struggle, using a word meaning "to wrestle" (cf. 2:1; Ephesians 6:12) (Vaughan 1978, 193). The hard work of preaching the gospel and maturing believers is carried out, not by personal effort, but through the empowerment of the Holy Spirit.

2.2.4
OBJECTIVE
Clarify why effective ministry is dependent upon the empowerment of the Holy Spirit.

Many people today think ministry is an easy profession. Paul did not see it in that way. It involved hard work and was a struggle (cf. 1 Corinthians 4:12; 15:10; 2 Corinthians 6:5; 11:23–27; 1 Thessalonians 2:9; 2 Thessalonians 3:8; 1 Timothy 4:10). The ministry *is* hard work, but when we feel we have no strength to continue, we discover the empowering resources of the Holy Spirit. Paul heard the Lord speak these words to him in his weakest moment: "My power is made perfect in weakness." He went on to testify, "For Christ's sake, I delight in weaknesses, in insults, in hardships, in persecutions, in difficulties. For when I am weak, then I am strong" (2 Corinthians 12:9–10).

I run a periodic marathon—26.2 grueling, often physically painful and mentally challenging miles. Many, like myself, who have run such a race, have experienced something called the *second wind*. This is a time when, unexplainably, new strength and vitality create a euphoria, making you feel like you could run forever.

10   What can you expect God to do for you when you are weary in service for the Lord?

The wonderful news is that God often comes in much the same way, by His Spirit, to those who serve Him. At their time of greatest weariness, discouragement, and testing, God provides the strength to continue. His strength is made perfect in weakness.

Do you long to be used by God in effective ministry? Is there something within you that cries out to make a lasting impact on your world? Think of those who have influenced your life for God. What characterized their lives? Likely, it was the traits and values Paul identified in this passage: selfless service to Christ and others, a clear sense of divine calling, a deep commitment to God's Word, a passion to help others mature in Christ, and complete dependency on the Holy Spirit. Are you willing to point your life toward those goals and prioritize those values in your service for the Lord?

A Warning about False Teaching (2:6–23)

Have you ever heard the saying, "That person is so heavenly minded, he or she is no earthly good"? If there was ever a passage in the Bible that directly addressed the truthfulness of this statement, it would be Colossians 2:6–23.

An attitude of superiority and intimidation had infiltrated the church in Colosse. Paul is writing to believers who have been belittled and intimidated by those who considered their spiritual experiences superior to those of the average Christian. He is deeply troubled by this attitude. It was polarizing and dividing the body of Christ, detracting from the supremacy of Christ, and ultimately leading to spiritual disaster. Similar attitudes trouble churches today.

Paul challenges the attitude of superiority and forcibly makes the point that every human **philosophy**, spiritual experience, or religious system that detracts from the supremacy and sufficiency of Christ is dangerous and should be resisted and rejected.

Continue the Walk In Christ (2:6–7)

First, Paul urges these believers to continue to walk in Christ. The word Paul uses here, translated "live" in the *New International Version*, is one of his favorite to describe practical Christian living. It literally means "to walk about." It emphasizes the fact that practical Christian living must be the natural outcome of the decision to become a Christian (O'Brien 1982, 106).

Paul uses three analogies to illustrate what the Christian life should involve:

1. being "rooted…in him" (Growth and fruit bearing)
2. being "built up in Him" (construction terminology)
3. being "strengthened in the faith" (legal terminology) (O'Brien 1982, 106–107).

All of this is to be carried out with a heart overflowing with thanksgiving. This kind of Christian living would help the Colossian believers withstand the intimidation and false teaching they faced.

A friend of mine is a mountain guide. He has an effective way of encouraging weary hikers to finish climbs they have started. When their legs get weary and they begin asking how much further they have to go, his answer is always, "It's not far now; just a little ways ahead." Christians can use the same encouragement. Do not give up when the going gets tough. Hear the encouraging voice of the Spirit and fellow believers who tell you to *walk on*.

Do Not Depend on Human Wisdom or Philosophy (2:8)

In addition to Paul's concern about whether these believers would continue walking with Christ was his fear that they would be deceived and taken captive by any humanistic philosophy of the day. Paul was not opposed to thoughtful reflection on the Christian life or being informed about philosophical views of the day. His point was that victorious and overcoming believers put Christ first in lives. Christ's example, teaching, and values become the basis for evaluating all else. The wise Christian will not allow any philosophical perspective to lead him or her away from a devoted relationship with Christ (Barton 1995, 188)

Philosophical perspectives, novel doctrines, and culturally popular beliefs abound today. Often these teachings and their proponents are like those who attend a costume party—they have all of the trappings of religion, they claim to be Christian and masquerade as spiritual people, but it all hides the true character, deceitful doctrine, and evil lifestyle of their teachers. What was Paul's advice? Do not be deceived. See to it that no one takes you captive.

Embrace the Complete Provision of Christ (2:9–15)

Paul warned the believers in Colosse about the dangers of humanistic philosophy, but he also urged them to embrace the abundant provision of salvation in Christ. In this passage he emphasizes four things:

---

11 What key point does Paul make regarding anything that detracts from the supremacy of Jesus?

2.3.1
OBJECTIVE
List and explain three analogies Paul uses to illustrate what the Christian life should involve

12 What does it mean to "walk" in Christ?

13 What three aspects of Christian life and growth does Paul emphasize?

2.3.2
OBJECTIVE
Explain Paul's warning about philosophy.

14 What should be the Christian's attitude toward philosophy?

2.3.3
OBJECTIVE
List the four ways Jesus provides all we need for salvation.

1. The Supremacy of Christ (2:9)

"In Christ all the fullness of the Deity lives in bodily form." Paul's statement is one of the greatest declarations of the deity of Jesus Christ found in the epistles. Jesus Christ is God in every way—undiminished Deity expressed through perfect humanity.

2. The Sufficiency of Christ (2:10)

In verse 10, Paul uses what was probably one of the favorite concepts of the false teachers in Colosse—*fullness*. These teachers may have claimed that fullness was beyond the grasp of the average Christian unless he or she were to give attention to the spiritual principalities and powers that filled the universe and follow the strict discipline, rituals, and rigorous self-denial prescribed by the teachers (O'Brien 1982, 113–114) Paul refutes their claim and announces that the fullness they seek is to be found in Christ.

When a person is away from God, his or her life is lacking. That person may try to fill it with possessions or various pursuits. But he or she always comes up empty. Still remaining is a gnawing desire for something these pursuits or possessions cannot provide. However, when that person comes to Christ, the void in his or her life is filled. That person is complete in Christ.

3. A Setting Apart or Sanctification by Christ (2:11–12)

The false teachers in Colosse may have incorporated Jewish ceremonies into their religious system and insisted that the members of this largely Gentile congregation be circumcised in order to be saved. Circumcision was an outward sign God commanded Abraham and his descendents to undergo to show their covenant relationship with Him (Genesis 17). Circumcision marked God's covenant people as being *set apart* to serve Him. It was an outward sign of an inward reality.

Paul declares to these believers that in Christ a greater spiritual reality exists—a circumcision of the heart completed by Christ, not by humans. It is a putting off of the sinful nature, through Jesus. Baptism, for the believer, corresponds in many ways to circumcision. Baptism is an outward sign of an inward change. We are not saved by baptism; salvation comes by faith alone (Ephesians 2:8–9). However, in baptism we identify with Christ.

4. Complete Salvation through Christ (2:13–15)

15 What does Christ do to our "indictment" or "list of indebtedness"?

Finally, Paul declares that complete salvation from sin and its power is available through Christ's victory at the Cross. Those once dead in sin—uncircumcised in their hearts—now experience eternal life, complete forgiveness, and liberating victory through Christ.

The imagery behind verses 14 and 15 most likely points to the ancient practice of either posting an indictment (the charge) against a prisoner or a list of indebtedness in a public place. Paul pictures the words *paid in full* or *forgiven* written across these documents (Vaughan 1978, 201–202). Because of Christ's death, those guilty of sin and victimized by powers and authorities are forgiven and set free. The forces of evil were disarmed and publicly shamed through Christ's victory on the Cross.

The search in the heart of people today is much like the effort to work a jigsaw puzzle. You fit together a piece here and a piece there. You put together the edge pieces and those that have the same color, and try to work with every piece until you can see the full picture. Each piece has its place. In a similar manner, people search and search for missing pieces to complete the life of purpose and fulfillment they envision. One piece after another is tried: this philosophy or that religion, this technique or that ritual, this goal or that pursuit. They may even try to force a piece to fit here and there. But try as they might, one critical piece—the one that would make the picture come together—is always missing. Where is it? How can one find it? The answer is: God provides it. It is found in salvation through Jesus Christ. He is the only One who makes life fulfilling and meaningful.

2.3.4
OBJECTIVE

Define legalism, asceticism, *and* mysticism, *and explain how they are a danger to today's church.*

Resist Every Substitute for Christ (2:16–23)

Throughout this passage Paul has identified at least six errors the false teachers were promoting in Colosse. Now he warns them about the dangers of legalism, asceticism, and mysticism.

Legalism is the religion of human achievement. It argues that true spirituality is based upon Christ *plus* human works. It obligates a person to keep a list of human rules in order to be spiritual. Believers were being judged by rules about what foods they could or could not eat as well as rules about the celebration of special holy days, including the Jewish Sabbath. Paul says such things are mere shadows. Jesus Christ is the reality, fulfilling what Old Testament practices and festivals pointed toward. The question implied by verses 16 and 17 is this: Why would a person fixate on shadow and neglect reality?

16 How have you seen legalism, asceticism, and/ or mysticism endangering today's church?

In verses 18 and 19, Paul expresses concern about the related issues of asceticism and mysticism. An ascetic is a person who practices rigorous self-denial. That person may take a vow of poverty, flagellate him- or herself, or abuse his or her body in some way to prove his or her spirituality or to attempt to reach some heightened level of spiritual experience. Mysticism, on the other hand, is the pursuit of a deeper or higher religious experience through subjective means. It evaluates everything on the basis of feelings or intuition. It denies the validity of the intellect or rational thought, labeling it as stiff or unspiritual.

Some in Colosse may have been practicing rigorous self-denial and fasting in an attempt to induce highly mystical experiences in which they either worshiped angels or worshiped with the angels (O'Brien 1982, 142–143). In either case, the emphasis was upon a highly mystical, super-spiritual experience. Paul claims such experiences only stimulated pride and led to unhealthy self-reliance. He goes further, saying that such practices ultimately result in severing a believer's relationship with Christ and His church.

Paul's question to the Colossian believers was pointed and direct. Why were they submitting to the world's understanding of spirituality—an approach that reduced spiritual reality to what could be handled, felt, tasted, or touched (2:20–21)? This whole approach appeared to be wise and holy by human standards, but had no power to transform lives or deliver from bondage (2:23).

Consumer protection has become big business. Its purpose is to protect the buyer from those who would deceive and exploit him or her. It is a business dedicated to protecting the consumer from substandard products, false claims, and hazardous materials. It is amazing just how vigilant some people are in protecting us from certain products, yet they remain ill-equipped and disinterested in protecting people from the spiritual substitutes for Christ-centered Christianity that are promoted daily. Effective churches and pastors understand they must serve as spiritual consumer protection agencies, all the while proclaiming Jesus Christ, the only "way . . . truth and . . . life" (John 14:6).

Test Yourself

Circle the letter of the *best* answer.

1. Concerning Christ's relationship to creation, which statement is correct?
a) By Him all things were created.
b) All things were created through Him.
c) All things were created for Him.
d) All of the above are true.

2. Which statement best describes the goal of creation?
a) By Him all things were created.
b) All things were created through Him.
c) All things were created for Him.
d) In Him all things hold together.

3. According to Colossians 1:22, the purpose of reconciliation is to
a) appease God's wrath.
b) present believers holy before God.
c) glorify God.
d) destroy the works of the devil.

4. Suffering in ministry is
a) to be avoided.
b) a result of sin.
c) to be expected.
d) a sign of pride.

5. According to Colossians 1:27–28, to whom did God want to make known the mystery of Christ?
a) Jews
b) Saints
c) Gentiles and all people
d) Romans

6. The tasks of preaching the gospel and the maturing of believers are accomplished through
a) hard work and determination.
b) the empowerment of the Holy Spirit.
c) programs and good organization.
d) personal sacrifice.

7. Paul uses the analogy of *being built up in Christ*, which is
a) construction terminology.
b) agriculture terminology.
c) legal terminology.
d) business terminology.

8. In Colossians 2:8, Paul warns the Colossians to not be taken captive by
a) lustful thoughts.
b) the pursuit of wealth.
c) hollow or deceptive philosophy.
d) complacency.

9. Being set apart to serve God is called
a) justification.
b) purification.
c) sanctification.
d) isolation.

10. Legalism is
a) the religion of human achievement.
b) the pursuit of a deeper religious experience through subjective means.
c) rigorous self-denial in attempt to reach a higher religious experience.
d) the pursuit of secret knowledge and wisdom.

Responses to Interactive Questions
CHAPTER 2

Some of these responses may include information that is supplemental to the IST. These questions are intended to produce reflective thinking beyond the course content and your responses may vary from these examples.

1 What did Paul mean when he said Jesus Christ was the image of God?

Jesus Christ perfectly and accurately shows us who God is and what He is like.

2 Why must believers keep Jesus as supreme in their lives?

Jesus was the fixed point of reference God appointed to guide the believers' personal lives, as well as the corporate life of the Church, and to protect them from spiritual shipwreck.

3 What five aspects of Christ's reconciling work does Paul present, and what does each include?

1. The Problem: All people need reconciliation to God.
2. The Plan: Jesus' work on the Cross has the power to reconcile all people to God.
3. The Price: Jesus' life for the lives of humanity.
4. The Purpose: "To present [believers] holy in His sight, without blemish and free from accusation" at the final judgment" (1:22).
5. The Proof: Faithful, holy lives.

4 What does effective ministry entail?

1. Selfless service to Christ and His Church as its motive,
2. A genuine call of God as its starting point,
3. The Word of God as its message,
4. Growth in Christ as its goal, and
5. The empowerment of the Holy Spirit.

5 What explanation exists for Paul's statement, "I fill up in my flesh what is still lacking in regard to Christ's affliction" (Colossians 1:24)?

Likely, Paul saw himself as somehow entering into a "fellowship of Christ's suffering" (Philippians 3:10–11). It is also possible that Paul is using a rabbinical concept of suffering—the birth pangs ancient Jews believed they were to suffer leading up to the last days. Paul saw Christ's sufferings as beginning a process that led to his own suffering as well as to the suffering of fellow Christians for the sake of Christ. Their suffering was simply a prelude to the glory to be revealed at Christ's coming.

6 In what sense may ministry mean suffering for believers?

Ministry involves suffering, such as doing without or being mistreated. Paul stated: "It has been granted to you on behalf of Christ not only to believe on Him, but also to suffer for Him" (Philippians 1:29).

7 How is the gospel a mystery in the biblical sense?

Paul uses the word to describe something God has now revealed "to the saints" and wants to make known "among the Gentiles." The mystery revealed is that the Jesus provides salvation and eternal life for all who believe.

8 What did Paul have in mind when he said he wanted to present every believer "perfect in Christ" (Colossians 1:28)?

The word "perfect" refers to maturity in Christ. Perfecting is a process which will be complete when believers stand before Christ.

9 In what five aspects did Paul want believers to mature?

1. That they might be encouraged.

2. That they might be united in their love.

3. That they would understand the mystery of Christ.

4. That they would be prepared to recognize and resist deception.

5. That their faith would be stable in Christ.

10 What can you expect God to do for you when you are weary in service for the Lord?

When we feel we have no strength to continue, the Lord says: "My power is made perfect in weakness." At times of greatest weariness, discouragement, and testing, God provides the strength to continue.

11 What key point does Paul make regarding anything that detracts from the supremacy of Jesus?

Every human philosophy, spiritual experience, or religious system that detracts from the supremacy and sufficiency of Christ is dangerous and should be resisted and rejected.

12 What does it mean to walk in Christ?

The word is one of Paul's favorites to describe practical Christian living. It literally means "to walk about." It emphasizes that practical Christian living is the natural outcome of the decision to follow Christ.

13 What three aspects of Christian life and growth does Paul emphasize?

1. Being rooted in Jesus; growing and bearing fruit

2. Being built up in Jesus

3. Being strengthened in the faith

All of this is carried out with a heart overflowing with thanksgiving.

14 What should be the Christian's attitude toward philosophy?

Christ's example, teaching, and values are the basis for evaluating all ideas and philosophies. The wise Christian will not allow any philosophical perspective to lead him or her away from a devoted relationship with Christ.

15 What does Christ do to our "indictment" or "list of indebtedness"?

The indictment against us is paid in full or forgiven. Because of Christ's death, those guilty of sin and victimized by "powers and authorities" are forgiven and set free. The forces of evil were "disarmed" and publicly shamed through Christ's victory on the cross.

16 How have you seen legalism, asceticism, and/or mysticism endangering today's church?

Answers will vary.

How Christians Should Live (Colossians 3:1–4:18)

As Christians, what we live daily really matters because it reflects what we believe, and what we believe is crucial to the witness of our lives. Our daily life should be the acknowledgment of what our heavenly Father has provided for us through His Son. And our lives should attest to the fact that the Holy Spirit's work is vital. But without these truths showing forth in the lives of believers, individually and corporately, all is futile.

That is why in this section of the epistle, Paul moves from the doctrinal to the practical. He has dealt with the false doctrine and those who taught it. He has prescribed the antidote for the error—a return to the simplicity of the gospel and the absolute supremacy of Christ. He has emphasized who Christ is and what He accomplished through His death, burial, resurrection, and ascension. Now he stresses the importance of seeing the evidence of these beliefs in the everyday lives of Christians. He addresses three key areas in which the Christ-life should be lived out:

1. in believers' relationships with one another and the world.

2. in their home lives.

3. in their workplaces.

Finally, he closes the letter by soliciting their intercessory prayer, highlighting several key people in the Lord's work, and giving some final instructions.

> • *Read Colossians 3:1–4:18 before you begin study in this chapter.*

Lesson 3.1   **Living the Christ-Life in Your Interpersonal Relationships (3:1–17)**

Objectives

3.1.1   Explain what it means to identify with Jesus Christ.

3.1.2   List what Paul said should be put off and put on in the Christian's life.

3.1.3   Explain what it means to do everything in the name of the Lord Jesus.

Lesson 3.2   **Living the Christ-Life at Home (3:18–4:1)**

Objectives

3.2.1   Compare biblical house codes to those of the ancient world.

3.2.2   Define the submission that in verse 18 Paul urges wives to practice.

3.2.3   Describe the kind of love in verse 19 that is expected of husbands.

3.2.4   Describe Paul's instructions to children.

3.2.5   Explain the responsibility of parents to children.

3.2.6   Define how Paul's challenge to slaves and masters would apply in today's culture.

Lesson 3.3   **Closing Challenges, Observations, and Greetings (4:2–18)**

Objectives

3.3.1   Explain what it means to devote oneself to prayer.

3.3.2   Explain the importance of prayer to the continued proclamation of the gospel.

3.3.3   Explain what Paul meant when he said, "Make the most of every opportunity."

3.3.4   List key people Paul mentions in 4:7–18, and describe their contribution to his ministry.

Living the Christ-Life in Your Interpersonal Relationships (3:1–17)

Jack was discouraged and frustrated. He was a new Christian who had enthusiastically committed himself to following Jesus with all his heart. But he faced some challenges. Not only did he have old friends who were putting pressure on him to go back to his old way of life, he also had fellow Christians in the church he attended who were trying to turn his newly found freedom in Christ into a competitive thing. Where was the joy and sense of exciting adventure he had first enjoyed in following Jesus?

Jack's problem is not unusual. It was the same problem Christians in Colosse faced in the first century. Paul had just addressed these very issues in Colossians 2, explaining that, "just as you received Christ Jesus as Lord, continue to live (or walk) in Him" (2:6). He also urged these believers, "to not let any one take you captive . . . judge you . . . or disqualify you" (2:8, 16, 18).

What can Christians do when they experience this kind of pressure? What can they do to overcome and live the Christian life victoriously? In Colossians 3:1–17 Paul gives three essential principles to guide them in achieving that victory.

Connect Fully with Christ's Death, Burial, and Resurrection (3:1–9)

Paul urged the believers in Colosse to identify completely with the death, burial, and resurrection of Jesus. Jesus died on the Cross for their sins, was buried, rose from the dead, ascended into the heavenlies, and was at the Father's right hand. Since this was the case, they needed to act upon it—they needed to consider it so in their lives.

First, they needed to put to death what belonged to their way of life before they experienced new life in Christ. Paul warns that those who continued to sin would experience God's wrath. Victory and freedom were to be found in fully identifying with their crucified and risen Savior (cf. Romans 6:1–14).

Then they needed to set their hearts and minds on things above, where Christ was. Their values, their behavior, their total orientation needed to be based upon and centered on eternal things. Jesus was their life. Their lives were securely hidden with Christ in God. The ultimate proof of God's approval of their lives would be that when Christ returned, they would appear with Him in glory.

Christians today face similar challenges. The answer is not to yield to the pressure and temptation to seek some intriguing new philosophy or mystical experience, nor to yield to legalism or rigid religious practices. Jesus crucified, buried, raised, and seated at the Father's right hand is enough.

Those who do well in the Olympic games know the value of correct mental focus. It is not uncommon to see Olympic athletes close their eyes for a brief moment before their performance. They are visualizing precisely how they want their routine to proceed. In the victorious Christian life, we focus not on ourselves but on Jesus. We fully identify with His death, burial, and resurrection. We make it our own: "Set your minds on things above, not on earthly things" (3:2). We remember that His death for our sin must become our death to sin. We recognize our life as "hidden with Christ in God." If we will fix our minds on Him we will experience freedom and victory.

Change Your Spiritual Clothes (3:9–16)

Paul draws upon a common metaphor of human experience: the changing of clothes. He may have been drawing upon the imagery of clothing oneself with

---

3.1.1
OBJECTIVE

Explain what it means to identify with Jesus Christ.

1   What did Paul mean when he urged believers to identify with Christ's death, burial, and resurrection?

2   What does it mean to *"set your mind on things above"* (Colossians 3:2)?

3   What did Paul mean when he urged Christians to change their spiritual clothing?

armor for battle or the imagery he frequently used of putting on spiritual clothing (Romans 13:11–14; Ephesians 4:20–24) (Keener 1993, 578). The language used for that generic experience easily provides a picture of the spiritual realities represented in baptism: taking off dirty garments before baptism and putting on clean ones afterward (Romans 6:1–14) (O'Brien 1982, 189–90).

3.12
OBJECTIVE

List what Paul said should be put off and put on in the Christian's life.

Some Things Need to be Taken Off

The practices of the old self that need to be taken off are listed in verses 5 and 8.

Sexual Sin (Vaughan 1978, 212)

1. Sexual immorality: illicit sex–sexual activity outside of marriage (Rienecker 1980, 578).

2. Impurity: moral impurity in thought and imagination (Vaughan 1978, 212).

3. Lust: sexual desire which does not rest until it is satisfied. Burning passion (Rienecker 1980, 578).

4. Evil desires: a broader word describing all kinds of evil desires (Rienecker 1980, 578).

5. Greed: within this context, the word picks up sexual overtones, but applies to insatiable selfish desires of any kind (Rienecker 1980, 578).

Sins of Attitude and Speech that Are Inconsistent with the Christian Life

1. Anger and rage: words that describe the deep-seated, burning anger which smolders and then flares up with the intensity of a raging fire (Barton et al. 1995, 208).

2. Malice: a vicious attitude that contemplates doing harm to another (Rienecker 1980, 579).

3. Slander: an attempt to belittle another or to damage his or her reputation by what we say (Rienecker 1980, 579).

4. Filthy language: indecent, crude, dirty, lewd, or abusive language (Rienecker 1980, 579).

5. Lying: wrong at any time but is especially damaging to the trust and unity that ought to characterize the body of Christ (Exodus 20:16; Leviticus 19:11; Ephesians 4:25).

Paul teaches that these things are out of character for the person who has fully identified with Christ in His death, burial, and resurrection. They represent the old, dirty, inappropriate clothing of a former life.

Some Things Need to be Put On

The spiritual garments, the wardrobe of those having new life in Christ, are identified in verses 12–15.

1. Compassion: Christlike sensitivity and heartfelt sympathy for the welfare of others (Barton et al. 1995, 217).

2. Kindness: a friendly, helpful attitude that seeks to meet the needs of others through gracious deeds (Rienecker 1980, 580).

3. Humility: an attitude that recognizes one's own weaknesses but acknowledges the power of God (Rienecker 1980, 580).

4. Gentleness: an obedient yielding (**submission**) to God and His will that displays itself in a gentle attitude and kind acts to others, even in the face of provocation (Rienecker 1980, 580).

5. Patience: the ability to bear up under injustice or unpleasant circumstances without giving in to inappropriate conduct or the urge to retaliate (Rienecker 1980, 580).

6. Forbearance: a tolerant attitude toward another person.

7. Forgiveness: the complete forgiveness exhibited by Christ to each redeemed sinner.

8. Unifying love: authentic Christian love is pictured as a belt or sash that holds all of the spiritual garments in place (Barton 1995, 217).

9. Peace: the peace that is to characterize the Christian comes from God and guards the heart of the believer, protecting it from all that would disturb it or flow from it (Proverbs 4:23; Matthew 15:19) (Rienecker 1980, 580).

10. Thankfulness: a strikingly attractive attitude of expressed gratitude that characterizes authentic Christians.

11. The indwelling Word: the message of Christ, which is the focus of God's Word that was to fill their hearts. It also needed to dwell among them richly as a church.

12. Sharing: the mutual instruction and encouragement that characterize an authentic Christian community and each Christian in it.

13. A Singing Heart: spiritual songs of all kinds overflow from hearts of thanksgiving among those redeemed by God's grace.

This passage does not give us everything that could make up our spiritual wardrobe. It does, however, give us a representative glimpse of the kinds of character qualities a truly spiritual person will put on every day (cf. Galatians 5:22–23).

How we dress can influence our lives. It can prepare us for success or failure. For example, if you are applying for a job in an office, you would dress for the interview in business clothes. If you were applying for a construction job, you may dress another way. You need to look the part. The point is that sincere Christians seek to look the part. Nothing is more damaging to the cause of Christ than for people to say they are Christians and then not live as if they are. If you are going to say you are a Christian, then you must look the part.

Carry Out Every Activity in Christ's Name (3:17)

In conclusion, Paul urged the Colossian Christians to do everything in the name of the Lord Jesus, with thankfulness to God the Father. Everything a Christian does must be in dependence upon the Lord, in full recognition of His Lordship. We are to be His devoted followers (Vaughan 1978, 216). What a way to live!

It is not uncommon to hear of successful athletes dedicating a particular performance or an entire season to significant people in their lives. This may be a loving parent, a teammate who has been injured or died, or another person close to them. That person becomes the inspiration for the athlete's effort, the motivation for his or her success. Jesus Christ is this for every Christian. He died for our sins and rose again to give us new life. He is now in heaven, in a place of honor and authority at our heavenly Father's right hand, acting on our behalf (Romans 8:31–34; Hebrews 7:25). Because of this Jesus is the inspiration of our lives, the motivation for everything we say or do!

Is Jesus the inspiration of your life? Is He the motivation for every activity? Perhaps you have not been changed inside out by His power and presence. Perhaps you have not visited the Cross where He died to have your old life crucified there with Him. Maybe you have not visited the tomb where He was

3.1.3
OBJECTIVE

Explain what it means to do everything in the name of the Lord Jesus.

4   To your life, how would you apply Paul's challenge to do everything in the name of the Lord Jesus?

buried on your behalf. Have you ever thought of the resurrection as His victory that brings you new life? In Christ, there is an old way to abandon and a new way to live. Today you have the opportunity to choose to live all of life in His honor. Thinking this way, believing this way, brings incredible freedom and victory!

3.2.1
OBJECTIVE

Compare biblical house codes to those of the ancient world.

5   How do the house codes in the Bible compare to other codes in the ancient world?

Living the Christ-Life at Home (3:18–4:1)

It has been said, "It is sometimes easier to live for Christ in the marketplace than to live for Him at home." It seems we put on our best behavior when we are away from home. All day we feel the pressure to treat others with courtesy and consideration. Sometimes, however, when we return home after a busy day, we relax, let down our guard, and let family members see the dark side of our characters. Often the hardest place to practice our Christianity is at home.

Paul taught that what a person believes should make a difference in how he or she lives everyday life. He believed that correct doctrine should result in right living. For him, the relationships of life were the testing ground of authentic Christianity.

The point of this passage is that real Christians fulfill, and even surpass, the domestic obligations of their culture. They do it, however, for a higher motivation: allegiance to Jesus Christ. A commitment to serve the Lord has a positive impact on our relationships in the workplace and at home.

Bible scholars often refer to these verses as a *house code* or *haustafel* (a German theological term). Many examples of these kinds of ethical lists exist in the ancient world. Ephesians 5:21–6:9 and 1 Peter 2:13–3:12 are also examples. These lists were given to govern moral conduct within the ancient household (as well as in other contexts). The reference to slaves and masters in the lists reflects the ancient practice of viewing slaves as a part of the household.

Paul's lists given in the Epistles are different from their secular counterparts in at least two ways: (1) They are reciprocal or mutually beneficial in nature. They deal with the responsibilities of wives and husbands, children and parents, and slaves and masters and (2) They appeal to a different dynamic or motivation.

"Paul does not attempt to overthrow established practices, but "guides believers in how they should live in obedience to Christ within these fundamental social structures. He writes against behaviors that would bring discredit to Christ and the gospel and advocates behavior that will advance the testimony and freedom of believers living within those social structures" (Payne 2009, 272).

The Christian's relationship to Jesus Christ and not mere duty is the basis of Paul's appeal (Vaughan 1978, 217). In these verses Paul tells how knowing Jesus Christ makes a difference in the home and workplace.

3.2.2
OBJECTIVE

Define the submission in verse 18 that Paul urges wives to practice.

In Christ, a New Way of Looking at Submission (3:18)

Great care must be taken when dealing with passages about the male-female relationships, both in the church and in the home. One must keep in mind the principles taught by Paul in his letter, being careful not to insert traditional, religious, and societal interpretations where none is intended. Indeed, scholars and theologians cannot agree on the meaning of these and similar passages (Hull 1987, 183). Understanding must therefore come not only from the passage at hand, but from Paul's overall teaching and behavior in these matters, as well as the general principles of Scripture as a whole. Care must also be taken to remember the cultures of the New Testament world were vastly different from our modern culture. The principles of Scripture instruct us in righteousness, not the features and values of the ancient cultures. With these things in mind, we will continue our study of Paul's instructions to the believers at Colosse.

We sometimes find it difficult to grasp how God's laws drastically change relationships tainted by sin. Sin puts people at odds with one another; people may seek power over other people. The results are class wars, gender wars, and race wars. Only the laws of God can break the barriers raised by our struggle to dominate and rule one another.

6 How did Christ's love change the way wives in ancient days related to their husbands?

The lifesaving change God's law brought to marriages in the time of the Romans was that of mutual love and submission, the same law that governed relationships within the church. When love is at work, barriers come down, and the desire for control and power ceases to be an issue in relationships. A couple who are *in love* is a good example of this law at work. Each cannot do enough to please and serve the other. Each lives for the happiness of the other (Grady 2000, 177).

Marriage in Jewish culture in the time of the Romans usually was not the result of romantic love, but an arrangement for survival, for business, for gain. A woman's survival depended on being married. In a culture that placed little value on women, the emotional needs of a wife to be loved and valued often went unmet. Her status, as well as her unfulfilled needs, could engender bitterness and resentment toward the person who controlled her world—her husband. Submitting to her husband was necessary, but not necessarily genuine.

Paul is introducing a dramatic change in the way marriage is lived out, *based on the laws of Christ.* He has just listed the characteristics of the Christian, a person living out the nature of God. Now he turns to more specific application of these truths. How does the Christian lifestyle play out in family relationships?

Paul begins with wives. Because God's Spirit lives within her, a wife's

1. feelings about her husband will be those of love and a desire to please and serve his best interests.

2. submission will no longer be that of a person forced, by necessity, to yield to a greater power. Instead, it will be the natural outcome of a heart overflowing with Christ's love, a love that wants the best for the object of that love—her husband (Grady 2000, 177).

3. relationship with her husband will reflect the Christ-life at work in her.

Christ's Love, a New Way of Relating to Wives (3:19)

3.2.3
OBJECTIVE
Describe the kind of love in verse 19 that is expected of husbands.

After addressing wives, Paul turned to husbands.

Most marriages in Roman times were of convenience, business arrangements. Marriage provided the woman with protection and a place to live. Marriage provided the man with his wife's dowry and a means of having children who could work in the family fields. Women were not viewed as objects of love, and men typically found companionship and mental stimulation with other men, not their wives (Hull 1987, 196).

7 How would husbands' attitudes toward their wives change according to Paul?

Paul was introducing to husbands a new way—a redeemed way—of relating to their wives. This way was founded on love, not business, convenience or self-service. Instead of seeing their wives as their property, husbands were urged to see who their wives really were—human beings, made in the image of God, created for a loving, supportive relationship with their spouses.

Lovingly relating to a wife instead of using her as a means to an end, brought God's life to marriage. Marriage became a partnership, in Christ, ruled only by mutual love and submission. Issues would not be about who was in charge, but about serving one another and seeking to find the mind of Christ in all their decisions (Grady 2000, 178). The two became one, as God had intended in the beginning (Gill and Cavaness 2004, 161–163).

An incident is related of a husband and wife team teaching at a marriage seminar on the topic of mutual submission. When the question was asked, "What do you do when you do not agree on an issue, but a decision *must* be made? Then who is in charge?" Their reply was that in the many years of their marriage, because of their mutual love and respect for one another, there had never been an occasion in which one of them had the last word. They talked it out, listened to one another, deferred to one another, and always sought God's mind in the matter. It was not always easy, but it was always the right way to make a decision (Gill and Cavaness 2004, 166–167).

Christ Helps Children Obey Their Parents (3:20)

3.2.4
OBJECTIVE
Describe Paul's instructions to children.

Paul's counsel to children in the Christian home is obedience to parents in everything. A loving Christian parent certainly would make this easier, but it does not lessen the responsibility of the child (Robertson 1931, 506) Paul does not envision a situation where the wishes of a parent would run counter to God's will and authority. In such a case the child would have to respectfully appeal to a parent. If that failed, the child would have to submit to the ultimate authority of God (Matthew 10:34–37; Luke 12:51–53) (Bruce 1984, 165).

8   How was the parent-child relationship different for new believers in the ancient world?

We have all encountered obnoxious, rebellious, disrespectful children. A direct connection exists between the lordship of Jesus and obedience to parents. A child who finds it difficult to submit to the authority of a parent will also find it difficult to submit to the Father in heaven.

Christ Helps Parents Care for Their Children (3:21)

3.2.5
OBJECTIVE
Explain the responsibility of parents to children.

Sometimes children exhibit an uncanny ability to frustrate and infuriate parents. Parents may retaliate with incessant nagging, belittling speech, angry voices, and even physical abuse. These things do nothing but embitter and discourage children. They lose their self-respect and give up.

Children raised in this way act like cowering puppies. They are afraid of everything. Their faith and confidence are fragile. They find it difficult to trust anyone, including God. Responding to their Heavenly Father's love is nearly impossible. Their lives are characterized by psychological wounds and deep spiritual damage. How different it is when they experience loving discipline and nurture. Again it is clear—Jesus makes a difference. His presence makes the difference in how we parent our children.

Christ Helps People Serve Faithfully (3:22–25)

3.2.6
OBJECTIVE
Define how Paul's challenge to slaves and masters would apply in today's culture.

Keep in mind that Paul's instruction is given in a cultural setting where slavery was institutionalized. Slaves were considered part of the household. Many served as educators, childcare providers, accountants, and in other strategic areas of responsibility. They held positions of responsibility, but had few rights (Vaughan 1978, 219).

Do not let the words *slave* and *master* throw you. They were simply terms used to describe the general employment situation of the time. The faithfulness and work ethic of these slaves were an important witness for Christ.

Notice four points Paul makes:

1. Christians in the workplace must demonstrate godly behavior.

Slaves were to obey their masters in everything. The only exception would be if they were asking them to do something that was illegal, immoral, or in direct violation of biblical teaching.

2. Christians in the workplace must do their work well.

Paul urged these workers to do quality work with sincere hearts. They should do quality work not only when they were watched, but at all times. They should do all their work to please the Lord. The way we work either validates or discredits the gospel.

3. Christians in the workplace must have the right attitude.

What we do must be done for the Lord, not just for other humans. "Sincerity of heart" speaks of integrity. "Reverence for Christ" implies being continually conscious of God. We must work with the right attitude.

4. Christians in the workplace must keep the heavenly reward foremost in their minds.

When we get to heaven, we will not receive a reward based only on what we did at church. We will also be rewarded for what took place on the job.

I worked in construction one summer. One of the guys on the crew worked only when the foreman was around. At other times he was usually goofing off. I did not listen to much of anything he had to say. He turned off everyone around him. Everyone resented him. It is no different for the person who claims to be a Christian but is a slacker on the job.

Christ Helps Bosses Supervise Considerately (4:1)

9 How does Paul's challenge to masters apply in your culture?

What about the masters of these slaves? How about bosses, period? Should Jesus make a difference in the way bosses supervise their employees? Yes. Paul urges them to keep two things in mind: (1) Though in the Roman world slaves had no rights, Paul did not hesitate to tell Christian masters they must do what was right by those who worked for them (Vaughan 1978, 219) and (2) He goes on to reminds these masters that they too have a master—a "Master in heaven." With Him "there is no favoritism" (Ephesians 6:9).

10 How would following the guidelines of mutual respect, love, and submission impact any contemporary culture for Christ?

Think of how these principles, if practiced consistently within a culture, would impact it. Christian marriages would be stronger than their secular counterparts. Christian homes would produce respectful, obedient, loving, emotionally healthy children with deep convictions and a sense of purpose. Christian employees would be sought after, and Christian employers would have the best applicants from which to choose. Jesus Christ would be honored and the gospel would spread. "In every way they will make the teaching about God our Savior attractive" (Titus 2:10). Jesus makes a difference in people's lives!

LESSON 3.3

Closing Challenges, Observations, and Greetings (4:2–18)

Paul's concern for the Christians in the small community of Colosse had run its full course. Although he had never personally met these believers, one of his converts, Epaphras, was their founding pastor. He had brought Paul a report of their spiritual stability as well as the challenges they were facing. Paul's letter to them is filled with apostolic concern. He tells them that he prays for their spiritual welfare daily. He does not want anyone to take advantage of them, bring them into bondage, or lead them astray. He deals with the key issues they were facing. Now he closes his apostolic letter to them with a few concluding challenges, final observations and closing greetings. His closing remarks to the church in Colosse remind us of four central components.

Prayer for One Another Is Important (4:2–3)

3.3.1
OBJECTIVE
Explain what it means to devote oneself to prayer.

Paul challenges these believers to devote themselves to prayer. The Greek word he uses here, translated "devote yourselves," is used ten times in the New Testament and emphasizes strength of resolve, persistence, and giving close attention to something (Vaughan 1978, 221). He does not simply urge them to practice devotional prayer, that is, prayer that contributes to one's own spiritual welfare; he urges them to participate in intercessory prayer—prayer as ministry, prayer for others. He urges them to be alert for opportunities for such prayer (cf. Ephesians 6:18) and encourages them to saturate their praying with thanksgiving (Philippians 4:6).

11   What does it mean to devote oneself to prayer?

How dedicated are you to intercessory prayer? What occupies your praying? Is it your needs and concerns (legitimate as they may be) or is it the cause of Christ, the needs of others, and the spreading of the gospel? Do you watch for intercessory opportunities? Is your heart filled with gratitude to God as you pray?

Dr. Delmer Guynes, a great missionary statesman, for years has challenged Christians to practice selfless prayer. He has also modeled it. I remember hearing him passionately plead with a congregation: "You can ask for a house; but you can't take that to heaven with you. You can pray for a car, but you will leave that behind, too." Then he wrapped his arms around a globe that he had brought to the podium, as he challenged his audience with these words: "Get your eyes off yourself. Pray for the needs of others. Intercede for the world. You can take them to heaven with you!"

Proclamation of the Gospel Is Critical (4:3–4)

3.3.2
OBJECTIVE
Explain the importance of prayer to the continued proclamation of the gospel.

Paul recognized the importance of the gospel being continually proclaimed without hindrance. Although he was in prison in Rome, he never felt the gospel was chained (2 Timothy 2:8–9). In fact, in his letter to the Philippians he claimed his imprisonment had actually provided an opportunity to reach "Caesar's household" with the gospel (Philippians 1:12–18). Then he asked the congregation in Colosse to pray that God would open new doors for the message of the gospel and that God would help him proclaim it clearly.

12   In what ways have you seen prayer impact the spreading of the gospel?

Nothing can hinder the gospel. In God's plan and purpose it will go forth. It breaks down barriers, demolishes spiritual strongholds, sets people free, and transforms lives, communities, and nations! How important it is that we pray for open doors for the gospel and the success of those who proclaim it.

13   What imagery does Paul use to emphasize the importance he places on making the most of every opportunity?

For years, faithful Christians asked God to destroy the iron curtain of communism that blocked open access to the gospel in the Soviet bloc. They asked God to sustain, protect, and enable believers to witness in that land. China, too, seemed an impenetrable barrier. Little was known about the welfare and vitality of the church there. The prayers of God's people were answered. A miracle took place and the walls came down. The Soviet bloc was opened to the gospel. Incredible reports of the success and vitality of the persecuted church in China were reported. God had again been faithful. It pays to pray.

3.3.3
OBJECTIVE

Explain what Paul meant when he said, "Make the most of every opportunity."

14 In what ways have you seen the daily lives of Christians help or hinder the spread of the gospel?

3.3.4
OBJECTIVE

List key people Paul mentions in 4:7–18, and describe their contribution to his ministry.

Public Life Is an Important Witness (4:5–6)

Paul also recognized the importance of the consistent Christian living and witness of the Colossian believers. He urged them to "make the most of every opportunity," seizing each for the sake of sharing the life-giving message of Christ Jesus. Paul also challenged the believers to be careful about their everyday conversation. He considered the quality of their lives and graciousness of their words as important to the success and spread of the gospel as his own apostolic mission.

Your daily life is important to the Lord. Unbelievers watch Christians closely. They listen to our words. If we are sensitive to the Spirit's leading, we will have daily opportunities to minister to needs and share Christ. Think of yourself as an ambassador for the King of kings, Jesus Christ (2 Corinthians 5:18–20). You represent Him and His kingdom. Your task is to make the most of every opportunity to further the cause of Christ in your neighborhood and world.

Personal Friends Encourage and Challenge Us (4:7–18)

In the final verses of this letter, Paul informs the Colossian congregation about the task he has given those who will deliver his letter. He passes on greetings from several key members of his ministry team, as well as a number of key leaders of the church in Colosse.

At the close of a movie, it is traditional to see the names of those who have played a role in its production scroll across the screen. Paul recognized that the success of his apostolic ministry depended on others. He knew the work of God was not a one-person show. It is almost as if he is rolling credits at the end of his letter. Paul spotlights ten individuals who have played a central role in the success of his ministry.

1. Tychicus—The Person with a Servant's Heart

On several occasions, Tychicus willingly tackled difficult assignments for the apostle Paul (Acts 20:1–5; Ephesians 6:21–22; 2 Timothy 4:12; Titus 3:12). In this case, we find him taking Paul's letter across many miles to Colosse and other churches in Asia Minor. There was no complaint, just the faithful expression of a servant's heart. Could it be that the apostle Paul accomplished so much for God because of people like Tychicus?

2. Onesimus—The Person with a Sinful Past

Onesimus had been a runaway slave. He had worked for a Christian in Colosse named Philemon. Onesimus wanted his freedom, so he stole money from Philemon and ran away. In ancient culture this was a serious crime. But in Rome, Onesimus met the apostle Paul and was saved. Now Paul calls Onesimus "a faithful and dear brother" (v. 9). When a person comes to Christ, their past is no longer an issue. You may have been the worst person in the world, but if you have come to Christ, God can use you.

3. Aristarchus—The Person with a Sympathetic Heart

Aristarchus was a Jewish believer from Thessalonica (Acts 19:28–29; 20:1–5; 27:1–2). Aristarchus stuck with Paul through thick and thin. For four years he stayed close to Paul in prison, encouraging him and ministering to his needs. Every Christian leader needs a faithful helper like Aristarchus.

4. Mark—The Person with a Second Chance

John Mark had a different beginning to his ministry career. He started out as part of Paul's ministry team, but apparently things got too tough for him. He left the team and returned home (Acts 13:5, 13). This angered Paul and he refused to take him along on the next missionary journey (Acts 15:36–40). Now several years later, we find Mark a changed man and restored to usefulness. Paul told the Colossians that if Mark came, they needed to listen to him. Perhaps you have made a glaring mistake in the past—you had your chance to succeed and failed. The good news is that God gives His servants second chances!

5. Justus—The Person with a Strong Commitment

Nothing is known about Justus other than the information we have in verse 11. It is possible he was one of the Roman Jews who believed Paul's message when he preached in Rome. Paul was severely criticized by the Jews. Justus was not afraid of criticism. He was a person of strong commitment. How encouraging it must have been to have someone like Justus on his team!

6. Epaphras—The Person with a Powerful Prayer Life

Epaphras was the founder of the Colossian church. Here he was with Paul in Rome, "wrestling in prayer" for those in Colosse and "working hard" on their behalf. The Greek word translated "wrestling" is *agonizomai* from which we get our English word "agony" (O'Brien 1982, 253). Every church needs individuals like Epaphras who pray fervently for the church and its needs.

7. Luke—The Person with Dedicated Talent

Luke was Paul's personal physician as well as his close friend. We do not know a lot about Luke's background. We do know Luke surrendered what might have been a lucrative practice to serve the Lord with his talent. In return, God gave him the privilege of writing a significant part of the New Testament (Luke and Acts). God may call you to sacrificially dedicate your skills or vocation to His work. What a privilege! What an opportunity! You never lose by serving God.

8. Demas—The Person with a Sad Future

Demas is listed as one of Paul's ministry associates. Later, this man turned out to be a disappointment to Paul (2 Timothy 4:9–10). He abandoned Paul; he defected because of his love for the world. The point is this: An individual can serve with great distinction and dedication at one point and still lose out. We must guard our hearts.

9. Nympha—The Person Who Was Willing to Open Her Home

Nympha is singled out by Paul because of her willingness to open her home to a small gathering of believers. Meeting in homes was a common practice in the early church (Acts 16:15; Romans 16:5; Philemon 1:2). Would you be willing to use your home for the Lord's work?

10. Archippus—The Person Who Needed Encouragement to Finish Well

Archippus started well. He was filled with enthusiasm and vision. God had given him a task and a calling. But Paul saw the signs and it concerned him. Archippus was letting up. Paul said, "Complete the work you have received in the Lord." In a race, awards are not for those who start fast but those who finish well.

15 What will you do to see that the gospel continues to be preached at home and around the world?

Are you willing to dedicate yourself to the Lord's work in your church and community? Will you give yourself to intercessory prayer? Will you do everything in your power to see that the gospel continues to be preached at home and around the world? Will you dedicate yourself to living a consistent Christian life and sharing the gospel with others as the Lord gives you opportunity? How do you think God wants to use your gifts and abilities to make the ministry of your pastor and church more effective? Everyone has a valuable part to play in the success of God's work.

Test Yourself

Circle the letter of the *best* answer.

1. Since the Colossian believers had been raised with Christ (Colossians 3:1–3), Paul instructs them to
a) flee the youthful lusts of the flesh.
b) stand strong in the face of affliction.
c) set their hearts and minds upon things above.
d) pray in the Spirit at all times.

2. According to the IST, compassion is
a) a friendly, helpful attitude that seeks to meet the needs of others.
b) an obedient submission to God and His will that leads to a good attitude and kind acts.
c) a Christ-like sensitivity and heartfelt sympathy for the welfare of others.
d) an attitude that recognizes our own weaknesses.

3. According to Colossians 3:16, what richness should dwell in the lives of believers?
a) The peace of Christ
b) Joy
c) The word of Christ
d) Gentleness

4. In Colossians 3:17, Paul instructs believers to do all things, whether in word or deed,
a) in the name of Jesus, with thanksgiving to God.
b) without mumbling or complaining.
c) for the glory of God.
d) for the sake of winning a crown.

5. The biblical house codes listed in Colossians 3 are different from those of the ancient world because they are
a) mutual in nature and listed in sequential order.
b) reciprocal and different in motivation.
c) listed in sequential order and different in motivation.
d) different in motivation and exclusive only to Christianity.

6. The greatest enemy of submission in the marriage relationship is
a) work.
b) sin.
c) cultural upbringing.
d) personality.

7. In Colossians 3, Paul's instruction to wives is to
a) love their husbands and try to submit.
b) respect their husbands in public.
c) serve their husbands for peace's sake.
d) submit to their husbands in the love of Christ.

8. In Colossians 3, Paul's instruction to servants is to
a) respect their masters.
b) work as though working for the Lord.
c) rejoice in their freedom in Christ.
d) peacefully fight for their freedom and deliverance.

9. Mark was a person with a
a) sympathetic heart.
b) strong commitment.
c) second chance.
d) servant's heart.

10. Who does Paul mention in Colossians as having had a powerful prayer life?
a) Tychicus
b) Epaphras
c) Justus
d) Archippus

Responses to Interactive Questions
CHAPTER 3

Some of these responses may include information that is supplemental to the IST. These questions are intended to produce reflective thinking beyond the course content and your responses may vary from these examples.

1 What did Paul mean when he urged believers to identify with Christ's death, burial, and resurrection?

Believers needed to put to death what belonged to their old life of sin and unbelief. Then they needed to set their minds on the things of God.

2 What does it mean to "set your mind on things above" (Colossians 3:2)?

Believers needed to base their values, behavior, orientation on eternal things.

3 What did Paul mean when he urged Christians to change their spiritual clothing?

The practices of the sinful self needed to be taken off or ended. Spiritual garments need to be put on. These refer to the character qualities of Christ, such as compassion, kindness, humility, gentleness, submission to God, patience, forbearance, and forgiveness.

4 To your own life, how would you apply Paul's challenge to do everything in the name of the Lord Jesus?

Answers may include: Jesus is the inspiration and motivation for everything the believer does.

5 How do the house codes in the Bible compare to other codes in the ancient world?

Many examples of lists for ethical behavior existed in the ancient world. They were developed to govern moral conduct within the ancient household. The lists in the Bible are different from their secular counterparts in at least two ways: They are reciprocal or mutual in nature, dealing with the responsibilities of both wives and husbands, children and parents, slaves and masters. The biblical lists also appeal to a different motivation for the behavior. The Christian's relationship to Jesus Christ, not mere duty, is the reason for abiding by the guidelines.

6 How did Christ's love change the way wives in ancient days related to their husbands?

In ancient cultures, women submitted to their husbands because they had no choice. They were considered inferior beings, basically their husbands' property. To survive, wives needed a husband to provide for her. When Christ filled her heart, a wife's submission grew out of love for her husband and a desire to meet his needs. Her willingness to defer to her husband was voluntary and spontaneous, the result of Christ's love.

7 How would husbands' attitudes toward their wives change according to Paul?

Instead of viewing his wife as his property and as a means to a dowry and children, the husband would love his wife. He too would be willing to defer to his wife to see that her needs for love and relationship were met.

8 How was the parent–child relationship different for new believers in the ancient world?

A child's value as a human being was greatly increased. While the child was to respectfully submit to his or her parents' tutoring, parents were to value the child and take care not to allow harshness to embitter the child.

9 How does Paul's challenge to masters apply in our culture?

Christians in the workplace must demonstrate godly behavior, do their work well, have right attitudes, and keep in mind their heavenly reward. Christian employers must do right by their employees. They should remember that they too have a Master in heaven who shows no favoritism.

10 How would following the guidelines of mutual respect, love, and submission impact any contemporary culture for Christ?

Christian marriages would be stronger than their secular counterparts. Christian homes would produce respectful, obedient, loving, emotionally healthy children with deep convictions and a sense of purpose. Christian employees would be sought after, and Christian employers would have the best applicants from which to choose. Jesus Christ would be honored and the gospel would spread. His teachings would be made attractive.

11 What does it mean to devote oneself to prayer?

Paul challenged the believers to strength of resolve, persistence, and close attention in intercessory prayer as ministry. He urges them to pray for the needs of others and the spreading of the gospel.

12 In what ways have you seen prayer impact the spreading of the gospel?

Answers will vary.

13 What imagery does Paul use to emphasize the importance he places on making the most of every opportunity?

Paul thought of each opportunity to share the gospel as a once in a lifetime purchase to be bought up for the Lord Jesus Christ.

14 In what ways have you seen the daily lives of Christians help or hinder the spread of the gospel?

Answers will vary.

15 What will you do to see that the gospel continues to be preached at home and around the world?

Answers will vary.

Introducing Philemon (Philemon vv. 1–25)

What goes through your mind when you see a homeless person or hear about a runaway? We hear about and see more and more of these individuals and we ask ourselves, "What circumstances in their lives caused their situations? Was it a bad childhood, poor choices, criminal activity, a life of addiction, lack of ability, or even personal choice?" Interviews with these people reveal a great variety of reasons for what has happened to them. There are family conflicts, personal failures, physical disabilities, and criminal behaviors, to name just a few.

The apostle Paul was considering the influence and impact of some very difficult circumstances touching a fellow believer when he wrote this letter to a man named Philemon, a Christian slave owner. It was neither an official letter nor a corrective letter; such as those Paul is known to have written to churches throughout the Roman Empire. This letter was quite different.

Of all Paul's writings, his letter to Philemon is the most intimate and personal (Fee and Stuart 1993, 46–49). Paul is appealing to Philemon on behalf of this master's runaway slave. His words are characterized by personal warmth and vulnerability, as well as the tact and diplomacy that distinguish them. Forgiveness and **restoration** are the key themes of this epistle.

- *Read Philemon before you begin study in this chapter.*

Lesson 4.1   Understanding Philemon (vv. 1–25)

Objectives
4.1.1   Summarize the key elements of the circumstances behind the epistle.
4.1.2   Describe the purpose of Paul's letter to Philemon.
4.1.3   List and explain the importance of the major themes in Philemon.

Lesson 4.2   Paul's Appreciation of Philemon (vv. 1–7)

Objectives
4.2.1   Describe how Paul emphasizes the importance of relationships within the family of believers in vv. 1–3.
4.2.2   Identify and explain the importance of the godly character qualities Paul gives thanks for in this passage.
4.2.3   Summarize what Paul is praying for in v. 6.

Lesson 4.3   Paul's Appeal on Behalf of Onesimus (vv. 8–25)

Objective
4.3.1   List and explain five principles of forgiveness taught in Paul's letter to Philemon.

Understanding Philemon (vv. 1–25)

People are separated by many barriers: race, color, culture, nationality, experience, economics, possessions, education, social status, gender, religion, abilities, or the lack thereof. These imposed categories become very real prisons of prejudice, stereotype, and expectation. We judge people based upon them, sorting them out and putting them in their places.

Jesus tore down all such barriers through His sacrifice on the Cross (Ephesians 2:14–16). He sought out, accepted, and forgave sinners. He ignored prejudice by associating with Samaritans. He welcomed outcasts. He loved the entire world.

Paul was like his Lord in that regard. He became the apostle to the nations (the Gentiles). He shared the life-changing message of the gospel with all types of people. He made the revolutionary declaration, "There is neither Jew nor Greek, slave nor free, male nor female, for you are all one in Christ Jesus" (Galatians 3:28).

Paul's letter to Philemon is probably one of the greatest biblical examples of the power of the gospel to break down barriers. It is a personal letter from Paul urging **reconciliation** and forgiveness between two of his friends who exist on opposite ends of the social ladder. It reveals a true Christian leader willingly filling the role of advocate and reconciler. It urges someone with power to demonstrate Christ-like forgiveness and **grace** to a person without power. It makes the point that Christ-like character is proven by Christian grace.

The Circumstances Behind Philemon

Philemon was a wealthy slave owner who lived in Colosse, a city of ancient Asia Minor. He had probably come to Christ under Paul's ministry to the church in Ephesus (v. 19). Paul and Epaphras had probably discipled him. He was a key leader in the church at Colosse, the church that met in his home (v. 2).

We do not know what prompted it, but Onesimus, one of Philemon's slaves, ran away. He apparently also stole household goods or money from his master (which may have been a substantial amount considering that Paul felt the need to write with his own hand a pledge of indebtedness for all that was lost to Philemon). In ancient culture this was a serious offense. Treatment of slaves varied widely, depending on the temperament of the slave-owner and the role of responsibility of the slave. Runaway slaves were sometimes branded on the forehead. Onesimus, if captured, could have been beaten severely, jailed, or even killed.

Slavery was institutionalized in the Roman world. The economy depended upon slave labor. Slaves fulfilled all kinds of roles in Roman society, from the most menial to those of great responsibility. They were field workers, cooks, accountants, educators, personal attendants, and managers of estates. Some estimate that as much as 85 to 90 percent of the inhabitants of Italy were slaves (Barton et al. 1995, 244). To lose a slave was to lose a sizable investment.

After escaping, Onesimus apparently wanted to lose himself in a large metropolitan area, and so he headed for Rome. We do not know how the paths of Paul and Onesimus may have crossed initially, but it could have been through Epaphras, pastor of the congregation in Colosse. Epaphras would have known both Philemon and Onesimus. Epaphras may have happened upon Onesimus in the city, recognized him, and brought him to Paul because he knew Paul would try to help him (Bruce 1984, 197).

4.1.1
OBJECTIVE
Summarize the key elements of the circumstances behind the epistle.

1   Who was Philemon? What was his relationship to Paul?

2   Who was Onesimus and what did he do?

3 What did Paul decide to do about Onesimus' situation?

At any rate, Onesimus heard the gospel from Paul. He received Christ's forgiveness and made Him Lord and Savior of his life (v. 10). Onesimus was discipled by Paul. He demonstrated his faithfulness and became a valuable aide in Paul's ministry.

Paul, however, faced a dilemma. He would have liked to have kept Onesimus in his service, but he had a social and legal obligation. Harboring a runaway slave was a serious offense. Paul talked with Onesimus about his responsibility as a Christian to return to Philemon. He then wrote a letter to Philemon, appealing for the forgiveness and **restoration** of Onesimus (vv. 17–21). It is believed that Paul sent Onesimus back with Tychicus along with this letter and the letter to the Colossians (Colossians 4:7–9).

The Purpose of Philemon

4.1.2
OBJECTIVE

Describe the purpose of Paul's letter to Philemon.

This letter to Philemon is unique among Paul's letters. It is a "letter of recommendation," the kind patrons wrote to social peers or inferiors on behalf of various individuals in order to ask a favor for them (Keener 1993, 644). Many examples of similar letters exist, both pagan and Christian, from the Graeco-Roman (also spelled Greco-Roman) world. Philemon is of the type used on behalf of a delinquent slave (Rupprecht 1978, 458).

Paul was the master of diplomacy and tact. The letter is filled with courteous and disarming language. He exhibits a knack for diversion when introducing his appeal in verse 10 and not completing it until verse 17 (Patzia 1993, 704).

Paul asks Philemon to forgive and reconcile Onesimus to his household without punishment. He also hints strongly that it would be nice if Onesimus were freed so he could be of ongoing service to Paul. But nowhere does Paul ask openly for that. Paul does not appeal to Philemon because he has the authority of an apostle, but because they both love Christ (v. 9) and they have a good relationship (vv. 17–19). Paul wanted to make a strong case, but he wanted the response to be voluntary (v. 14). He wanted Philemon's decision to be one of conviction, not compulsion (Patzia 1993, 704).

Philemon's response to Paul's appeal for Onesimus is unknown. But it is fair to believe that this letter would not have been preserved by the church if it had not achieved its intended goal (Bruce 1984, 200).

The Key Themes of Philemon

4.1.3
OBJECTIVE

List and explain the importance of the major themes in Philemon.

This small, but personal, letter from Paul emphasizes at least three key themes:

1. The Power of the Gospel to Break Down Barriers (vv. 10–16)

The most unique aspect of this situation, though a common occurrence in Paul's day, is the particular approach the apostle asks the owner to take as his response. Paul, an apostle, was in prison. He wrote to Philemon, a wealthy landowner, asking that he forgive, restore, and perhaps free his runaway slave who had stolen some of his property. The social dynamics of that ancient culture would have made such a request absurd, even ludicrous. But Paul made his appeal within the dynamics of another culture—that of the life-transforming and wall-shattering power of the gospel.

In Christ we are one family. No walls of racial, economic, political, social, or gender differences can be permitted to divide us. Christians must recognize this and work to remove such barriers. Paul did not directly seek to end slavery, but the gospel and the values it brought to people's lives eventually did.

2. The Importance of Complete Forgiveness and Restoration (vv. 17–21)

4   Based upon Roman law, what could Philemon have done to Onesimus?

Philemon had certain rights under Roman law. His servant had run away, absconding with his property. He had every right to pursue him, capture him, and punish him. Paul, upon finding Onesimus, had a responsibility under Roman law to turn Onesimus in to the authorities or see to it that he was returned to his owner. Philemon had the power; Onesimus was powerless. Philemon was the one wronged; Onesimus was the guilty party.

Paul's appeal to Philemon was counter to Roman lifestyle. In the Christian lifestyle his appeal fit how believers lived. Paul asked for complete forgiveness and restoration. He even went so far as to imply Philemon should free Onesimus.

When we have been wronged, it is culturally normal to protest, "This is wrong! I have rights!" But Christ's example and the dynamics of the gospel call for complete forgiveness and restoration. Who has wronged you? What will you do?

3. The Value of Mutual Friendship and Respect Within the Church (vv. 4–9, 21–25)

5   How was the way Paul dealt with Philemon a good example for us to follow?

Paul was responsible for Philemon's coming to Christ. He was a spiritual father to Philemon. It was likely that Paul's modeling had influenced Philemon's role as a Christian leader. But he had also come across his runaway slave and personally prayed with that slave to receive Christ. Paul's friendship with Philemon and his influence upon him are critical issues in this letter. Paul chose the route of influence and appeal over apostolic coercion, setting a marvelous example for the church today.

Interpersonal relationships, the *one another* dimension of the gospel, are vitally important. We must recognize how essential our relationships are in Christ. We must value them, nurture them, and use them redemptively and wisely.

Pastor Randy Frazee tells a story that has some of the dynamics found in Paul's letter to Philemon.

> I remember seeing a picture of a husband and wife in a gentleman's office. I said, "Nice picture," and when I turned around and looked at the man, I noticed that he had tears in his eyes. I asked him, "Why are you crying?"

> He said, "There was a time in our marriage when I was unfaithful to my wife, and she found out about it. She was so deeply hurt and injured she was going to leave me and take the kids with her. I was overwhelmed at the mistake I had made, and I shut the affair down. I went to my wife in total brokenness. Knowing I did not deserve for her to answer in the affirmative, I asked her to forgive me. And she forgave me.

> "This picture was taken shortly after that. When I see this picture, I see a woman who forgave me. I see a woman who was willing to stand with me in this picture. So when you see this picture you say, 'Nice picture.' But when I see this picture, I see my life given back to me again (Frazee 2001)."

May we have the grace to forgive as Philemon did, the courage to ask forgiveness as Onesimus did, and the leadership to work for reconciliation as Paul did.

As we look more closely at this unique letter we consider the following breakdown of the contents of *The Epistle to Philemon* and hopefully discover why this epistle has been crowned as one of the greatest examples of the power of the gospel to break down barriers found in the Bible.

The Outline of Philemon

I.   Christian Greetings to a Friend and His Family (vv. 1–3)

II. Thanksgiving and Prayer for a Christian Friend (vv. 4–7)

III. An Appeal for Forgiveness and Restoration (vv. 8–22)

IV. Final Greetings (vv. 23–25)

Paul's Appreciation of Philemon (vv. 1–7)

The local church is a fellowship of believers. Christians separated by miles, nations, cultures, color, gender, and even denominations are part of a divine fellowship (1 John 1:3–7). The New Testament uses the language for family relationships to describe relationships between believers, that is, in Christ we are made *brothers* and *sisters*. Consequently, we dare not overlook the importance of interpersonal relationships in the Lord (1 John 4:19–21). At any and every point of disharmony, reconciliation becomes a prominent issue (Matthew 5:23–24). Jesus declared that the world at large would know we were His disciples because of the quality of our love for one another (John 13:34–35). Time spent fostering love and unity among fellow Christians is never wasted.

At the outset of Paul's letter to Philemon on behalf of Onesimus, the strong relationships he has developed within the body of Christ become evident. The quality and depth of these relationships is the basis for Paul's appeal to Philemon for the forgiveness and reconciliation of Onesimus, the runaway slave who has wronged his owner.

Paul opens his letter by blessing Philemon, his family, and the Christians who worship with them. He thanks God for their godly character. He prays for the practical expression of their faith in ways that demonstrate authentic fellowship to the world. In verses 1–7 of this short letter, Paul demonstrates an important truth: Christian friends genuinely appreciate one another and want God's best for each other.

Paul's words show us that as fellow Christians we should do some very definite things to maintain Christian fellowship.

Bless One Another with Christian Greetings (vv. 1–3)

OBJECTIVE

Describe how Paul emphasizes the importance of relationships within the family of believers in vv. 1–3.

6 How should Christians demonstrate authentic fellowship toward one another?

Each of the phrases in verses 1 and 2 emphasizes the value Paul places on relationships within the family of believers. He begins by taking a secular greeting (which would have been expressed as "greetings" in Greek and "peace" or *Shalom* among Jews) and *Christianizes* it so it summarizes what they enjoy together in Christ, "Grace and peace to you from God our Father and the Lord Jesus Christ."

These people are dear to Paul. He loves them, and they enjoy a fellowship in Christ that is worth nurturing and fighting for. Paul describes himself as a prisoner for the cause of Christ. Timothy, Paul's close associate, is described as "our brother." Philemon is characterized as "a dear friend and fellow worker." Apphia, probably Philemon's wife or a close relative who helped manage his household, is greeted as "our sister." Archippus, who may have been Philemon's son or an elder in the Colossian church (cf. Colossians 4:17) is described as "our fellow soldier" in spiritual warfare. And finally, the entire church "that meets in your house" is greeted.

As fellow Christians we should always acknowledge the deep and unique relationship we have in Christ. Our relationship runs deeper than natural family ties. It is a relationship of the Spirit brought about by our shared family bond "in Christ" (Matthew 12:48–50; Ephesians 2:11–22, especially verse 19). We, appropriately, have uniquely Christian ways to greet and bless one another when we meet, correspond, or share fellowship.

I remember a hiking vacation my wife and I enjoyed in the Colorado Rockies. It was wonderful! Every morning we would leave our cabin and spend as much time as we could exploring the marvelous trails near Cuchara, Colorado. We spent time just taking in the breathtaking scenery, wonderful wildlife, and refreshing mountain air—what could be better? How about Christian fellowship? One morning we were trying to find a picturesque mountain lake we had heard was nestled among the trees. We stopped to ask directions from a couple we met on the trail. There was something about the way they greeted us that caught my attention. I felt prompted to ask if they were believers, and they were! What refreshing and uplifting fellowship we enjoyed with a brother and sister in Christ that morning!

Thank God for Each Other's Godly Character (vv. 4–5, 7)

4.2.2
OBJECTIVE

Identify and explain the importance of the godly character qualities Paul gives thanks for in this passage.

7 What character qualities in Philemon's life does Paul give thanks for? Why are these qualities important?

Paul sets an example in the letter to Philemon with his repeated expressions of thanksgiving offered to God for the godly character that is shown in the lives of fellow believers. He responds with, "I always thank my God . . . because I hear about *your faith* in the Lord Jesus and *your love* for all the saints" (emphasis added). Paul had received a good report about Philemon. He also knew Philemon's character firsthand. Faith and love are core character qualities of a believer worthy of giving thanks for.

Verse 7 continues the thought of verses 4 and 5, giving further information about what has prompted Paul's thanksgiving. Paul does not explain what "deeds of love" Philemon has done. He simply describes the effect—it had "refreshed" the hearts of God's people on many occasions (O'Brien 1982, 282). Philemon's love for others has brought "great joy and encouragement" to Paul who is far off in prison in Rome. Paul probably emphasizes these qualities in hope that they will be expressed to Onesimus (O'Brien 1982, 282).

Christians experience joy, not only when they are benefited or blessed by others but when they witness the expression of godly character in the lives of others. They rejoice at faith that stands strong in personal crisis, faith that trusts God through difficulty, faith that endures through disappointment. They rejoice in love shown to an enemy, love that gives life and possessions to spread the gospel, the self-giving love of a parent and spouse, the unconditional love of a friend, and the forgiving love given freely in spite of wrongs suffered.

Albert Einstein stated: "A hundred times a day I remind myself that my inner and outer life depends on the labors of other men, living and dead, and that I must exert myself in order to give in the measure as I have received and am still receiving" (Einstein n.d.).

Paul recognized and responded to this great truth in his thanksgiving for Philemon. Let us recognize and respond to it when we observe the godly character flowing out of the lives of so many fellow Christians to enrich and bless us all.

Pray for the Practical Expression of Our Faith to Others (v. 6)

4.2.3
OBJECTIVE

Summarize what Paul is praying for in v. 6.

8 What did Paul pray that God would do in Philemon's life?

Finally, in a verse that is notoriously difficult to translate, Paul prays for the practical expression of Philemon's faith to others. A comparison of several translations will reveal the challenge of translating this verse. The New International Version reads: "I pray that you may be active in sharing your faith, so that you will have a full understanding of every good thing we have in Christ." A literal translation of the Greek text might read: "So that the fellowship of your faith may become effective in the full knowledge of every good thing in us for Christ."

After all the interpretational issues have been considered and sorted out, Paul's prayer is that Philemon's faith will show itself practically in an expression of *koinonia* (the Greek word for true fellowship and sharing) within the body of Christ. This will either lead to or lead from an awareness of every good thing that is ours in Christ.

James teaches us that faith without works is dead. Faith is to be demonstrated by our works (James 2:14–18). Paul believed that faith needed to express itself within the fellowship of believers and through the fellowship of believers. Paul prayed that Philemon would experience what he had prayed for other believers in several of his other epistles: "A full understanding of every good thing we have in Christ" (cf. Ephesians 1:18; Philippians 1:9; Colossians 1:9). This understanding could either be the cause of the good works or the result of them. Onesimus was about to return home. He wanted Philemon to forgive, restore, and even free Onesimus as the practical expression of his faith and love. The results could only be positive—a deepened grasp of all we have in Christ!

9 In what practical ways are you expressing your faith to others?

We have an obligation to demonstrate our faith to others, even those who have wronged us, within the context of true Christian fellowship. Paul taught that faith expresses itself through love (Galatians 5:6). For Philemon that expression was first to be manifested through genuine forgiveness and restoration. But it may also be manifested through acts of compassion and provision. For the believer today, an expression of faith can be as simple as a word of encouragement or as risky as opening your home to someone in need, as inexpensive as a cup of cold water or as costly as paying someone's hospital bill. Faith and works go together.

As commonly told, when Abraham Lincoln died, Secretary of War Edward M. Stanton pulled a sheet over the body and said, "Now he belongs to the ages." Lincoln and Stanton had first met in 1855. Both were to represent a man in a law suit, but Stanton had an intense dislike for Lincoln and excluded him. The arrogant Stanton publicly described Lincoln as a "giraffe" or "gorilla." Stanton later became the Attorney General, losing that position when Lincoln became president. Stanton called him the "embecilic" president and it was no secret in Washington of Stanton's low regard for Lincoln (Oates 1977, 278). In the early days of the Civil War, Abraham Lincoln appointed an "astonished" Stanton as the Secretary of the War Department. Instead of hating each other, historian Stephen Oates describes how "they developed a lasting respect for one another" (280). Martin Luther King, Jr. described the story in his sermon "Loving Your Enemies" in which he adds, "But through the power of love Abraham Lincoln was able to redeem Stanton" (King 1998, 55).

Our attitudes toward others impact our relationship with God. Attitudes toward a brother or sister in the Lord can help or hinder our relationship with God (Matthew 5:23–24; 6:14–15; 1 John 4:20–21). Christ-like people genuinely appreciate one another and want God's best for each other.

Paul's Appeal on Behalf of Onesimus (vv. 8–25)

On December 1997, about a dozen students were gathered for their daily prayer meeting before class at Heath High School in Paducah, Kentucky. Classes would start in a few minutes, so one of the students closed in prayer. The final

Amen hung in the air as the sound of gunshots shattered the peace. A 14-year-old boy had walked up and fired on the group. Three of the students died, while five others were seriously wounded. The story made headlines for weeks.

In the midst of this tragedy, an amazing story of forgiveness emerged. One of the injured girls was 15-year-old Missy Jenkins. As she lay in the hospital less than a week after the shootings, fully aware that the damage to her spinal cord was so severe she would probably never walk again, she sent this message through a friend to the boy who had deliberately tried to kill her: "Tell him I forgive him" (Gupton 1998, 70).

We live in a society that knows little about that kind of forgiveness. In fact, our culture conditions us to be unforgiving. It celebrates and exalts people who are unwilling to forgive. It glamorizes the violent. Our heroes come from Quentin Tarantino and Martin Scorsese movies—people who murder out of vengeance. People of our culture sue others for every conceivable reason. Law schools today have higher enrollments than all other graduate schools combined. Endless number of lawyers will take care of an endless number of lawsuits as people retaliate for every miniscule miscue and major issue of life. And what will be our results? We will become increasingly hostile, angry, and bitter—a culture that knows little of forgiveness.

So Paul counseled Onesimus and persuaded him to return to Philemon. Then Paul wrote a letter, appealing to Philemon to forgive and restore Onesimus. Paul's message in this little epistle is powerful. It teaches that authentic Christianity expresses itself in the forgiveness, acceptance, and restoration of those who have wronged us! Five principles about real forgiveness should be noticed and remembered.

OBJECTIVE

List and explain five principles of forgiveness taught in Paul's letter to Philemon.

10 What principles about forgiveness can be learned from Paul's letter to Philemon?

Real Forgiveness Receives the Offending Person Back into One's Life (vv. 10–12)

The first principle of forgiveness Paul addresses is that of Philemon's taking back into his life the slave who had wronged him. What would Philemon do? Punish Onesimus? Jail him? Throw him off the property in a fit of rage? Or forgive him and accept him back?

Accepting back into our lives a person who has wronged us is usually the last thing we want to do. We would rather build a wall and shut that person out. But Jesus asks us to accept that person (Romans 15:7). Onesimus returned to his legal owner and asked for forgiveness. But we are to take others back and forgive them even if they do not ask for forgiveness! Why? Because that is what Jesus did. He hung on the Cross and said, "Father, forgive them, for they do not know what they are doing" (Luke 23:34).

Many parents have been deeply hurt by a rebellious, hateful child. Some almost shut their child out of their lives for emotional protection. But then Jesus dealt with their hearts by His Holy Spirit and they forgave that child. They realized they had to welcome their child back into their home.

Real Forgiveness Realizes that God Is at Work Even through an Offense (vv. 11, 15–16)

Paul assured Philemon, "Formerly he [Onesimus] was useless to you, but now he has become useful both to you and to me" (v. 11). He said, "Perhaps the reason he was separated from you for a little while was that you might have him back for good—no longer as a slave, but better than a slave, as a dear brother" (vv. 15–16). If Philemon was going to be successful at forgiving, he needed to focus on what God was working out through the situation.

We must realize that God is at work even in the bad things that happen to us. God is at work in the midst of situations where people have wronged us through actions or words. God is sovereign, and He can take evil and bring good out of it. We can either focus on what has been done to us in the past or we can focus on what God can do through what has happened to us.

One of the incredible things about Missy Jenkins's story is her perspective. In her own words she says, "Nothing happens without a reason—even this, so God will somehow make good come from it. I believe that. I believe this happened for a reason. A lot of people have told me my good attitude has been an inspiration to them. I think that's my purpose" (Gupton 1998, 70). This young lady really believes that God is at work through this offense!

Real Forgiveness Releases the Person
from Obligation to Us (vv. 17–19)

Philemon, if he were going to forgive, had to release Onesimus from his obligation. Paul recognized this when he said, "If he [Onesimus] has done you any wrong or owes you anything, charge it to me. I Paul, am writing this with my own hand. I will pay it back—not to mention that you owe me your very self" (vv. 18–19).

Emotionally, we must release people who have wronged us so that in our minds they no longer owe us a debt. In fact, we will see them as people who owe us nothing, not even an apology—if real forgiveness has taken place. We will wish them no evil and will not watch for them to *get what is coming to them.*

My friend Earnest told me the following story. A family member had ripped him off, borrowed a large sum of money, and then left the area. He was angry. Then to top it all, the person distorted the story, so Earnest appeared to be a mean scoundrel to a lot of people. Oh, how he wanted to retaliate! Bitterness was eating Earnest alive. All he could think about was how to get even. One day, Earnest realized he had to do something about the situation. The Lord helped him devise a plan and he wrote a letter, forgave the person, and completely and forever cancelled the debt. He began to pray for the person daily, asking God to bless him (Luke 6:27–31; Romans 12:14). The results were amazing: for the first time in months, Earnest was free!

Real Forgiveness Recognizes the Personal
Obligation Owed to Others (v. 19)

Paul reminded Philemon of something important. He acknowledged that Philemon had a legal claim against Onesimus. But he also reminded Philemon that he owed Paul an even greater debt. He owed him a debt because Paul had led Philemon to the Lord.

If someone wrongs us, we can choose to cancel his or her debt. We have had a much greater debt canceled. Forgiven people should willingly forgive. It is a terrible thing to have been forgiven a great debt and to then refuse to forgive someone who owes us a debt.

Jesus told a story to illustrate God's view of unforgiveness in Matthew 18:23–35. A man owed an enormous debt, much greater than he could pay. The king to whom he owed the debt ordered that the man's wife, children, and all he possessed be sold to pay off the debt. The man begged for forgiveness and the king cancelled the debt. But the man turned right around and found an individual who owed him a small debt. He harshly demanded his money and threw the person into jail when he could not pay it. When the king learned what had happened, he was angry and ordered that the man be turned over to jailers to be tortured until he paid his debt. Jesus concluded, "This is how my heavenly Father will treat each of you unless you forgive your brother from your heart" (Matthew 18:35). Forgiven people have an obligation to others.

Real Forgiveness Refreshes Others by Exhibiting a Readiness to Forgive (vv. 20–21)

Finally, Paul writes, "Refresh my heart in Christ" (cf. 7). Paul had asked Philemon to forgive Onesimus and accept him back as a fellow believer. But verse 21 alludes to the fact that Paul may have been thinking about the possibility of Philemon's freeing Onesimus so he could enter service with Paul on an ongoing basis. Paul expresses his confidence in Philemon's character and leaves the final decision to him. Paul does not coerce; he persuades (O'Brien 1982, 305–308).

11 Can you think of instances where witnessing real forgiveness has refreshed the lives of others? Describe them.

How refreshing to see an example of true Christ-like forgiveness. When we forgive as Christ forgave us, others are refreshed. There is love, unity, and joy. Unforgiveness and bitterness poison relationships (Hebrews 12:14–15). Forgiveness refreshes the heart.

As I read the story of Missy Jenkins, I was moved by her forgiving attitude. She said this:

"I believe hating Michael is wasted emotion. I know it is not what Jesus would do. Hating Michael will not make me walk again or bring my schoolmates back to life. I do feel sorry for Michael. Unlike him, I can get on with my life. I have lots of friends supporting me every day. I will live my life and be happy. I'm not mad at him. I can forgive him.

The people in the media want to know how we could forgive Michael. But as Christians, it's what God expects us to do. Besides, I've always had a hard time being mad at anyone. It's a whole lot easier to forgive than to be mad. I would really hate the feeling of carrying an awful grudge in my heart." (Gupton 1998, 70)

Missy, I want to tell you, you really remind me of Someone I love and admire. His name is Jesus. You challenge me. I, too, want to be like Him.

Paul closes his letter by sharing his plans to visit Philemon as soon as circumstances allow. He asks Philemon to prepare a guest room. Then he sends greetings from the believers and his fellow workers in the Lord's service in Rome. He prays for the marvelous grace of Jesus to be with their spirit.

Test Yourself

 CHAPTER 4

Circle the letter of the *best* answer.

1. What was Paul's particular role as the apostle to the Gentiles?
a) He did not preach to the Jews.
b) He communicated exclusively in Greek.
c) He encouraged Gentiles to observe the Law.
d) He preached to all types of people.

2. Paul's letter to Philemon is identified as what kind of letter?
a) An occasional letter
b) A doctrinal treatise
c) A letter of recommendation
d) An expression of thanks

3. On what basis did Paul want Philemon to respond to his request?
a) Paul wanted Philemon's response to be voluntary.
b) Paul invoked his apostolic authority.
c) Paul reminded Philemon of his obligation as a friend.
d) Paul told Philemon to obey as a son

4. Why was Paul's request to Philemon so unusual?
a) Paul was a prisoner, requesting amnesty for a lawbreaker.
b) Paul made his appeal with respect to the values of the gospel.
c) The request would be seen as a direct attack on the institution of slavery.
d) Onesimus was guilty of a crime under Roman law.

5. What role did Philemon have in the Colossian church?
a) The church met in Philemon's house.
b) Philemon was a ruler, possibly the chairman of the board.
c) Philemon's son was an elder.
d) Philemon was a prominent teacher.

6. What should we give thanks for in our Christian life?
a) For our Christian family: brothers and sisters in Christ
b) For the good things that we receive from the church
c) For the absence of conflict in our church relationships
d) For the opportunities to meet new people

7. Identify a characteristic of *koinonia* with one another in the church.
a) Our attitudes toward each other have an effect on our individual relationships with God.
b) Confrontation and conflict should be avoided at all costs.
c) We should not have special favorites in the church.
d) Leaders in the church should be accorded special respect and honor.

8. What evidence does our author offer that our society knows little about forgiveness?
a) We have retained the death penalty in our legal system.
b) Law schools have higher enrollments than all other graduate schools combined.
c) The American Civil Liberties Union opposes religiously-oriented decisions.
d) Americans are intensely individualistic.

9. Identify a principle of forgiveness that is found in the letter to Philemon.
a) Though one forgives, it is often not possible to forget the offense.
b) Forgiveness of others is a way to repay God for forgiving us.
c) God will judge us more severely if we do not forgive.
d) Real forgiveness releases the offender from all obligations.

10. Following Paul's example, how should we encourage others to forgive those who have offended them?
a) Church leadership should take no official notice of private offenses.
b) Both parties should appear before the church board so that they may resolve the problem.
c) Forgiveness should be gently encouraged, but not demanded or forced.
d) Serious problems should be handled with legal counsel.

Responses to Interactive Questions
CHAPTER 4

Some of these responses may include information that is supplemental to the IST. These questions are intended to produce reflective thinking beyond the course content and your responses may vary from these examples.

1 Who was Philemon? What was his relationship to Paul?

Philemon was a wealthy slave owner who lived in Colosse, a city of ancient Asia Minor. He had come to Christ under Paul's ministry. He was a key leader in the church at Colosse.

2 Who was Onesimus and what did he do?

Onesimus was one of Philemon's slaves. He ran away, stealing household goods or money from his master.

3 What did Paul decide to do about Onesimus' situation?

Paul talked with Onesimus about his responsibility as a Christian to return to Philemon. He then wrote a letter to Philemon, appealing for the forgiveness and restoration of Onesimus.

4 Based upon Roman law, what could Philemon have done to Onesimus?

Philemon had the right to pursue Onesimus, capture him, and punish him. Runaway slaves were sometimes branded on the forehead, beaten severely, jailed, or even killed.

5 How was the way Paul dealt with Philemon a good example to follow?

Paul chose the route of influence and appeal over apostolic coercion.

6 How should Christians demonstrate authentic fellowship to one another?

Christians demonstrate authentic fellowship by greeting and blessing one another when we meet, corresponding, or sharing fellowship. We may always acknowledge the deep and unique relationship we have in Christ.

7 What character qualities in Philemon's life does Paul give thanks for? Why are these qualities important?

Faith and love are core character qualities of a believer worthy of giving thanks for. Deeds of love refresh the hearts of God's people and bring joy and encouragement to them. They rejoice in love shown to an enemy, love that gives life and possessions to spread the gospel, the self-giving love of a parent and spouse, the unconditional love of a friend, and the forgiving love given freely in spite of wrongs suffered. Expressions of faith also encourage and bring joy to fellow believers.

8 What did Paul pray that God would do in Philemon's life?

Paul prayed that Philemon's faith would show itself practically in an expression of koinonia (true fellowship and sharing) within the body of Christ. This would either lead to or lead from an awareness of every good thing that is ours in Christ.

9 In what practical ways are you expressing your faith to others?

Answers will vary.

10 What principles taught about forgiveness can be learned from Paul's letter to Philemon?
   1. Real forgiveness receives the offending person back into one's life.
   2. Real forgiveness realizes that God is at work even through an offense.
   3. Real forgiveness releases the person from obligation to us.
   4. Real forgiveness recognizes the personal obligation owed to others.
   5. Real forgiveness refreshes others by exhibiting a readiness to forgive.

11 Can you think of instances where witnessing real forgiveness has refreshed the lives of others? Describe them.

Answers will vary.

UNIT PROGRESS EVALUATION 1

Now that you have finished Unit 1, review the lessons in preparation for Unit Progress Evaluation 1. You will find it in Essential Course Materials at the back of this IST. Answer all of the questions without referring to your course materials, Bible, or notes. When you have completed the UPE, check your answers with the answer key provided in Essential Course Materials. Review any items you may have answered incorrectly. Then you may proceed with your study of Unit 2. (Although UPE scores do not count as part of your final course grade, they indicate how well you learned the material and how well you may perform on the closed-book final examination.)

Ephesians

Ephesians is definitely a seminal statement of Paul's theology. So, clearly, is the book of Romans. This is true of Romans because of its emphasis on justification—how sinful humanity can become right with God through faith in Christ. I would argue, however, that Ephesians should be regarded as one of Paul's strongest and most clearly spelled out theological statements because it fully spells out the dominant theme of all of his writings, the believer's position in Christ. In Ephesians Paul tells us (1) what it means to be in Christ and (2) how that plays itself out in our daily lives.

Paul faced a daunting challenge in writing Ephesians. By the time of its writing, Colossians had probably been completed. In the meantime, however, he seems to have become aware of the fact that the doctrinal errors that plagued the Colossians were much more pervasive. They had infected all of the churches in ancient Asia. How do you deal with a situation like that from long distance (when you are imprisoned)? Paul wrote an apostolic letter. And we are forever grateful! The message of Ephesians has enriched and instructed Christians down through the centuries.

Although Ephesians lacks the vivid immediacy and concrete descriptions found in the smaller letter to the Colossians, together they provide us with a fairly clear picture of the situation that caused Paul to write it. Colossians gives us the apostle's first response to a disturbing situation. Ephesians is the follow-up document, written like a comprehensive treatise designed to instruct and correct the situation in the churches of the Lycus Valley.

The first half of Ephesians (chapters 1–3) systematically emphasizes what Christ has accomplished through His death, burial, resurrection, and ascension. It stresses who Christians are and what is available to them in Christ. It paints a vivid picture of what it means to be lost and the rich blessing of being forgiven, restored, and included in Christ.

The second half of the epistle (chapters 4–6) points out the practical outcome of being in Christ. It reveals the difference that He makes within a local church, our personal lives, and our homes. It challenges believers to be engaged in the spiritual conflict and assures them of victory through the power of the Holy Spirit, the complete armor of God, and prayer!

Introducing Ephesians (1:1–23)

Early in my Christian experience I heard an illustration I have never forgotten. It communicated so much truth about the way Christians sometimes live below their privilege. A man and his wife had worked hard, scrimped, saved, and finally purchased tickets for a long awaited trip on a wonderful cruise. After purchasing the tickets, however, they had little money left. The wife was an enterprising person and purchased cheese, lunch meat, bread, and other items for meals on the trip. Day after day, while other passengers went to the formal dining room and dined upon sumptuous fare, this couple would slip away to eat cold sandwiches and snack items. The captain noticed this unusual behavior and inquired why they were not eating in the dining room with the other passengers. They self-consciously admitted they could not afford it. The captain was shocked and showed them their ticket. All meals were included in the price of passage. They had been living far below their privileges.

Ephesians was written to the churches of the Lycus Valley in ancient Asia near Ephesus. It informed believers of their blessings and benefits in Christ. Paul did not want these believers to live below their privilege. He did not want anyone to intimidate them. He wanted them to know who they were and what they had in Christ.

The rich bounty that was theirs had come to them through the death, burial, resurrection, and ascension of Jesus. They needed to be aware of their position and privilege. Paul opened this letter with praise to God for every spiritual blessing in Christ. Then he fell to his knees and asked God to open the spiritual eyes of the believers to grasp who they were and what they had in Christ Jesus. Christians today need the same enlightening experience. It is tragic to live below your privilege.

• *Read Ephesians 1:1–23 before you begin study in this chapter.*

Lesson 5.1   Introductory Matters (1:1–23)

Objectives

5.1.1   Identify the central theme of Ephesians and the verse that supports it.

5.1.2   Discuss the importance of Ephesus in the ancient Roman world.

5.1.3   Discuss the common concerns that induced Paul to write both the Colossian letter and the Ephesian letter.

5.1.4   Summarize Paul's purpose in writing the letter to the Ephesians.

5.1.5   List and briefly explain the eight themes of Ephesians.

Lesson 5.2   Praise for Every Spiritual Blessing In Christ (1:1–14)

Objectives

5.2.1   Explain how the believers were being distracted from Christ's sufficiency.

5.2.2   Explain the significance of Paul's use of the word chosen *in referring to the Ephesian believers.*

5.2.3   Compare adoption as we know it with its meaning in the ancient Greco-Roman world.

5.2.4   Explain the relationship between the words redemption *and* forgiveness *in Ephesians 1:7.*

5.2.5   Explain the mystery of His will as it is used in Ephesians 1:9–10.

5.2.6   Explain God's purpose for Jews and Gentiles in Christ.

5.2.7   Explain what is meant by the sealing of the Holy Spirit.

Lesson 5.3   Paul's Apostolic Prayer (1:15–23)

Objectives

5.3.1   Explain the importance of prayer in dealing with church problems.

5.3.2   Summarize Paul's prayer in Ephesians 1:15–23.

5.3.3   Identify three things Paul asked God to do for the believers to whom he was writing.

5.1.1
OBJECTIVE

Identify the central theme of Ephesians and the verse that supports it.

1   What is the theme of Ephesians and the key verse that supports it?

Introductory Matters (1:1–23)

Many Bible scholars consider this epistle to the Ephesians a crowning literary and theological achievement. Written by the apostle Paul, it is a masterpiece articulating his distinctive theological themes (Bruce 1985, 229). Others have questioned whether Paul actually wrote the epistles and have tried to pick it apart, alleging he borrowed heavily from other sources (Keener 1993, 538–539). This commentary operates on the premise that no good reason exists to question the claim that the apostle Paul is the author (1:1).

Paul wrote this letter from prison, most likely in Rome (3:1; 4:1). Although other locations have been suggested (Ephesus and Caesarea), the evidence favors house arrest in Rome as the location from which this epistle was written (Acts 28:30). During this time Paul was able to receive guests, others were able to come and go to meet his needs, and he was able to devote significant time to the writing of the prison epistles (Wood 1978, 13–15).

Along with the letter to the Romans, Ephesians stands as a foundational expression of Pauline theology. As God's Word, it has molded the beliefs of countless Christians. Just as Romans has contributed so much to our belief in justification by faith, Ephesians has contributed to our conviction that everything the believer needs is to be found in Christ. In fact, the central theme of Ephesians is that God has graciously provided everything necessary for an effective life in Christ (1:3).

5.1.2
OBJECTIVE

Discuss the importance of Ephesus in the ancient Roman world.

2   How important was Ephesus in the ancient Roman world?

The Importance of the City of Ephesus

Ephesus was a key city in the ancient Roman world, the leading city of Asia. It would have compared to New York City, London, Paris, or Tokyo in today's world. It was the metropolitan center from which Paul and his converts succeeded in evangelizing Asia and planting churches all over the Lycus Valley (Acts 19:10, 26–27). Ephesus was an important commercial center and stood at an intersection of important trade routes. It was a cultural and religious center for the ancient world. The pagan temple of the Roman goddess Diana (or Greek Artemis), one of the wonders of the ancient world, was located there (Acts 19:23–41). Ephesus was a pagan stronghold, a melting pot of cultures and ideas within the ancient world (Arnold 1993, 249–251).

5.1.3
OBJECTIVE

Discuss the common concerns that induced Paul to write both the Colossian letter and the Ephesian letter.

3   What are the probable reasons for the similarities that exist between Paul's letter to the Ephesians and his letter to the Colossians?

The Circumstances Behind Ephesians

This commentary is written in the belief that the similarities between this letter and Colossians indicate that Paul probably wrote both letters within the same general time frame and to a common situation that the churches in the Lycus Valley in ancient Asia were facing. It is likely that Epaphras, the founding pastor at Colosse, brought an early report of the welfare of that church to Paul in prison. Much was to be commended, but there was also dangerous and disturbing news. Paul, with apostolic and pastoral concern, quickly responded with the letter we call Colossians. Not long afterwards, however, other reports came that made it clear the problems were not isolated to Colosse. Other churches were struggling with similar issues. In response to this broader concern, Paul wrote Ephesians. This view is strengthened by the fact that the words in Ephesus are missing in a number of early manuscripts. The general nature of the letter, the lack of direct references to particular situations, and the absence of personal greetings also point in this direction (Keener 1993, 541; Wood 1978, 9–12). Consequently, an understanding of the situation behind Colossians provides an excellent background against which to interpret Ephesians.

5.1.4
OBJECTIVE

Summarize Paul's purpose in writing the letter to the Ephesians.

4   Why did Paul write to the church at Ephesus?

The Purpose of Ephesians

Paul writes to deal with the errors infecting the churches of the Lycus Valley, emphasizing key theological themes to enable them to deal with the crisis. In keeping with Colossians, he underscores the centrality of Jesus Christ and points out the incredible resources every believer has in Christ. He addresses the spiritual nature and unity of the church, stressing the importance of living out their relationship to Christ in every dimension of their lives. He encourages them in the power of the Holy Spirit to "put on the full armor of God" to resist the spiritual attacks they face (6:10–17).

5.1.5
OBJECTIVE

List and briefly explain the eight themes of Ephesians.

The Key Themes of Ephesians

Christ's Provision and Christian Responsibility

This theme dominates Ephesians. It influences how the epistle is structured and all of Paul's logic. It is sometimes called the **indicative–imperative motif** (see glossary). This is based on two verbal **mood**s that Paul uses throughout the letter. The *indicative mood* is used to describe reality or facts from an objective perspective. In Ephesians (as well as Paul's other epistles) it is used to describe who Christ is, what He has done, and all God provides for His people as a result. The *imperative mood* is used to command or to appeal to people. Paul uses this mood in dealing with Christian responsibility in light of what Christ has done and who all believers are in Him. Chapters 1–3 emphasize Christ's provision and Christian identity in Him. Chapters 4–6 emphasize Christian responsibility in light of who we are and what we have in Him.

God's Plan and Purpose

5   What are the key themes of Ephesians?

Ephesians portrays God as fulfilling His plan for humanity's salvation and Christ's glorification. The people of God, the church, are integral to that plan (1:3–14, 18–23; 2:6–10).

The Exalted Position of Christ

6   What is meant by the *indicative–imperative motif* and how is it expressed in Ephesians?

Ephesians, with breathtaking clarity, portrays an all-powerful Christ. His power is unlimited, His sovereignty universal. Christ has conquered and is exalted over all His enemies. All spiritual beings (principalities and powers) are defeated and under His control. He will bring all things, including history itself, to completion. He is head of all things, in particular, the body of Christ, His church. Yet all of this is presented in stark contrast to the suffering, passion, and redemption of the Cross (1:9–10, 19–23; 2:11–22; 3:10–11, 20–21; 4:7–16).

The Status of Believers in Christ

Paul's favorite way of portraying believers in Ephesians is to describe them as *in Christ*. This phrase (or its equivalent) occurs thirty-four times in Ephesians. Paul sees Christians as closely identified with Christ, both personally and collectively. This spiritual identity is sometimes referred to as *the mystical union*—our salvation is founded *in Him*; our purpose is rooted *in Him*; our fulfillment is centered *in Him*; the depth of our fellowship is founded *in Him*; and our future is anchored *in Him*.

The Already–Not Yet Dimensions of Salvation

Ephesians seems to emphasize the *already dimension* of salvation. It would be a mistake, however, to say that the *not yet* or the future (normally called the **eschatological** dimension) is neglected (1:9–10; 2:7). This *already* emphasis is sometimes called realized eschatology. Salvation and its benefits are available in Christ to those who will accept them. Christians are described as being raised and exalted with Christ (2:6). We look forward, however, to a marvelous future fulfilled in Christ (1:3, 13–14, 18–23; 3:7–12, 20–21).

The Unity of Jew and Gentile in Christ

Paul declares that Christ has brought about a reconciliation between Jew and Gentile. He accomplished this through His *flesh*, that is to say, His death on the Cross (2:16; 3:6). In fact, Jesus is pictured as tearing down every barrier between any believer of any people in the world and creating a new identity for each member of humanity who through belief is in Christ (2:12–18). Because of this, Paul repeatedly stresses the inclusiveness and unity of the church. All redeemed people, regardless of their cultural or racial differences, have equal access in Christ to God the Father (2:1–3:14; 4:1–6).

The Nature of the Church

Ephesians has a great deal to say about the church. The church for Paul was an organism (the living, growing body of Christ), not simply an organization or institution. Three images are used for the church, each rich with significance:

1. A building or temple—the household of God (2:19–22);
2. A growing body vitally connected to its head (1:23; 4:16; 5:23);
3. A bride in intimate submission to her husband (5:25–32).

The church is Christ's body, representing Him and carrying on His ministry in the power of the Holy Spirit. Each member of the church has been given spiritual gifts and has a contribution to make to the health and growth of the Body. There are no hierarchies. Each member is important. In the church no one is a stranger, an alien, or a foreigner (1:2–23; 2:1–22; 4:1–16).

Spiritual Warfare

Believers in the Lycus Valley lived in a culture where evil spiritual forces were active and real. These forces had bound, controlled, and tyrannized the members of the church before their conversion. The cult of Artemis was powerful. Fear of evil spirits still affected the believers. More than any other letter, Ephesians addresses the issue of spiritual warfare. Satan was attacking believers and Christ's church. Confronting the situation, Paul emphasizes the ultimate victory and superiority of Christ. Through the power of God, the victory of Christ, unity among believers, and the putting on and use of spiritual armor, they would be able to overcome (1:17–23; 4:8–10; 6:10–20) (Barton et al. 1995, xx–xxv; Arnold 1993, 246–48).

The Outline of Ephesians

I.   Christian Greetings (1:1–2)

II. Who Christians Are and What they Have in Christ (1:3–3:21)

   A. Praise for Every Spiritual Blessing in Christ (1:3–14)

   B. An Apostolic Prayer Begun in Light of These Blessings (1:15–23)

   C. Salvation by God's Grace–Before and After (2:1–22)

   D. The Mystery of Christ (3:1–13)

   E. An Apostolic Prayer Concluded (3:14–19)

   F. A Doxology in Light of Who Christ Is and What He Has Accomplished (3:20–21)

III. What God Desires–Christ Fully Expressed in the Various Contexts of Life (4:1–6:20)

   A. Christ Fully Expressed in the Local Church (4:1–16)

   B. Christ Fully Expressed in the Christian's Personal Life (4:17–5:21)

   C. Christ Fully Expressed in Our Homes (5:21–6:9)

   D. A Final Charge to the Christian Involved in Spiritual Warfare (6:10–20)

IV. Concluding Remarks and Benediction (6:21–24)

Praise for Every Spiritual Blessing in Christ (1:1–14)

Have you ever met someone who always wants another something new or different although his or her life is filled with so many *things* that many are still unused? That kind of attitude leads to discontent and poverty right in the midst of plenty.

In the Christian life, it is possible to do this also. Some Christians continually pursue deeper or higher spiritual experience while overlooking or minimizing what is already available in Christ. The tragedy is that in the pursuit they lose sight of the sufficiency of Christ, develop spiritual pride, and become susceptible to deceptive teaching. That is what was happening in the churches of the Lycus Valley near Ephesus.

OBJECTIVE

Explain how the believers were being distracted from Christ's sufficiency.

7   What pattern does Paul follow for describing each blessing in Christ?

Paul has an antidote for the problem. He joyfully proclaims, "Praise be to the God and Father of our Lord Jesus Christ, who has blessed us in the heavenly realms with every spiritual blessing in Christ" (1:3). Here Paul uses a *berakhah*, a poetic form of blessing God used in Jewish synagogue worship (Bruce 1984, 253). The assurance Paul gives is based on the same source he points to in his letter to the Philippians: "My God will meet all your needs according to His glorious riches in Christ Jesus" (4:19). All of the abundant blessings of the Christian life come through Christ out of God's unlimited treasure house.

Paul then enumerates six spiritual blessings that are representative of God's unlimited treasure in Christ. Paul follows a similar pattern each time he lists one of these blessings. First, he identifies the blessing in Christ. Then he points out how the blessing comes to believers. Finally, he reveals the purpose of the blessing.

In Christ We Are a Chosen People (1:4)

OBJECTIVE

Explain the significance of Paul's use of the word chosen *in referring to the Ephesian believers.*

8   What was the significance of Paul's use of the word *chosen* to describe the Ephesian Christians?

- The blessing is that believers, many of whom were Gentiles, were *chosen* or elected by God, just as much as Israel was chosen. In fact, the Greek word Paul uses in describing the choosing of the Ephesian Christians is the same one used in the Septuagint (Greek Old Testament) in connection with God's choosing of Israel (Wood 1978, 24).

- The means or choosing of the believers was in Christ.

- The purpose of their choosing was so that they could and would reflect God's character in their daily lives, that is, that they might be blameless.

Have you ever been the last to be chosen as a member of a team? Then you know the pain rejection can cause. But God has chosen you *in Christ* as His very own.

In Christ We Have Full Rights as God's Children (1:5–6)

OBJECTIVE

Compare adoption as we know it with its meaning in the ancient Greco-Roman world.

9   In what sense can it be said that every believer is adopted by God?

- The blessing is that God determined ahead of time that this largely Gentile congregation would be adopted as His children. Adoption in the ancient world was used in a broader sense than we know it. Slaves could be adopted. Adoption referred to the legal process whereby one person brought another person into his family, giving that person all the status and privileges of a biological son or daughter. It literally meant to "place as a son" (Romans 8:15–17, 23; Galatians 4:1–7; Reese 1979, 53).

- Paul says the believer's adoption into the family of God comes through Jesus Christ.

- God's purpose was to make believers His sons and daughters because He loves all humankind. Each and every adoption into His family gives God great pleasure.

A child has certain privileges. Wise parents, however, know when they should receive their full inheritance. God in His love has already insured our inheritance; we are predestined to receive it in Christ Jesus. In fact we enjoy many of its benefits now (Romans 8:15–17, 23; Galatians 4:1–7).

In Christ We Are Redeemed and Forgiven (1:7–8)

OBJECTIVE

Explain the relationship between the words redemption *and* forgiveness *in Ephesians 1:7.*

- The blessing of redemption has to do with the purchasing of slaves or prisoners for the purpose of setting them free. Before we found freedom in Christ, we were slaves of sin and self. Our redemption was costly; it cost Jesus His life (1 Peter 1:18–19). Forgiveness is the consequence of redemption. The Greek grammatical construction of verse 7 shows that these two things, redemption and forgiveness, are in apposition to each other (placing a word beside another so the second word explains the first). Redemption results in and leads to our forgiveness (Salmond 1990, 254).

- As before, these blessings are all in Christ. The price for redemption has been paid *through His blood.* The abundant riches of God's grace determine the degree of His sacrifice (Romans 5:7–8, 20; John 1:16).

- The words "with all wisdom and understanding" indicate that God does not provide this blessing indiscriminately. He knew what He was doing and considered it a wise investment of His lavish grace.

Most of us have no idea what it would be like to be a slave—in bondage, with no rights, without identity, forced into hard labor, subject to cruel treatment, and without hope. Yet sin and Satan enslave millions with the same results. Jesus redeems, frees, and forgives us. What a blessing! What good news!

10 In what ways were you in slavery before you found freedom in Christ?

In Christ We Receive Insight into God's Eternal Purpose (1:9–10)

5.2.5
OBJECTIVE

Explain the mystery of His will as it is used in Ephesians 1:9–10.

- It is a blessing to Christians that God reveals *the mystery of His will:* His plan for all eternity, to His people.

- God revealed His plan through His Son, Jesus.

- God's ultimate purpose is to bring everything together in Christ. Followers of the mystery religions of Paul's time sought diligently to discover the unifying principle of the cosmos. Paul declares that Jesus is the unifying principle of the universe, and that the simplest believer has access to Him. At the end of time, Christ will be recognized as the sum total of everything (Romans 8:18–21; 1 Corinthians 15:24–28; Philippians 2:6–11; Colossians 1:15–20) (Wood 1978, 26).

Many people struggle like mice in a maze. They spend all their efforts, energy, and ingenuity trying to make sense of life. Their efforts prove futile. God sent His Son to restore life to what it was meant to be—the relationship of God with His people and His people with one another. Jesus gives purpose to life. He is the key that causes it to all to make sense.

In Christ We Are Included in God's Plan (1:11–13)

5.2.6
OBJECTIVE

Explain God's purpose for Jews and Gentiles in Christ.

- Jewish believers (v. 12, "we, who were the first to hope in Christ") and Gentile believers (v. 13, "you also were included in Christ when you heard the word of truth") are included in Christ. Both groups "were chosen, having been predestined" according to His plan. All barriers are removed, and Jews and Gentiles *become one body in Christ.*

- The blessing comes through God's working out His will in Christ.

11 What does Paul say is God's plan for Jews and Gentiles?

- God's purpose is that together, as one body, the body of Christ, we would praise Him (cf. 1:6, 12, 14). This is the believer's reason-for-being (1 Peter 2:9–10).

A beautiful tapestry has much more than just one color. It is the intricate weaving, by a gifted artisan, of a variety of colors into a marvelous design. God, the master artisan, is weaving an incredible tapestry with the variety of human lives He has redeemed. When He finishes, the redeemed of all ages, from every age, race, gender, and culture will be brought together in glorious splendor. Even now the beauty of His handiwork can be seen within the church, Christ's glorious bride (3:8–11; 5:27).

In Christ We Are Sealed by the Holy Spirit (1:13–14)

5.2.7
OBJECTIVE

Explain what is meant by the sealing of the Holy Spirit.

- In Christ all believers are sealed by the Holy Spirit. In ancient culture, an official seal was put on documents to guarantee their genuineness. It was also put on goods in transit to identify the owner and insure their safe delivery (Wood 1978, 27).

12 What does Paul mean by the "sealing of the Holy Spirit" mentioned in Ephesians 1:13–14?

- This blessing came by God's promised Holy Spirit. He is the One who bears witness, giving us inner assurance, that we are heirs with Christ. He seals us. He is the down payment (the earnest or deposit) guaranteeing we will receive our full inheritance in Christ (Romans 8:15–17).

- Once again the refrain is heard, "To the praise of His glory" (cf. 6, 12,14). The ultimate purpose of God's marvelous spiritual blessings is that our lives and lips would praise Him.

In some ways, this sealing is like certifying or guaranteeing a package for delivery. The price guaranteeing delivery has been paid—the precious blood of Jesus that redeems us. The Holy Spirit sets us apart, putting God's seal of ownership on us like a heavenly address label. God, our Heavenly Father, oversees, watches, and cares for us through His agent, the Holy Spirit, until we arrive safely at our heavenly destination "to the praise of His glory" (Philippians 1:6; Colossians 1:21–23; Jude 24–25).

Paul's heart could not help but erupt in praise as he contemplated all of the rich, wonderful blessings of God in Christ. Paul's list of six blessings is not exhaustive, but representative of the many wonderful things God provides. The fact is, God has abundantly blessed His people with every blessing they will ever need in Christ Jesus (John 1:16; 2 Peter 1:3). Reflect on each of these wonderful blessings. No amount of money or effort can provide them. They are graciously provided to every Christian in Christ. The key or the secret is knowing Christ. "In [Him] are hidden all the treasures of wisdom and knowledge" (Colossians 2:3).

Paul's Apostolic Prayer (1:15–23)

If I faced a crisis, I know certain people I would want praying for me. They are people of spiritual passion and power. They are people who, over the years, have demonstrated they are on speaking terms with God. They are people of faith and character. Whom would you want praying for you?

The apostle Paul would not be a bad choice. At the beginning of this letter, which was probably sent to several churches near Ephesus, we catch a glimpse of the apostle's heart. Reports had reached his ears about the character of these churches and the challenges they faced. Paul was in prison when he first heard the reports from Epaphras (Colossians 1:7). Later, other people reinforced what he had learned in the first report.

5.3.1
OBJECTIVE

Explain the importance of prayer in dealing with church problems.

Some of what Paul heard was encouraging and prompted thanksgiving. Their faith in Christ was strong. The love they had for each other and God's people everywhere warmed his heart (1:15). But there were other things: reports of dangerous doctrines that detracted from Christ's supremacy, an unhealthy interest in unusual spiritual experiences, a legalistic emphasis upon works, as well as spiritual pride. These things burdened Paul's heart with deep concern. These things drove Paul to his knees in unceasing intercession for these congregations. Then after praying (even while he was praying), Paul wrote this letter.

13 What should spiritual leaders always do first when they are facing problems in the church?

Sometimes spiritual leaders, faced with church problems, are tempted to reverse Paul's order. They quickly fire off letters or impulsively speak out of a heart blazing with concern. But when we do that, we are always at risk. A spiritual safeguard is to first bathe our concern in prayer and then to deal with the problem. Prayer provides the objectivity, the spiritual perspective, and the opportunity to hear from God before responding. This is an essential lesson for spiritual leaders to learn.

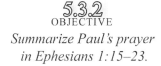
OBJECTIVE

Summarize Paul's prayer in Ephesians 1:15–23.

What did Paul pray for the churches in and around Ephesus? Verse 17 summarizes his prayer. Verses 18 to 23 list his specific requests. Paul's prayer, in general, was that God would give them the Spirit of wisdom and revelation so that they would know Him better. Paul's prayer was **trinitarian**. He addresses the Father as a true Hebrew would, noting the Father's relationship to the Son, Jesus Christ, and emphasizing the Holy Spirit's role in revelation as well.

Although some have translated the word *spirit* in Paul's prayer to mean attitude or capability, the context demands this word to mean the Holy Spirit. The fact that *revelation* is involved and that the language used is drawn from Isaiah 11:2 indicates that Paul is referring to the Holy Spirit (Fee 1994, 674–679). Paul's prayer was that the Holy Spirit would produce within the believers a level of spiritual insight that would result in a deepened understanding of God's work in Jesus Christ. Paul uses one of his favorite words, a word for knowledge intensified by a preposition (*epignōsis),* to emphasize the deep, accurate, personal, Spirit-generated level of knowledge (Fee 1994, 674). He realized that the greatest need for Christians facing the challenges these believers faced was to know beyond doubt who they were in Christ and what the Father had provided in Him. This is also one of the greatest needs of believers today. This knowledge would solve most spiritual problems.

Paul continues his prayer in verses 18–23, identifying three things he wanted these believers to know. These verses express three passions of an apostolic heart.

Christians Need to Grasp the Grandeur of Their Hope (1:18)

5.3.3
OBJECTIVE

Identify three things Paul asked God to do for the believers to whom he was writing.

We have little idea of the wonder and grandeur of our future as those God has called. Hope, as used in this context and elsewhere in Scripture, is not of an uncertain desire or dream, such as the expression, "I hope something happens or comes to pass," but a confident expectation anchored in the promises, provision, and faithfulness of God. In Paul's writing, hope is often presented as a work of the Spirit during times of suffering and affliction (Dunn 1998, 357, 437–438). Paul, quoting Isaiah 64:4, wrote, "No eye has seen, no ear has heard, no mind has conceived what God has prepared for those who love him" (1 Corinthians 2:9–10). We need the Holy Spirit to *open the eyes of our heart* so we can perceive the wonderful salvation that we have in Christ.

14 What did Paul ask God for on behalf of the believers at Ephesus?

When I was a young man, my father took me on many hikes in the Rocky Mountains. I fondly remember his voice calling, "Son, come over here and look at this." I would go to where he was standing on a high mountain precipice and look out over an incredibly beautiful mountain range filled with beautiful lakes, waterfalls, wildlife, and lush green foliage. My experience pales next to the apostle John's when he heard the Father summon him, "Come up here," and he was given a glimpse of God's throne room and heaven's glories (Revelation 4:1). The Holy Spirit is the One who makes our future hope vivid and real in our hearts.

Christians Need to Become Aware of Their Glorious Inheritance (1:18)

God has invested so much in us. What Jesus purchased for us through His death, burial, and resurrection is beyond imagining. This is the second of five times that Paul uses the word *riches* in this letter (1:7; 2:7; 3:8, 16). In Romans, Paul put it this way, "He who did not spare his own Son, but gave him up for us all—how will he not also, along with him, graciously give us all things? (8:32). All God's wealth is available to believers in Christ.

As I reflect on this verse, I visualize a large, heavenly treasure chest filled with God's "riches in glory" (KJV) or "glorious riches" (Philippians 4:19). The chest contains everything needed to live the Christian life victoriously. One by one, I see our heavenly Father pick them up, display them, and say, "Here son or daughter, look at what is yours in Christ Jesus." He truly has given us "everything we need for life and godliness through our knowledge of him who called us by his own glory and goodness" (2 Peter 1:3).

Christians Need to Experience and Appropriate God's Power (1:19–23)

Finally, Paul prayed that these believers would grasp just how incredibly great the power of God was on their behalf. He describes this power as being *incomparably great*. Only Paul uses this Greek word in the New Testament. The word is *huperballon* and is compounded. The Greek word *ballon* means "to throw." With the addition of the preposition *huper,* the word takes on the added meaning of throwing "above or beyond" (Wood 1978, 30). Perhaps the concept can be illustrated by imagining someone putting a ball into the hands of a great athlete and asking that person to throw the ball as far as humanly possible. That would be *ballon*. However, if the ball were placed into the hands of Almighty God, and He were to throw it, that would be *huperballon*–"incomparably great." This is power beyond human comprehension, power in a completely different realm, incomparably great power for us who believe!

Like a capable wordsmith or literary master, Paul searches for the right words to express this power's potential. The Holy Spirit guiding Paul's writing is limited by human language, so the words used for power multiply in this passage—four different Greek words (*dunamis, energeia, kratos,* and *ischus*). Gordon Fee observes, "There is nothing else in the Pauline corpus quite like this especially high concentration of power terminology" (Fee 1994, 678).

Paul says this is the same power that raised Jesus from the dead, that resulted in the ascension, that led to Christ's exaltation at the Father's right hand, and the power by which He rules and sustains everything (Colossians 1:15–18). This is incredible power. It is cosmic power that is available to the humblest believer for living the Christian life.

It is not enough for Christians simply to have an intellectual awareness of their hope and inheritance or a theological understanding of God's power. Paul prayed for a personal, experiential knowledge. It is not sufficient to simply know about these things, rather we need to personally know Christ in whom they are to be found. Are you coming to know Him better every day?

Test Yourself

Circle the letter of the *best* answer.

1. What is the theme of Ephesians?
   a) The supremacy of Christ
   b) The priesthood of the believer
   c) The humanity of Christ
   d) God's complete provision for effective Christian life

2. What verse captures the central theme of Ephesians?
   a) 1:3
   b) 1:6
   c) 2:1
   d) 3:6

3. Ephesus was the leading city in the Roman Province of
   a) Asia.
   b) Achaia.
   c) Macedonia.
   d) Bithynia.

4. Ephesus had a pagan temple dedicated to the Roman goddess
   a) Aphrodite.
   b) Diana.
   c) Athena.
   d) Demeter.

5. What two verbal moods does Paul use throughout the letter of Ephesians?
   a) Subjective and indicative
   b) Optative and imperative
   c) Subjective and imperative
   d) Imperative and indicative

6. Paul lists six spiritual blessings in Ephesians 1. What are two of them?
   a) In Christ, believers are justified and sealed by the Holy Spirit.
   b) In Christ, believers are chosen and are purified by the power of the Holy Spirit.
   c) In Christ, believers are chosen and sealed by the Holy Spirit.
   d) In Christ, believers are adopted and anointed for ministry.

7. The Greek word Paul uses for *adoption* literally means "to
   a) be one."
   b) place as a son."
   c) accept."
   d) be chosen."

8. In Ephesians 1, what does Paul mean by saying believers are sealed by the Holy Spirit?
   a) Believers are anointed by the Holy Spirit for ministry.
   b) The Holy Spirit is the down payment guaranteeing what is still yet to come.
   c) Believers have received God's stamp of approval.
   d) Believers have been sanctified and set apart for ministry.

9. In Paul's prayer for the Ephesians, context demands that the term *spirit* refers to
   a) attitude.
   b) capability.
   c) the Holy Spirit.
   d) revelation.

10. The Greek word *huperballon* means
    a) "super-exalted."
    b) "incomparably great."
    c) "majestic."
    d) "holy and set apart."

Responses to Interactive Questions

CHAPTER 5

Some of these responses may include information that is supplemental to the IST. These questions are intended to produce reflective thinking beyond the course content and your responses may vary from these examples.

1   What is the theme of Ephesians and the key verse that supports it?

Just as Romans contributes so much to our belief in justification by faith, Ephesians contributes to our conviction that everything the believer needs is to be found in Christ. In fact, the central theme of Ephesians is that God has graciously provided everything necessary for an effective life in Christ (1:3).

2   How important was Ephesus in the ancient Roman world?

Ephesus was an important city in the ancient Roman world–the leading city of Asia, comparable to modern-day New York City, London, Paris, or Tokyo. Ephesus was an important commercial center and stood at an intersection for trade routes. It was a cultural and religious center for the ancient world. The pagan temple of the Roman goddess Diana (or Greek Artemis), one of the wonders of the ancient world, was located there. Ephesus was a pagan stronghold, a melting pot of cultures and ideas within the ancient world. It was also the metropolitan center from which Paul and his converts succeeded in evangelizing Asia and planting churches all over the Lycus Valley.

3   What are the probable reasons for the similarities which exist between Paul's letter to the Ephesians and his letter to the Colossians?

The similarities between Ephesians and Colossians indicate that Paul probably wrote both letters within the same general time frame and to a common situation faced by the churches in the Lycus Valley. After Paul responded to concerns at the Colossae church, other reports made it clear that other churches were struggling with similar issues. In response to this broader concern, Paul wrote Ephesians. This view is strengthened by the fact that the words in Ephesus are missing in a number of early manuscripts. The general nature of the letter, the lack of direct references to particular situations, as well as the absence of personal greetings also point to this.

4   Why did Paul write to the church at Ephesus?

Paul wrote to deal with the error infecting the churches of the Lycus Valley, He underscores the centrality of Jesus Christ and points out the incredible resources every believer has in Christ. He addresses the spiritual nature and unity of the Church, stressing the importance of living out their relationship to Christ in every dimension of their lives. He encourages them, in the power of the Holy Spirit, to put on the full armor of God to resist the spiritual attacks they face.

5   What are the key themes of Ephesians?

Christ's provision and Christian responsibility

    God's plan and purpose

    The exalted position of Christ

    The status of believers in Christ

    The already/not yet dimension of salvation

    The unity of Jew and Gentile in Christ

    The nature of the church

    Spiritual warfare

6   What is meant by the indicative/imperative motif and how is it expressed in Ephesians?

This is based on how Paul uses two verbal moods in the Greek language. The indicative mood is used to describe reality or facts from an objective perspective. In Ephesians (as well as Paul's other epistles) it is used to describe who Christ is, what He has done, and all God provides for His people as a result. The imperative mood is used to command or to appeal to people. Paul uses this mood to explain Christian responsibility in light of what Christ has done and who we are in Him.

7   What pattern does Paul follow in describing each blessing in Christ?

Paul identifies the blessing. Then he points out how the blessing comes to believers. Finally, he reveals the purpose of the blessing.

8   What was the significance of Paul's use of the word chosen to describe the Ephesian Christians?

The believers, many of whom were Gentiles, were chosen or elected by God, just as much as Israel was chosen. In fact, the Greek word Paul uses is the same one used in the Septuagint in connection with God's choosing of Israel.

9   In what sense can it be said that every believer is adopted by God?

God determined ahead of time that this largely Gentile congregation would be adopted as His children. Adoption referred to the legal process whereby one person brought another person into his family, giving that person all the status and privileges of a biological son or daughter. It literally meant to "place as a son."

10 In what ways were you in slavery before you found freedom in Christ?

Answers will vary.

11 What does Paul say is God's plan for Jews and Gentiles?

Jewish and Gentile believers are included in Christ. Both groups "were chosen, having been predestined" according to His plan. All barriers are removed so Jews and Gentiles become one body in Christ.

12 What does Paul mean by the "sealing of the Holy Spirit" in Ephesians 1:13–14?

In ancient culture, an official seal was put on documents to guarantee their genuineness. It was also put on goods in transit to identify the owner and insure their safe delivery. The sealing by the Holy Spirit identifies believers as belonging to God and insures their safe arrival in heaven.

13 What should spiritual leaders always do first when they are facing problems in the church?

A spiritual safeguard is to first bathe our concern in prayer and then deal with the problem. Prayer provides the objectivity, the spiritual perspective, and the opportunity to hear from God before responding to the problem.

14 What did Paul ask God for on behalf of the believers at Ephesus?

Paul prayed that the believers would grasp the grandeur of their hope, that they would become aware of their spiritual inheritance, and that they would both experience and make use of God's power.

CHAPTER 6

What God Has Accomplished in Christ (Ephesians 2:1–3:21)

The theme of Christ's provision and Christian responsibility dominates Ephesians. This pattern is sometimes called the indicative–imperative motif (see Chapter 5 in this IST). This terminology is based on how Paul uses two verbal moods in the Greek language. The indicative mood is used to describe reality or facts from the perspective of someone looking at things objectively. In Ephesians the indicative mood is used to describe who Christ is, what He has done, and all the spiritual provision and realities that flow out of that. In the part of Ephesians we are dealing with in this chapter, the indicative mood dominates. The imperative mood is used extensively in chapters 4–6 of Ephesians. Paul uses this mood to deal with how Christians should live in light of what Christ has done and who they are in Him. Without fail, Paul moves logically from the indicative to the imperative—first emphasizing Christ's provision and then dealing with Christian responsibility in light of that provision. In other words, chapters 4–6 of Ephesians flow out of what Paul has established, doctrinally, in chapters 1–3.

Chapter 2 of Ephesians is built on a before-and-after pattern. In the first part of chapter 2, Paul reminds the Ephesian Christians of what Christ has done for them personally through salvation. He has reconciled them to God in Christ. In the second part of Ephesians 2, Paul emphasizes reconciliation through Christ on an interpersonal and collective level. In Christ, all are accepted and included as God's covenant people, regardless of their background. Chapter 3:1–13 amplifies this theme around the concept of the mystery of Christ. And finally, Paul prays that these believers would become aware of and appropriate all they have and are in Christ. The section ends with a powerful doxology of praise to God for all He is able to do in the lives of Christians personally and within the church collectively.

- *Read Ephesians 2:1–3:21 before you begin study in this chapter.*

Lesson 6.1   The Before and After of Those In Christ: Part 1 (2:1–10)

Objectives

6.1.1   Describe four aspects of the human condition without Christ as described by Paul in Ephesians 2:1–3.

6.1.2   Define salvation *and* grace *as used in Ephesians 2:8–9.*

6.1.3   Describe the four results of being saved and in Christ identified in Ephesians 2:4–10.

Lesson 6.2   The Before and After of Those In Christ: Part 2 (2:11–22)

Objectives

6.2.1   Define reconciliation, *and describe what it includes in Ephesians 2:11–22.*

6.2.2   List five spiritual conditions Paul identifies that describe people before they meet Christ.

6.2.3   Name the four things Christ accomplished in the reconciliation He provided for us in Ephesians 2:14–18.

6.2.4   Give the three analogies Paul used to describe the lasting results of the reconciliation Christ accomplished on our behalf.

Lesson 6.3   **The Revelation of the Mystery of Christ (3:1–13)**

Objectives

6.3.1   Explain the difference between mystery *as it is commonly understood and the way it was used by Paul in his letter to the Ephesians.*

6.3.2   Describe what is included in the mystery of God.

6.3.3   List the four responsibilities Christians have in light of the mystery of Christ.

6.3.4   State the two purposes of the fulfillment of the mystery of Christ.

Lesson 6.4   **Prayer and Doxology (3:14–21)**

Objectives

6.4.1   Explain how Paul's great apostolic prayer starts, is interrupted, and then is completed in Ephesians.

6.4.2   List the four things Paul prays for in Ephesians 3:14–19.

6.4.3   Describe Paul's worship at the end of the first half of Ephesians (3:20–21).

The Before and After of Those in Christ: Part 1 (2:1–10)

When the self-concept of individuals has been distorted or destroyed, how do you help them? How do you help rebuild their sense of self-worth? How do you help a person struggling with guilt? How do you help a person with an inferiority complex develop confidence?

Paul demonstrates an effective process for restoring an individual's self-concept with the great truths of the gospel. It was a process that dealt realistically with a person's past, recognized the life-transforming power of God's grace, and built confidence and hope about the future. The process involved salvation by grace through faith. Paul wanted believers to remember what happened to them when they came to Christ.

These same truths work today. The good news is that God imparts salvation and completely changes the lives of people today by grace through faith.

Before Salvation Our Situation Was Hopeless (2:1–3)

OBJECTIVE

Describe four aspects of the human condition without Christ as described by Paul in Ephesians 2:1–3.

1   What four aspects of the human condition without Christ are described in Ephesians 2:1–3?

Fundamental to any lasting change in our self-concept is a realistic appraisal of what our spiritual condition is like without Christ. Paul writes to these believers in ancient Asia Minor and reminds them of what their former life was like without their Savior. What Paul said to them is still true for Christians today. Without Christ our situation was as hopeless as theirs.

We Were Dead in Sin

Paul describes the lifestyle of the person without Christ as sinful. In Romans, Paul declared, "The wages of sin is death" (6:23). Without salvation through Christ, Paul says we are all "dead in sin." Spiritual deadness is the state of all people without Christ, and in the future, eternal death is all they have to look forward to.

We Were Lost

People without Christ are lost. According to Paul, they follow "the ways of this world" (v. 2) and its spiritual leader, Satan. When we were without Christ, the world determined our values and set the agenda for our lives. Behind the world system is the "god of this world," Satan (2 Corinthians 4:3–4). Allowing the world and the "god of this world" to set the agenda for our lives means we are truly lost.

We Were Headed for God's Judgment

Paul says that "by nature" we all deserve God's wrath (cf. Romans 1:18–21; 2:5–11). Interestingly, he contrasts what we deserve with what we receive *by grace*—salvation (Ephesians 2:8).

We Were Out of Control

Paul describes life without Christ as a life out of control. It is a life lived purely to satisfy our sinful cravings. We follow our self-focused, godless thinking. Because of this, a sense of guilt, alienation, and impending judgment characterizes our lives. One has put it this way: "We are at the mercy of the tyrant self and its rash impulses" (Wood 1978, 34).

Throughout history, many famous and affluent individuals report intense emptiness and despair at the very time they are publicly exhibiting a carefree and self-indulgent lifestyle. These people are often the envy of millions, seeming to have everything a human could possibly desire. Inside, however, these men and women are out of control, spiritually bankrupt and experiencing deteriorating mental and emotional health. Very few of these folks ever turn to God in humility and repentance to seek forgiveness and healing, but those who do find meaning and wholeness within.

6.1.2
OBJECTIVE
Define salvation *and* grace *as used in Ephesians 2:8–9.*

2   What are the meanings of the words *saved* and *grace*?

God's Grace Imparts Salvation by Faith (2:5, 8–9)

Some of the most wonderful words in Scripture follow the tragic picture painted of the human condition. They are the words "but God." The good news is that God stepped in when things were hopeless. He provided salvation for sinful, lost humanity through Jesus Christ. In these verses Paul proclaims that God graciously offers salvation to all who will receive it.

God's Grace Imparts Salvation

First, Paul reminds the believers of how salvation had come into their lives. *Salvation* is a broad, comprehensive term in the Bible. In this context, it is equivalent to the word *justification* that Paul uses in Romans (3:21–24, 27–30; 4:4–5; 4:25–5:11, 15–19; 8:33; 10:9–13). It describes how God takes guilty sinners and declares them righteous because of what Jesus has done for them (Bruce 1984, 286; Kittel 1985, 1135). Because of Christ, guilty sinners are acquitted.

Paul says this salvation from sin comes through God's grace—His gracious, unmerited favor in Christ. Completely apart from anything we attempt to merit it, God gives salvation as a gift to those who receive it by faith.

God's Grace Also Sustains Salvation

Although these verses (Ephesians 2:5, 8–9) are often used to lead people to Christ as Savior, this is not their primary purpose. Paul's purpose in writing them to the Christians in the area of Ephesus was to remind them of the salvation they already had in Christ. In fact, as the tense of the Greek verb used here indicates, they were written to remind believers of how to stay saved. The Greek verb translated "saved" in verses 5 and 8 is actually a perfect passive participle. An attempt to reproduce this in English would go something like this: "By grace you presently stand as one having been saved." In other words, if they were saved at the time of Paul's writing, it was because of God's grace in the past, God's continual grace, and God's grace presently. Salvation had come, at the beginning, by grace through faith. That salvation was being sustained by grace. Salvation is by grace, not works, from beginning to end (cf. John 1:16–17; Romans 5:1, 2; 1 Corinthians 15:10; 1 Peter 5:12; 2 Peter 3:18) (Wood 1978, 35, 37).

During a British conference on comparative religions, experts from around the world debated what belief, if any, was unique to Christianity. They began eliminating possibilities. Incarnation? Other religions had different versions of gods appearing in human form. Resurrection? Again, other religions had accounts of return from death. The debate went on for some time until C.S. Lewis wandered into the room. "What's the rumpus about?" he asked, and heard in reply that his colleagues were discussing Christianity's unique contribution among world religions. Lewis responded, "Oh, that's easy. It's grace" (Yancey 1997, 11).

OBJECTIVE

Describe the four results of being saved and in Christ identified in Ephesians 2:4–10.

3 What are the four results of being saved that Paul identifies in Ephesians 2:4–10?

At Salvation Our Lives Are Changed (2:4–7, 10)

Paul reminds the believers of four things that result from the salvation they enjoy, that is, four consequences of being in Christ.

1. We Have Life

First, Paul says that even when we were dead in sin, God gave us life when He raised Jesus from the dead (cf. 2:1). With salvation (with Christ) comes the gift of eternal life (John 3:16; Romans 6:23; Colossians 2:13; 1 John 5:11–12).

2. We Have Hope

Second, Paul says we are raised with Christ (2:6). Because of Christ's resurrection we have hope in this life, hope beyond this life, and hope beyond the grave (1 Corinthians 15:16–22).

3. We Have Position

We also have been given position along with Christ. God "has seated us with him in the heavenly realms in Christ Jesus (2:6)." Christ is not only raised from the dead, He has been exalted to the Father's right hand in a place of authority and honor. His position is somehow shared with us—we "reign in life" (Romans 5:17). Christ has taken His place at the right hand of the Father (1:20–21). We are seated with Him now. We share in His victory now. This should help us face the challenges of daily living with confidence and hope (Barton et al. 1995, 44).

4. We Have Purpose and Potential

Finally, we have purpose and potential. This is emphasized in two dimensions–the present and distant future. God wants to make us a demonstration of His abundant grace and kindness in Christ. He wants to hold us up to the universe in the coming ages as a case study in what God's grace can accomplish (2:7).

But right now, in the present, Paul claims we are God's "workmanship" (His artistic creation, His work of grace, art) created specifically through new birth to do good works in our world (Wood 1978, 36).

Author, pastor, and former atheist Lee Strobel says:

How can I tell you the difference God has made in my life? My daughter Allison was 5 years old when I became a follower of Jesus, and all she had known in those five years was a dad who was profane and angry. I remember I came home one night and kicked a hole in the living room wall, just out of anger with life. I am ashamed to think of the times Allison hid in her room to get away from me.

Five months after I gave my life to Jesus Christ, that little girl went to my wife and said, "Mommy, I want God to do for me what he's done for Daddy." At age 5. What was she saying? She'd never studied the archeological evidence [regarding the truth of the Bible]. All she knew was her dad used to be this way: hard to live with. But more and more her dad is becoming this way. And if that is what God does to people, then sign her up. At age 5 she gave her life to Jesus. God changed my family. He changed my world. He changed my eternity. (Strobel 2004)

How is your spiritual self-concept? Are you overcome with guilt? Do you struggle with feelings of inferiority because of the dramatic experiences of others? Do they seem more spiritual than you? Have others tried to put legalistic demands on you and reduce your walk with Jesus to keeping a list of rules?

This passage directs you to look to Jesus, to think about the wonderful salvation He has provided by grace through faith, to reflect on who you are and what you have *in Christ*. Remember, our salvation is not merited; we did not receive it because of our works. Rather, our standing with God comes by faith. It comes by God's grace and is sustained by God's grace from beginning to end.

The Before and After of Those in Christ: Part 2 (2:11–22)

As long as nations have existed on the earth, feuds also have existed between various groups. Think of the things that divide people: Place of birth, gender, race, religious background, politics, education, marital status, location, money, and opinions. In Christ Jesus it is different. Paul declared, "There is neither Jew nor Greek, slave nor free, male nor female, for you are all one in Christ" (Galatians 3:28).

6.2.1
OBJECTIVE

Define reconciliation, *and describe what it includes in Ephesians 2:11–22.*

4   What is the meaning of the word *reconcile* as used in Ephesians 2:11–22?

Reconciliation—a Key Theme

Reconciliation is the major, unifying theme of Ephesians 2. Reconciliation is the bringing together of two parties that are somehow divided. First, it is Christ's bringing God and mankind together through salvation. But it also includes reconciliation between individuals and groups of people as a result of the gospel (Erickson 1986, 140). In verses 1 through 10, the emphasis is upon how Christ reconciles individuals to God. Here (2:11–22), the stress is on how God reconciles people to each other because of Christ. We are united "in Christ." The good news of this passage is that anyone on the face of the earth can be reconciled through Christ, accepted by God, and made one of His chosen people. What an important message in a world torn by racial and ethnic strife!

6.2.2
OBJECTIVE

List five spiritual conditions Paul identifies that describe people before they meet Christ.

Without Christ We Experience the Consequences of Alienation (2:11–12)

Paul challenges the Christians of the Lycus Valley to remember five things about the condition of their lives before they met Christ. They can be summed up under the word *without*.

Without Christ they were "separate from Christ."

They had no *Messiah* or *Savior* to give them hope. Apart from Christ, they were headed for judgment. This is true of everyone before he or she come to Christ.

5   How did Paul describe the spiritual condition of people before they were reconciled to God through Christ?

Without citizenship they were "excluded from citizenship in Israel."

The people Paul addressed were largely Gentiles by birth and had none of the rights of spiritual citizenship enjoyed by God's people Israel. They were called *uncircumcised* by those who called themselves *the circumcision*. You can almost hear the disdain in the voice of a proud child of Abraham as he or she spoke these words.

Without covenants they were "foreigners to the covenants of the promise."

These Gentiles were not entitled to any of the benefits of the covenant community. They were viewed as aliens by Jews and had no rights to covenant promises.

Without identity they were "without hope."

Without Christ, without citizenship, and without God's covenant, they were devoid of hope (1 Thessalonians 4:5, 13). Their hopelessness was not simply because they did not share the hope of Israel; it was also the hopelessness of not sharing in the resurrection that comes through Christ (1 Corinthians 15:14–19). Without the "God of hope" (Romans 15:13) there is no real hope in this world. (Bruce 1984, 294).

Without the living God they were "without God in the world."

These Gentiles had many gods, but they were without the One true God–the living God. It was not that God would have nothing to do with them. Their condition had been caused by their own sinfulness (Romans 1:18–19), as is true for all of us.

Imagine being a refugee from another country. After surviving your flight, you land, destitute and without housing, on the shores of what you hope will be your new homeland. No one is present to welcome you, you cannot speak the language, you have no friends, and what little money you have, you do not know how to use. You are not a citizen and have no legal rights. You feel lonely, fearful, uncertain, and alienated. This is a lot like the spiritual condition of people without Christ.

Remember that the situation Paul describes for these people is true for most of us. As Gentiles, we needed an act of God to be included in God's wonderful reconciliation. The sad fact is, whether we are Jews or Gentiles, we all are sinners and need Christ's reconciliation (Romans 3:9–18, 23–24).

OBJECTIVE

Name the four things Christ accomplished in the reconciliation He provided for us in Ephesians 2:14–18.

6   What four things did Christ accomplish when He reconciled us to God?

Christ Himself Reconciled Us (2:14–18)

The words "but now," in verse 13, point to four things Christ accomplished on our behalf.

1. He Brought Us Near (2:13)

These words are Hebrew expressions used by Jews in the ancient world to describe the relative distance a person lived from Jerusalem. Paul makes the point that God acted through what Christ did on the Cross to bring us near to Him.

2. He Brought Peace (2:14–15)

Where there was no peace, Jesus brought peace. The words *He himself* are placed in such a way in the Greek as to make clear that the reconciliation was brought about by the initiative and activity of Jesus himself—through His death (*in his flesh*). Josephus, the Jewish historian, describes a barrier in the Jerusalem temple that separated the court of the Gentiles from the temple proper. Located along this barrier were signs that read, "No foreigner may enter within the barricade which surrounds the sanctuary and enclosure. Anyone who is caught doing so will have himself to blame for his ensuing death." When Jerusalem was destroyed by Titus in AD 70, that wall came down. Paul teaches here that this "dividing wall of hostility" (14) was actually dismantled much earlier by Christ, through His death (Wood 1978, 39).

3. He Brought Unity (2:15–17)

Jesus brought unity between Jew and Gentile. He brought into being a new kind of person–not Jew or Gentile, but *Christian*. Through His body, given sacrificially on behalf of both groups, reconciliation came about. He brought us together. He is "the Savior of the world" (1 John 4:14–15). Consequently, peace through Christ can be proclaimed to all—both Jew and Gentile. We are all one *in Christ*.

4. He Brought Access (2:18)

Finally, Jesus gave both Jews and Gentiles access to the presence of the Father by the Spirit (Hebrews 4:14–16; 10:19–22).

How did Christ accomplish this reconciliation? Notice the number of phrases Paul uses to show how Christ accomplished our reconciliation: He did it "through the blood of Christ (2:13); "in his flesh" (2:15); "in himself" (2:15); "through the cross" (2:16), and finally, "through him" (2:18). What a wonderful Savior! He accomplished what all the wars, the peace treaties, and the alliances of the ages have failed to do. He brought people of the world together (Jew and Gentile) *in himself.*

In 1987, an IRA bomb went off in a town west of Belfast. Eleven died; sixty three were wounded. Gordon Wilson, a cloth merchant and devout Methodist, was buried with his twenty–year–old daughter under five feet of concrete and brick. "Daddy, I love you very much," were Marie's last words as she grasped her father's hand. Later, from his hospital bed, Wilson said, "I've lost my daughter, but I bear no grudge. I shall pray every night that God will forgive them." Once recovered, Wilson crusaded for reconciliation. He met with the IRA, personally forgave them, and asked them to lay down their arms. When he died in 1995, all Ireland and Britain honored this ordinary citizen for his uncommon forgiveness (Yancey 1997).

Why did Christ do what He did? Reconciliation was His objective. First, reconciliation of humanity to God (2:1–10). Then reconciliation between individuals and groups of people through Christ (2:11–22). Christ's purpose was a new order of humanity. "His purpose was to create in himself one new person out of the two, thus making peace, and in this one body to reconcile both of them to God through the cross" (2:15–16).

Through Christ We Experience the Benefits of Reconciliation (2:13, 19–22)

OBJECTIVE

Give the three analogies Paul used to describe the lasting results of the reconciliation Christ accomplished on our behalf.

What are the results of the reconciliation Christ brought about? We are no longer excluded from God's covenant, promises, or provision. Together, we are the people of God (cf. 1 Peter 2:9–10). Paul makes this point using three analogies:

1. We Are Fellow Citizens in God's Kingdom

Paul used a political metaphor the people would understand. People born and raised in a country are citizens of that country. They belong, as do all born into that country. Christians are *fellow citizens* with the people of God from all ages—Jew and gentile.

2. We Are Fellow Members of God's Family

7   What three analogies does Paul use to describe the results of Christ's reconciliation?

Not only does Paul draw upon a political analogy, he uses the warmth and closeness of family relationships to make his point. No distance exists here. We are family.

3. We Are Built Together Into a Temple

We are a dwelling place in which God lives by His Spirit. Two ideas would come to the mind of these Ephesian believers. First, their thoughts would go to the enormous, opulent temple of Artemis, void of the presence of any living god. Second, they would think of the Jewish temple in Jerusalem. Paul's point is stunning and revolutionary. The dwelling place of the living God was not constructed of marble and mortar. It was being built of redeemed, reconciled human *stones* who were *in Christ*. The presence of God is what constitutes a temple, not lavish architecture or ritual. Anyone who had visited the small gatherings of believers throughout Ephesus and the surrounding countryside knew God manifested His presence among them. These believers, Jew and Gentile, were being "built together to become a dwelling in which God lives by his Spirit" (2:22).

Imagine trying to place a personal call to the president of our country. Your call probably would not be put through. Or visualize going up to the White House gates, shaking them, and ordering the guards to let you in. They would probably put you in a little, white van and make you wear a funny-looking jacket as they hauled you away. But One greater than the president will accept you and allow you to enter His presence as part of His family. You can call on Him any time. You can knock and be invited in. You will not be an outcast; He will make you a citizen. You will not be a stranger. You will be a member of His family!

God loves the whole world. Jesus died for the sins of whole world. The reconciliation He provides for us is both vertical and horizontal in orientation. Christ's reconciliation first brings those who accept it into right relationship with God. But it also reconciles people to each other. Consequently, there is no place for racial, cultural, or gender prejudice among Christians. Feelings of superiority over other people for physical, emotional, intellectual, social, national, educational, or financial reasons are caused by sinful pride and a failure to understand the nature of God's grace. Since God, through His love, is the supreme reconciler, we also should be reconcilers. "Accept one another, then, just as Christ accepted you" (Romans 15:7).

LESSON 6.3

6.3.1
OBJECTIVE

Explain the difference between mystery *as it is commonly understood and the way it was used by Paul in his letter to the Ephesians.*

The Revelation of the Mystery of Christ (3:1–13)

I enjoy reading a good mystery novel: one that keeps my attention with a captivating plot, draws me in and keeps me on the edge of my chair to the very end. You never really know how it is going to turn out. I can hardly put such a book down. That is how we tend to think about a mystery. It is a whodunit, a puzzle, a problem for us to solve, something for humans to discover by their ingenuity.

To some degree, the above description is the way people in the Greco-Roman world thought of mystery. The word was well-known to people involved in the mystery religions of the time. For them, religious truth, such as the secret of the ages or the *mystery* of the cosmos, was available only to a select few who had been initiated into the deep things of their religion. They had to work hard to achieve this level of knowledge.

Paul's use of the term, however, is different. He used the word *mystery* as someone with a Jewish background would use it. The Jewish view was that *mystery* (3:9) was a truth, once hidden, but now made known. It was something incredible, but true. It was a truth made known by revelation. It could not be uncovered by human effort or ingenuity. It was an *open secret*. Paul declares that God himself had revealed the mystery in Christ (3:11) and now it was to be proclaimed to *all nations* or all peoples of the world (Ladd 1974, 93–99; O'Brien 1993, 621–623).

The Mystery Has Been Revealed (3:1–5)

The first thing Paul wanted the believers to understand was why he was in prison and why he was writing to them. Although he had been arrested on Jewish charges, he did not consider himself a prisoner of the Jews. Although Roman authority had imprisoned him, he did not consider himself a Roman prisoner. Although he had appealed to Caesar, he was not ultimately in Caesar's jurisdiction. He was where he was because of Jesus Christ, and he was serving the needs of others at the Lord's command (cf. Philippians 1:12–13). An exemplary approach to difficult circumstances!

Paul saw himself as a steward or administrator of *the mystery of Christ*—God's revelation to all humanity. The wonderful thing was, the mystery was no longer hidden. In the past, although glimpses of it had been revealed to the patriarchs and prophets, the Holy Spirit had now revealed it *in Christ* in a clear and wonderful way.

The key to an effective mystery story is timing. The stage needs to be set, the plot introduced, the characters developed, the suspense built and built and built, and then the revelation. Timing was everything for the revelation of God's mystery, too. Scripture says, "When the right time finally came, God sent his own Son. He came as the son of a human mother and lived under the Jewish Law, to redeem those who were under the Law, so that we might become God's sons" (Galatians 4:4–5, TEV).

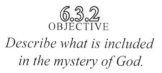

OBJECTIVE

Describe what is included in the mystery of God.

The Mystery Includes All Nations (3:6)

In verse 6, Paul describes the content of *the mystery of God*. His description is really a summary or restatement of the wonderful truth of Ephesians 2:11–22. Paul said the mystery of Christ is that Gentiles are welcomed into the body of Christ along with Jewish believers.

It is easy to miss the significance of the Greek word translated "Gentiles" in our New Testament Bibles (*ta ethnē*). It literally means "the nations" or "the peoples of the world" (Gingrich 1983, 55). Paul would be the first to acknowledge and reaffirm God's historic and ongoing plan for Israel, clearly taught in the Bible. He does this in Romans 9 through 11. But he would also passionately argue that the mystery of God (God's marvelous redemptive plan) includes the nations as well, irrespective of race, culture, gender, or status in life. In fact, people from all nations of the world, people called and redeemed by God's grace, are included on an equal footing with Jewish believers as *God's very own, elect people*.

God makes no distinction between Jewish and Gentile believers. In fact, the words Paul uses to describe their relationship in Christ emphasizes the togetherness of their relationship. Each word is a compound created with a Greek preposition meaning "along with." Paul proclaimed that Jewish and Gentile believers were:

"Heirs Together with Israel"

The covenant promises made to Abraham, Isaac, and Jacob are confirmed and passed on to all those who possess the faith of Abraham (Romans 4:16–25). We share in these promises because of Jesus Christ (Romans 8:17; Galatians 3:26–29).

"Members Together of One Body"

How wonderful that Christ's reconciliation makes us members of one body with the incredible privilege and responsibility of being called "the body of Christ" (Romans 12:4–5; 1 Corinthians 12:12–27; Ephesians 4:11–16; 5:22–30; Colossians 1:18). How marvelous that God takes the diversity that makes up the *body of Christ* and brings unity *in Christ*, both personally and collectively.

"Sharers Together in the Promise in Christ Jesus"

Paul also wrote, in 2 Timothy 1:1, about "the promise of life that is in Christ Jesus." God fulfills those promises, irrespective of race, culture, gender, age, or any other factors that divide people. All of the promises of God find their "yes" in Christ (2 Corinthians 1:19–20).

We are not unique, but we have had the privilege of adopting three Native American children as our own. We certainly are not perfect parents, but when we decided to adopt the children, we agreed we would do everything in our power to treat them as our own. They are as much a part of our family as our birth daughter. They are included equally in our inheritance; we love them dearly and receive them as our children in every sense of the word. Perhaps, in a small way, we have been able to mirror "the mystery of God" (v. 6).

6.3.3
OBJECTIVE
List the four responsibilities Christians have in light of the mystery of Christ.

8   How does the message of Ephesians 3:6 apply to your church, your community, and our world?

The Mystery Involves Responsibilities (3:2, 7–9)

Paul recognized the benefits that came to all nations—all peoples of the world—because of God's revealing "the mystery of Christ" and bringing it to pass through the sacrifice of Christ. But he also recognized that the mystery involved responsibilities. He identifies at least four areas of responsibility:

1. The Responsibility of Stewardship for God's Grace (3:2)

Paul spoke in verse 2 of "the administration of God's grace that was given to me for you." The word used here is one that relates to the administrative responsibility given a person assigned to manage the finances and affairs of a household, such as a steward (Rienecker 1980, 524). Paul viewed the gospel as God's grace extended to the world. Paul's responsibility was one of stewardship (1 Corinthians 4:1–2; 9:16–17; Colossians 1:25–28).

2. The Responsibility of a Servant (3:7)

Paul then adopts one of his favorite words for describing Christian service, *servanthood* (from the Greek word, *diakonos*, meaning "servant" or sometimes "table waiter"). From Paul's perspective, being a minister of the gospel was the highest imaginable honor—an undeserved blessing (Bruce 1984, 316–317). He believed being a servant of the Lord could be adequately carried out only "through the working of His power."

3. The Responsibility to Proclaim Christ (3:8)

What a marvelous, undeserved privilege to proclaim the *unsearchable riches of Christ* to the world. The word Paul uses here is the one found in the Septuagint to describe the inscrutability of God's ways (cf. Romans 11:33). It describes the unlimited riches to be found in Christ. He who had once viciously persecuted the church (1 Corinthians 15:9–11) now proclaimed the gospel. What grace! What responsibility!

4. The Responsibility to Teach Clearly (3:9)

And finally, Paul emphasizes the importance of a teaching ministry. He saw it as his responsibility to *make plain* to others what God had now revealed and provided for all humanity through the gospel. Those involved in teaching ministry will understand the joy that comes from helping people understand what God has provided *in Christ*. This, in fact, was the theme of Paul's apostolic prayer (1:17–19).

Missionary David Grant tells the following story:

My Dad was a wonderful provider. He saw to it we had everything we really needed. But we had responsibilities. When Dad had to leave for the day, he would leave a list of things to be done. When he returned, he expected those things to be accomplished. One of these days our loving, generous Lord is going to return. Will we have accomplished what He commissioned us to do? (Grant 2004)

The Mystery Expresses God's Purpose (3:10–13)

This marvelous mystery of Christ had both a grand and practical purpose. First, Paul said God wanted to make known His multifaceted wisdom through the church. He wanted to hold up the redeemed of all nations as a demonstration of what God's grace in Christ can accomplish.

Second, there was a very practical purpose of the mystery of Christ being fulfilled in prayer. In the Old Testament, the high priest could approach God's presence in the *Holiest of All* of the temple only once a year with a blood sacrifice. To come at any other time meant death. But Paul now declares that "in Him and through faith in Him we may approach God with freedom and confidence" (cf. 2:18; Hebrews 4:14–16; 10:19–22). Regardless of our background, our position in life, our gender or color, we can boldly approach God through Christ in prayer (Wood 1978, 48).

What an electrifying moment I experienced at *Celebration 2000* in Indianapolis as redeemed people from nearly every nation on earth paraded into the large stadium. Equally electrifying was the moment the voices of believers from every part of the globe were lifted in a mighty chorus of fervent prayer. Scenes like this have been repeated over the years and in every case they deeply move those experiencing them. They will be nothing, however, compared to the scene in heaven when the redeemed from every nation, tribe, people, and language stand before the throne of the Lamb and raise their voices in worship (Revelation 7:9–10).

What marvelous news. Paul called it a mystery, a truth once hidden, but now openly revealed. The good news of this mystery is that you are included. I am included. All are included who believe. "God so loved *the world* that he gave his one and only Son, that *whoever* believes in him shall not perish but have everlasting life" (John 3:16; emphasis added). "You are a chosen people, a royal priesthood, a holy nation, a people belonging to God, that you may declare the praises of him who called you out of darkness into his wonderful light. Once you were not a people, but now you are the people of God; once you had not received mercy, but now you have received mercy" (1 Peter 2:9–10). "You are all sons of God through faith in Christ Jesus" (Galatians 3:26). Through the gospel, God has brought about a new order of humanity, not Jew or Gentile, but Christian.

Prayer and Doxology (3:14–21)

Have you ever been interrupted? Was that a point of frustration or a welcome event? It appears as though Paul's prayer resumes after a long interruption (2:1–3:14). He began his apostolic prayer in chapter 1 with the words "For this reason" (1:15–23). He prayed that the Father would give the Christians in and around Ephesus a Spirit of wisdom and revelation so they would know Christ in a deeper, more personal and accurate way. He wanted them to know the hope they had been called to receive, the riches of their inheritance in Christ, and how incredibly great was God's power at work within them. Paul then, however, felt compelled to remind the believers of what they were like before they experienced Christ and how their lives had changed after meeting Him (2:1–22). Then it appears he briefly attempted to continue his prayer at the beginning of chapter 3 with the phrase, "For this reason" (v. 1), but began to explain his stewardship of the mystery of Christ—that all people of the world, regardless of background, race, culture, gender, or situation in life, could be included in God's family in Christ (3:2–13). What wonderful digressions! What inspired interruptions! Now at last, at the end of chapter 3, Paul finishes the prayer he began in chapter 1 (note the telltale "for this reason" in 3:14).

This passage also functions like an exclamation mark at the end of the first part of the epistle. In the first part, Paul emphasized God's provision in Christ, which was the indicative part of the motif (see Chapter 5, Lesson 1). He reminded these believers of who they are and what they have in Christ. He informs them of what Christ has accomplished, what He is doing, and what He will do in their lives. He systematically pumps into their spiritual awareness a reminder of *every spiritual blessing* they have in Christ. The prayer, at the close of the first half of the epistle, is like a fanfare ending the first movement of a spiritual symphony the Apostle is writing. The trumpets blare, the cymbals crash, the drums roll. Everything builds to this point.

Believers Need Everything God Provides in Christ (3:14–19)

Thus far the Ephesian believers have been re-awakened to what they have in Christ as their provision for Christian life and living. "The God and Father of our Lord Jesus Christ . . . has blessed us in the heavenly realms with every spiritual blessing in Christ" (1:3) and "for this reason," Paul can now kneel and pour his heart out to the Father in intercession. He wants these believers to understand who they are and what they have. Paul's heart longs for and prays specifically for four things that every believer needs.

1. For the Believers to be Strengthened Within by the Holy Spirit (3:16)

Christians, in and around Ephesus, faced circumstances that sorely tested their faith. They struggled with spiritual adversaries whose tactics sapped their spiritual strength (6:10–12). They needed inner strength sufficient to withstand the pressures they faced. That is precisely what Paul prayed for. The word *strengthen* used here is opposite of the word *discouraged* used in verse 13 (Wood 1978). This is precisely what Christians need today to be overcomers—the empowering of the Holy Spirit within.

2. For Christ to Be *At Home* in Their Hearts (3:17)

Second, Paul prayed that Christ would be more and more *at home* in the hearts of these believers. This is the natural result of the Holy Spirit dwelling within. In fact, it is facilitated by the Spirit (Romans 8:14–16; Galatians 4:5–7) (Fee 1994, 696). This at-home-reality, that is the growing awareness of Christ's presence within, is facilitated by the Holy Spirit and sustained through faith.

3. For a Deeper Knowledge of Christ's Love (3:17–19)

Paul was convinced that one of the greatest needs in the life of believers was the constant awareness and growing realization of how much God loved them. He prays that the roots of their spiritual lives be deeply embedded in God's love. Then he prays for a growing comprehension of that love. The terminology Paul uses creates a breathtaking paradox: "To know this love that surpasses knowledge" (3:19).

What is Paul saying? He is acknowledging that the Christian life is to be one ongoing, ever-deepening discovery of God's love (Lamentations 3:22–23; Romans 8:35–39). It is theologically and factually accurate to declare, "You have no idea how much God loves you." Yet we need to become more and more aware of that every day.

9 What four responsibilities does every Christian have in light of the mystery of Christ?

10 What four things does Paul pray for in this passage (Ephesians 3:14–21)?

6.4.2
OBJECTIVE

List the four things Paul prays for in Ephesians 3:14–19.

11 How do these four things relate to your Christian life?

A great hymn of the church put it this way:

Could we with ink the ocean fill, and were the skies of parchment made,

Were every stalk on earth a quill, and every man a scribe by trade,

To write the love of God above would drain the ocean dry.

Nor could the scroll contain the whole, though stretched from sky to sky.

O love of God, how rich and pure.

How measureless and strong.

It shall forever more endure the saints and angels song. (Lehman 1976)

4. For Them to Be Filled with God's Fullness (3:19)

Finally, Paul sums it all up by praying, "That you may be filled to the measure of all the fullness of God" (v. 19). This does not mean our being filled diminishes God's fullness in any way. His fullness is inexhaustible and unending. Neither does it mean that our being filled with His fullness makes us *little gods*. It simply means that God, in Christ, has made available to us divine resources for living the Christian life.

I remember someone telling me about visiting an aging parent and discovering, to his dismay, that the parent was living like a pauper. Closets were filled with threadbare clothes, the cupboards were bare, and the refrigerator was empty. The house was in disrepair. The parent would not visit a doctor because of a lack of money. An examination of the parent's finances, however, revealed something quite different. A loving spouse had provided more than enough to care for all needs. The living spouse was unaware of what was available. The same is true of those who have an inheritance *in Christ*. We need everything God provides. Here Paul prays, "O Father, help them realize and claim who they are and what they have in Christ."

6.4.3
OBJECTIVE
Describe Paul's worship at the end of the first half of Ephesians (3:20–21).

God Provides More than We Can Imagine in Christ (3:20–21)

Paul's heart seems to overflow as he rehearses the spiritual blessing available to believers (1:3). God has provided more than we can imagine in His Son. He is able to do far more than we can imagine. As a result, Paul fairly explodes in worship.

Anyone who has had to do much writing knows what it is to have a concept or idea so grand it is difficult to put into words. You search your vocabulary bank for the right words; you rummage in the thesaurus; and you talk with trusted colleagues about phraseology. The quest is to do the concept justice. That is the challenge Paul faced. His only recourse was to use many superlatives (extreme words), phrases, and images in an attempt to describe the spiritual bounty available in Christ. The Holy Spirit gave Paul inspiration, and the result is one of the most majestic, grand, awe-inspiring expressions of praise in the Bible.

12 According to Paul, to what extent is God able to work in believers' lives and how?

1. What Is God Able to Do?

"God is able to do immeasurably more than all we ask or imagine" (v. 20). We are accustomed to wanting more than we dare ask. Our dreams exceed our resources. But here that concept is turned on its head. Our imagination or our dreams cannot exceed God's provision in Christ.

2. How Is God Able to Do It?

God is able to accomplish all of this "according to His power that is at work within us" (v. 20, second part) That is the same power Paul says resurrected Jesus from the dead, that resulted in the ascension, that led to Christ's exaltation at the Father's right hand, and the same power by which He rules and sustains everything (1:19–22; Colossians 1:15–18). Incredible power for everyday living is at work within the humblest believer in Christ.

3. Why Is God to Be Glorified?

The Living Bible beautifully captures the character and spirit of Paul's praise: "Glory be to God who by his mighty power at work within us is able to do far more than we would ever dare to ask or even dream of—infinitely beyond our highest prayers, desires, thoughts, or hopes. May he be given glory forever and ever through endless ages because of his master plan of salvation for the church through Jesus Christ" (3:20–21, LB).

Have you discovered Jesus? Have you experienced life abundant in Christ? Have you grasped the possibilities of what God can do in your life? Have you begun to imagine the mighty things God is able to do within and through your church by the Holy Spirit? Let it be said again, with inspired emphasis—He is able!

Test Yourself

Circle the letter of the *best* answer.

1. Without Christ, people are
a) poor, lost, out of control, and headed for God's judgment.
b) lost, dead in their sin, out of control, and headed for God's judgment.
c) tormented, lost, dead in their sin, and out of control.
d) poor, dead in their sin, lost, and headed for God's judgment.

2. According to the IST, four results of being saved and *in Christ* are
a) life, hope, position, and purpose/potential.
b) prosperity, position, hope, and purpose/potential.
c) persecution, life, hope, and purpose/potential.
d) position, prosperity, hope, and life.

3. Before people accept Christ, Paul describes them as without
a) hope, God, purpose, Christ, and a future.
b) Christ, citizenship, hope, covenants, and God.
c) purpose, destiny, citizenship, hope, and God.
d) Christ, citizenship, covenants, purpose, and significance.

4. Believers are reconciled in Christ, bringing them
a) hope, joy, purpose, and access to God.
b) access to God, hope, unity, and prosperity.
c) hope, peace, purpose, and prosperity.
d) near to God, peace, unity, and access to God.

5. A benefit of reconciliation is that believers are
a) fellow citizens of God's kingdom.
b) fellow members of God's family.
c) built together into a temple, a dwelling place for God's Spirit.
d) all of the above.

6. Paul used the word *mystery* as it was commonly used by the
a) Greeks.
b) Romans.
c) Jews.
d) mystics.

7. The Greek word *ethnos,* usually translated as "Gentile" in the context of the New Testament, literally means "the
a) heathen."
b) nations."
c) uncircumcised."
d) outsiders."

8. Four responsibilities believers have in light of the mystery of Christ are to
a) be a steward of God's grace, be a servant, proclaim Christ, and teach clearly.
b) suffer, be a servant, proclaim Christ, and be hospitable.
c) be hospitable, be a servant, proclaim Christ, and teach clearly.
d) give generously, be a servant, proclaim Christ, and be hospitable.

9. In Ephesians 3:7, Paul refers to himself as a servant, which in the Greek literally means
a) "second class."
b) "bound to another."
c) "a table waiter."
d) "humbled one."

10. In Paul's prayer for the Ephesians (3:14–19), he prays that they may
a) know the joy of the Lord and His love that surpasses knowledge.
b) be strengthened by the power of the Holy Spirit and know His love that surpasses knowledge.
c) be rooted and built up, and have the joy of the Lord.
d) be filled with the fullness of God and have a peace that passes all understanding.

Responses to Interactive Questions

CHAPTER 6

Some of these responses may include information that is supplemental to the IST. These questions are intended to produce reflective thinking beyond the course content and your responses may vary from these examples.

1 What four aspects of the human condition without Christ are described in Ephesians 2:1–3?

Before they come to Christ, people are dead in sin, lost, headed for God's judgment, and out of control.

2 What are the meanings of the words saved and grace?

Salvation describes how God takes guilty sinners and declares them righteous because of what Jesus has done for them. Grace is God's unmerited favor toward us because we are in Christ. Completely apart from anything we do to try merit it, God gives salvation as a gift to those who receive it by faith.

3 What are the four results of being saved that Paul identifies in Ephesians 2:4–10?

When we are saved, we receive life, hope, and position, and we have purpose and potential.

4 What is the meaning of the word reconcile as used in Ephesians 2:11–22?

To reconcile is to bring together two parties that are somehow divided. First, it is Christ's bringing God and humanity together through salvation. But it also includes reconciliation between individuals and groups of people as a result of the gospel.

5 How did Paul describe the spiritual condition of people before they were reconciled to God through Christ?

Before salvation, people are separate from Christ, without citizenship, without covenants, without hope, and without God.

6 What four things did Christ accomplish when He reconciled us to God?

Christ brought us near, brought peace, brought unity, and brought access to God.

7 What three analogies does Paul use to describe the results of Christ's reconciliation?

Through Christ we are fellow citizens in God's kingdom, members of God's family, and are being built together into a temple, a dwelling place in which God lives by His Spirit.

8 How does the message of Ephesians 3:6 apply to your church, your community, and our world?

Answers will vary.

9 What four responsibilities does every Christian have in light of the mystery of Christ?

Every believer has his or her responsibility to serve as steward of God's grace, to minister by serving, to proclaim Christ, and to teach clearly.

10 What four things does Paul pray for in this passage (Ephesians 3:14–21)?

Paul prays for the believers to be strengthened within by the Holy Spirit, that Christ would be at home in their hearts, for them to have a deeper knowledge of Christ's love, and for them to be filled with God's fullness.

11 How do these four things relate to your Christian life?

Answers will vary.

12 According to Paul, what is God able to work in believers' lives and how?

God can do immeasurably far more than we could ask or even imagine by His power that is at work within us.

Paul's Appeal and God's Goal: Christ Fully Expressed (Ephesians 4:1–5:21)

This emphasis in this passage (really ranging from 4:1 to 6:9) beautifully illustrates a characteristic pattern found in Paul's letters that students of the New Testament refer to as Christ's provision and Christian responsibility or the indicative-imperative motif (see Chapter 5, Lesson 1). The pattern is first to establish who Christ is, what He has accomplished, and who believers are in Him (the indicative part). Then comes a focus on Christian responsibility or application. Paul urges Christians to be what they are in Christ. He challenges them to live out their daily lives in keeping with these spiritual realities (the imperative part). It was God's desire that Christ would be fully expressed by His children living out their lives as changed people. Paul specifies that Christ should be fully expressed in at least three broad contexts:

1. Christ expressed in and through the Church (4:1–16)
2. Christ expressed in and through the lives of believers (4:17–5:21)
3. Christ expressed in the home and work place (5:21–6:9)

Paul begins this section of Ephesians with a powerful Greek word that forms a turning point in the epistle. It is translated "I urge you" (4:1). It is then followed by a word that dominates the entire section of Ephesians—the Greek word translated "live" (NIV) or "walk" (KJV). It is Paul's favorite word for dealing with issues of Christian behavior in Ephesians (4:1,17; 5:1, 8, 15). It literally means "to go about, to walk about, to conduct one's life, to live" (Gingrich 1983, 157). In Ephesians, Paul says, "I urge you" to

- live a life worthy of the calling you have received (4:1).
- live no longer as the Gentiles do (4:17).
- live a life of love [imitate God . . . just as Christ] (5:1).
- live as children of light (5:8).
- be very careful how you live (5:15).

Paul was concerned that these believers, living in a pagan world, surrounded by pagan values, live as Christians, Christ-centered, Christ-oriented people, whose lives were being transformed inside out. God wants us to be new and transformed people because of Jesus.

- *Read Ephesians 4:1–5:21 before you begin study in this chapter.*

Lesson 7.1   Christ Fully Expressed through the Church (4:1–16)

Objectives

7.1.1   Explain why Paul placed such emphasis on the need for unity in the local church.

7.1.2   Explain how God uses the variety of people in a church.

7.1.3   Identify the responsibilities assigned by God to church leadership.

7.1.4   Describe God's goal for individual believers.

Lesson 7.2　　**Christ Fully Expressed in Our Personal Lives: Part 1 (4:17–32)**

Objectives

7.2.1　List five behaviors Paul indicated Christians should put off.

7.2.2　List five characteristics Paul indicated Christians should put on.

Lesson 7.3　　**Christ Fully Expressed in Our Personal Lives: Part 2 (5:1–7)**

Objectives

7.3.1　Explain how believers are to imitate God.

7.3.2　Compare the lifestyle of the Christian and the non-Christian.

7.3.3　Explain how Christians are able to demonstrate true love within their culture.

Lesson 7.4　　**Christ Fully Expressed in Our Personal Lives: Part 3 (5:8–21)**

Objectives

7.4.1　Identify how Paul uses the concepts of light and darkness to compare the life of the nonbeliever to that of a Christian.

7.4.2　Identify ways Paul defines walking in darkness.

7.4.3　Define what it means to live as children of the light.

Christ Fully Expressed through the Church (4:1–16)

Paul reminds the Ephesian believers that he was in prison for Jesus' sake, a "prisoner for the Lord" (v. 1) in Rome. He was there serving the needs of others at the Lord's command and will (cf. Philippians 1:12–13). Paul also reminds them that God has a high calling for them, even in their present circumstances. He has a mission for the local church. God's desire is that Christ be fully expressed through the church, the "body of Christ."

7.1.1
OBJECTIVE
Explain why Paul placed such emphasis on the need for unity in the local church.

The Church Must Be Unified to Be Effective (4:1–6)

Paul urges these Christians to live or walk worthy of their high and holy calling. They are called to be *the church*, the "body of Christ" (v. 4) in their culture. How are they to accomplish that? They must be unified. The first six verses of Ephesians 4 emphasize unity. This is summarized by the words in verse 3: "Make every effort to keep the unity of the Spirit through the bond of peace." To achieve this goal Paul emphasizes four things:

1　What is God's purpose for the church as the body of Christ?

1.　The Character Qualities that Contribute to Unity

Paul identifies four character qualities that contribute to unity: humility, gentleness, patience, and forbearance. In short, they were to allow the fruit of the Holy Spirit to dominate their relationships with each other (Galatians 5:22–23). These qualities are needed in every local church.

2.　The Recognition of What They Share in Common

Tragically, what Paul intended to be a reminder of what Christians share in common has often become a hotbed of theological debate (2:4–6). Debates have raged over in what sense there is "one Lord, one faith, one baptism" (5). But this type of debate misses Paul's point. His purpose was to point out what believers share in common and urge them to focus on these things, not the things that divide them. Focusing on points of contention only drives a wedge between Christians.

3. The Model or Example of the Trinity

Paul draws on the unity found in the Trinity into the discussion: "One Spirit . . . one Lord . . . one God and Father." Just as the Trinity is unified, yet its members are distinct, so believers are to be individually different, yet unified.

4. The Role of the Holy Spirit in Producing Unity

Finally, Paul stresses the role of the Holy Spirit in creating and sustaining unity. This type of unity cannot be produced by the believers. It exists because of the Holy Spirit's work within and among them. Their responsibility is to "keep it" (v. 3), to appreciate and nurture the unity the Holy Spirit creates (Fee 1994, 698–705).

No church can adequately be the "body of Christ" (v. 4) representing Jesus in its culture, without unity. My father was a farmer from an earlier era. I remember him describing, with glowing admiration, the beauty of a matched team of workhorses pulling together under expert leadership. He would explain how each horse had to fulfill its role and the cooperation and coordination of the horses required to accomplish tasks. In the same way, how beautiful, how powerful is a unified congregation within a community. They function as the body of Christ, fulfilling His ministry and accomplishing the work of God.

7.1.2
OBJECTIVE

Explain how God uses the variety of people in a church.

2   How can the church function effectively when people have such differing gifts?

The Church Is Made Up of Different People with Different Gifts (4:7–10)

Not only did Paul emphasize the importance of unity in the church, he acknowledged the differences that exist within it. Verse 7 begins: "But to each one." Paul points out that each person is different. Each Christian has been uniquely gifted by God. Christ, in His wisdom, is the giver of these different gifts through the Spirit (1 Corinthians 12:4–11; 1 Peter 4:10). He is the One who graces every believer (John 1:16; Romans 12:6).

In verses 8 to 10, Paul draws upon the language and imagery of Psalm 68:18. The Lord is pictured as returning in triumph after the overthrow of His enemies and those of His people. As was common with ancient conquerors, He had taken His enemies captive and brought with Him the spoils of battle. As a conqueror, He had received gifts He could give away. "When you ascended on high, you led captives in your train; you received gifts from men, even from the rebellious" (Psalm 68:18). But now, in Ephesians 4:8, Paul purposefully changes the wording to show that this victory has already taken place through Christ's death, burial, and resurrection. The Lord has engaged in a battle with cosmic proportions. He has won and returned with the spoil of battle. Now He gifts His people and gives them back to the church (Foulkes 1979, 114–115).

We are all different. We are the *spoils* of the battle waged through His death, burial, and resurrection. His redeemed people have been gifted and given back to the church to do His work in the world.

Jerry Cole fits this scenario. During the hippie movement, he lived in a commune, used drugs, lived a promiscuous life, and was lost. A fearless, godly lady preacher was God's agent to visit that commune, persistently demonstrate Christ's love in face of their rejection, and ultimately rescue those who lived there from sin for the Savior. They were the spoils of Christ's victory. The Lord redeemed Jerry, gifted him, and gave him back to the church as an effective pastor. Praise the Lord!

7.1.3
OBJECTIVE
Identify the responsibilities assigned by God to church leadership.

3   What is meant by each of the leadership functions Paul identifies in Ephesians 4:11–12?

The Church's Leadership Is to Equip and Mobilize Believers for Christ (4:11–12)

Paul now talks to the congregations about the purpose and role of church leadership. The leadership of the local church is actually made up of gifted people whom Christ has redeemed and then called to serve the fellowship of believers.

They include the following:

Apostles—Those agents of Christ authorized to declare the gospel and further God's purposes, especially in unreached areas.

Prophets—Those inspired, anointed individuals who powerfully speak a message from God.

Evangelists–Those individuals called and gifted to proclaim the gospel, both in personal and public contexts (Keener 1993, 547; Rossier 1989, 137).

Pastors and teachers—These two positions of service are grouped in the Greek text in such a way as to suggest they are complementary and often combined in the same person. One shepherds God's flock; the other disciples and trains them (Wood 1978, 58).

Others—This is not an exhaustive list of spiritually gifted leaders, but a representative and suggestive one (Fee 1994, 707).

4   What is the purpose of church leadership?

The task of church leaders, according to Paul, was to "prepare God's people for works of service" (v. 12). They were to help them identify their gifts and calling. They were then to train, empower, and release them into ministry. The ministry of Christ is fulfilled within a community and around the world by an empowered, trained, and fully mobilized church. A few superstars cannot accomplish the task! All are gifted, all should be trained and prepared, and all should be involved in ministry. The responsibility of church leaders is to fully equip and mobilize redeemed people for ministry.

In verse 13 Paul spells out the ultimate purpose for church leaders and the interdependent ministries of the local church. First, the church is to grow in unity in what they believe (that is, "the faith" often refers to what is believed). Second, they are to grow in their personal knowledge of God (that is, come to know the Lord better). And ultimately, the church is to become the mature, full expression of Christ, both individually and collectively.

I remember the shock I experienced when I first understood my job as a leader in the church. I was not hired by a congregation merely to marry, bury, visit the sick, and pray at public events. In fact, I was not to view myself as *hired* at all. I came to realize that my role was much like that of a player-coach. I was called to equip believers for ministry in keeping with their gifts and calling, and mobilize them as "the body of Christ" (v. 12) within the community and around the world. All of us were to be His hands, His feet, His voice, and His healing presence in the power of the Holy Spirit. God did enable us, pastor and people, to accomplish that. I praise Him!

7.1.4
OBJECTIVE
Describe God's goal for individual believers.

The Church Is to Express Fully Christ in the World (4:13–16)

In verses 13–16, Paul challenges the church to live out God's purpose in the world. God's ultimate purpose is that the church would fully express Christ in the world.

Then Paul describes a progression that ought to characterize every Christian and congregation. First, immature, inconsistent behavior would go. They would no longer be swayed by every "wind of doctrine" (v. 14) that blew. They would not be easily deceived. Instead, there would be ongoing growth and development like that of a healthy human body. Christ would be the head and each member of the church would function as a part of His body on earth. Loving truthfulness would characterize interpersonal relationships; Christlike love would bind all together. Every part of the body would be mobilized and functioning, in every way becoming more like Christ.

Nothing is more beautiful than a child growing into a mature, productive adult. I am a parent and I will jump at the chance to show you the pictures of my children. I am proud of them. Equal pride and satisfaction comes with beholding a growing, maturing, effective church that is becoming more and more the expression of Jesus to the world.

Jesus has a purpose for your life. You are important to Him. He cared enough to give His life to rescue you from sin. Apart from Him you will waste your life. With Him your life counts. He wants to include you in what He is doing in the world through the church. Will you commit yourself to Him and His purposes for your life? Will you develop your gifts and invest your best efforts to serve Him in and through the church–the body of Christ on earth?

Christ Fully Expressed in Our Personal Lives: Part 1 (4:17–32)

Governments sometimes offer something called a witness protection program for those willing to testify against elements of organized crime in their society. In exchange for incriminating testimony, the witness is given a new name and identity for his or her protection. In some cases, the historical record of that person is destroyed. In essence, they become *a new person*. Something similar happens when a person is born again (John 3:3, 6–7). Paul put it this way in another epistle: "If anyone is in Christ, he is a new creation; the old has gone, the new has come!" (2 Corinthians 5:17).

Christians are new and different people. Not different in terms of being weird or odd, but different because their lives have been radically transformed because of Jesus Christ. This influences their values and behavior. It impacts the way they think, talk, live, and respond to the issues of life.

Paul emphasizes the word live in verse 17. He challenges believers, "I tell you this, and insist on it in the Lord, that you must no longer live as the Gentiles (or unconverted) do."

Those Who Are in Christ Should Not Live Like the Unconverted

Paul solemnly insists that Christians must not live their lives as the unconverted do. Paul is writing to a largely Gentile church. Therefore, his use of the word Gentile in verse 17 is not used in a racial way, but rather to indicate those who are not people of God (Keener 1993, 548). The challenge for these Christians was the same faced by new believers today. They must leave their old way of life; they must no longer live as they did before finding Christ.

Paul emphasizes the role our thought life plays in our behavior. He says the thinking of non-Christians is "futile" (v. 17) or vain. Their understanding is darkened and their hearts are hardened, leading to spiritual ignorance (vv. 17–18). The minds, hearts, and lives of the unconverted are actually in the process of "being corrupted" (4:22). The consequences of this spiritual condition are tragic, leading to separation from the eternal life God provides, loss of all moral sensitivity, and involvement in every kind of sinful, sensual behavior (4:18–19; cf. Romans 1:18–32).

This type of thinking and living ought not to be a characteristic of the Christian lifestyle. Consequently, Paul urges Christians to "put off" (v. 22) their old selves—their former way of life. He identifies five characteristics of pre–Christian living to be *put off*:

7.2.1
OBJECTIVE

List five behaviors Paul indicated Christians should put off.

5   What five behaviors does Paul say Christians should put off?

1. Put Off Falsehood (4:25)

We live in a day when truth is scarce. Much of our society is built on fabrications. Every day people shade the truth, cheat, exaggerate, flatter, betray confidences, and tell half-truths. Falsehood has no place in the Christian life. Tragically, studies have shown that church attendance makes little difference in many people's attitudes and practices in these areas.

2. Put Off Sinful Anger (4:26–27)

Righteous indignation has its place, according to Paul. But with it comes the temptation to view our anger as being righteous and the other person's as being unrighteous. The anger Paul says to put off is characterized by exasperation and resentment (Robertson 1931, 541). James 1:20 states clearly, "Man's anger does not bring about the righteous life that God desires."

3. Put Off Stealing (4:28)

Stealing is common in our culture. Business analysts report that financial losses due to employee theft eat significantly into profits and have dramatically increased the costs of goods. Falsifying cost overruns, embezzlement, reporting more hours than worked, and lack of diligence on the job all qualify as stealing. Paul reaffirms the eighth commandment for Christians (Exodus 20:15). Stealing is not to be part of a Christian's life.

4. Put Off Unwholesome Speech (4:29)

The word translated "unwholesome" points to that which is to be viewed as morally rotten. It is not simply bad language but includes gossip, slander, and conversation that injures others and drives a wedge between people (Wood 1978, 65). Ephesians 5:4 adds speech that is obscene, course, and vulgar to the list of what is inappropriate for Christians.

5. Put Off Negative Attitudes (4:31)

Our attitudes are very important; they are the wellspring from which everything in our lives flows (Proverbs 4:23). Paul warns against attitudes such as bitterness, rage, and anger. In fact, every kind of bad feeling toward others should have no residence in the life of Christians. These attitudes exhibit themselves in slander and unrighteous outbursts. We need to carefully guard our hearts. What can come out of them is frightening (Mark 7:21–23).

The analogy Paul uses in addressing what a Christian is to "put off" is that of old, worn out, inappropriate clothing in order to put on new, becoming clothing (22, 24). An individual cannot wear old and new garments at the same time. Attempting to do so is uncomfortable and unattractive. The Christian has no alternative. Putting off the old way of life is essential to a new, effective life of spiritual influence and victory.

Those in Christ Should Live Changed Lives as Authentic Disciples of Christ

Paul indicates that when a person comes to Christ in salvation, a dramatic transformation takes place.

6 How have you changed since believing on Jesus?

First, our sins are forgiven (v. 32) and we are changed within. A process of transformation begins that should be visible in our daily living. A reorientation of our thinking takes place which is a renewing of our mind (v. 23, cf. Romans 12:1–2). This renewed inner self is designed for godliness and leads to "true righteousness and holiness" (v. 24).

Paul also indicated a process of instruction and discipling had taken place in the lives of these Christians. The word translated "come to know," in verse 20, is a verbal form of the noun translated "disciple" elsewhere in Scripture. These Christians had been *discipled*, or taught, to pattern their behavior after Christ's. Every Christian needs discipling.

Verse 25 indicates that Christians are part of the body of Christ. As a result, they have responsibilities to each other.

Verse 30 emphasizes that the Holy Spirit *seals* us for a future time when we will experience what Christ has purchased for us—eternal life in heaven (see comments on 1:13–14).

Christians should live their daily lives in keeping with these spiritual realities. Paul also says there are things for believers to *put on* (24).

1. Put On Truthfulness (4:25)

7.2.2
OBJECTIVE

List five characteristics Paul indicated Christians should put on.

Truth characterizes God and ought also to distinguish His people. Paul says each believer should "speak truthfully to his neighbor." His rationale is this, "We are all members of one body." To lie to fellow Christians is to sin against the body of Christ. Do you know what would happen if, for just one day, everyone in the world told the truth? Our entire system would collapse—so much of it is based on a framework of lies. Truthfulness is to characterize Christians. But do not be brutal with the truth; speak it in love (4:15).

7 What are believers to put on?

2. Put On Righteous Anger (4:26)

Although not explicitly stated, verse 26 implies there is such a thing as righteous anger. Both God and Jesus were angry (Wood 1978, 64). Anger has its place. Injustice and unrighteousness should arouse our anger. We should be bothered when God's name is profaned and biblical principles are belittled. Moral depravity, godless humanism, liberal theology, and social injustice ought to make us righteously indignant. But we must beware allowing our anger to get out of control, resulting in un-Christlike behavior more directed toward selfish interests than God's cause.

3. Put On a Positive Work Ethic (4:28)

Without Christ, a person's goal of life easily becomes materialism. Because of this, people steal. Paul teaches that once we come to Christ, we should work hard so we can give to those in need. We are to go from stealing to sharing. The Bible emphasizes the importance of a positive work ethic (Acts 20:35; Colossians 3:22–24; 1 Thessalonians 4:11–12; Titus 3:14). The ancient church followed this rule, "If a man will not work, he shall not eat" (2 Thessalonians 3:10). Christians unwilling to work diligently are a poor testimony.

4. Put On Wholesome Speech (4:29–30)

These verses provide guidelines regarding character of speech. Paul gives this checklist: a Christian's speech is to be wholesome, uplifting, sensitive to needs, appropriate to the occasion, and beneficial. It should also reflect sensitivity to the Holy Spirit, remembering the admonishment, "Do not grieve the Holy Spirit of God, with whom you were sealed" (v. 30). *Watch your mouth* is good advice for Christians (cf. James 1:26; 3:2–12).

5. Put On Positive Attitudes (4:32)

Finally, Paul urges Christians to guard their attitudes. In contrast to the negative attitudes that characterized their lives before finding Christ, he urges Christians to be kind, compassionate, and forgiving of one another. In other words, we should go from *vice* to *nice*. Our model of forgiveness is our Savior who, while hanging on the Cross, prayed, "Father, forgive them" (Luke 23:34).

Can you not envision casting off the rags of a former existence and "putting on" the new, fresh, clothes becoming of a new life in Christ? That is the picture Paul captures in the following words: "You were taught, with regard to your former way of life, to put off your old self, which is being corrupted by its deceitful desires . . . and to put on the new self, created to be like God in true righteousness and holiness" (4:22–23).

Christ Fully Expressed in Our Personal Lives: Part 2 (5:1–7)

7.3.1
OBJECTIVE
Explain how believers are to imitate God.

Something caught my eye. I looked over just in time to see my toddler daughter struggling to hold her fork like Daddy does at the dinner table. I felt a surge of pride at her clumsy attempts to imitate me—holding her fingers just right, and that little finger had to be held just so.

Paul gives a tall order in verse 1 of this chapter. He says, "Be imitators of God, therefore, as dearly loved children and live a life of love, just as Christ loved us and gave himself up for us" (5:1–2). The love Jesus showed for us becomes both the pattern and motivation for our love. He helps us love in a way that pleases God.

This passage is structured around a stark contrast, that is, real love, the kind demonstrated by Jesus Christ and false love, the kind glamorized by the pagan culture around us. The challenges we face are much like those of the Ephesian Christians. Their challenge was to imitate the true God within a pagan culture—especially in the area of "living a life of love" (5:2). Paul uses the word translated "live" for the third time in Ephesians with this specific challenge for their lifestyle. "Live," he says, "a life of love" (cf. 4:1, 17; 5:8, 15).

7.3.2
OBJECTIVE
Compare the lifestyle of the Christian and the non-Christian.

Those in Christ Must Reject the Concept of Love Expressed in Local Culture

Paul did not soft-pedal God's will on this issue. He did not say to these Christians living with immorality all around them, "I understand. Just try to stay as morally pure as you can. God will understand. I'm sure He'll overlook a little moral defilement."

No. Paul knew God's standard for moral behavior was high and uncompromising. He said, "Among you there must not be even a hint of sexual immorality, or of any kind of impurity" (5:3). The degrading, sensual topics of the pagan world should not be acceptable topics of casual conversation among God's holy people (Bruce 1984, 370). The greed Paul speaks of probably picks up sexual overtones and points to sexual desire out of control. Paul's language is straightforward and terse: "These are improper for God's holy people" (5:3). God wants His people to replace culture's distorted concept of love with righteous lives.

Not only should Christians shun immoral behavior; Paul says Christians should be known for the purity of their speech. "Nor should there be obscenity, foolish talk or course joking, which are out of place" (5:4). Obscenity refers to filthy language. Foolish talk, in addition to its association with sinful sexual themes, includes senseless conversation and mindless humor (the Greek word is *mōrologia*, translated foolish or stupid speech). The final term refers to words or phrases with double meanings, especially when one is *risqué*–the double-entendre (Wood 1978, 68). Paul says these things have no place among Christians.

With these instructions comes a sober warning with three aspects (4:5–7). First comes a somber declaration: You can be sure that people who live immoral lives and think immoral thoughts will not inherit the kingdom of God. They are no different than idolaters. Then comes a warning about deception: Do not let anyone fool you. The penalty for immoral living is God's wrath. These are frightening words to be directed at professing Christians (1 Corinthians 6:9,10; Galatians 5:19–21; Colossians 3:6; Revelation 21:8; 22:15). And finally comes a strong exhortation: Do not get involved in an immoral lifestyle or develop improper relationships with those living in immorality.

The creation of computer sites for the publishing of illicit materials of almost every kind are on the rise. One has to walk very wisely to avoid unexpected exposure as he or she moves about using domains that were once unrelated to immorality (and pop-ups that are so commonly attached when you visit a site). This is what many in society offer as *love*. What a sad commentary on how our culture views love.

7.3.3
OBJECTIVE
Explain how Christians are able to demonstrate true love within their culture.

8   How can believers demonstrate the true meaning of love?

Those Who Are in Christ Must Demonstrate God's Love in Their Relationships

In stark contrast to what the popular culture called *love*, Paul urged his audience to "imitate God" as they "live a life of love." This was love patterned after that which Christ demonstrated at the Cross. Love was to be shown in their relationships with each other (John 13:34–35), their compassion for others, and in their homes and marriages (5:25–33).

Imitating God's love becomes achievable when we simply share with others the love we have received. God loved us while we were still sinners. We could not and did not earn God's love. It was freely given. Look at what the Bible says about what God did for us through Christ Jesus: "When we were utterly helpless, Christ came at just the right time and died for us sinners. Now, no one is likely to die for a good person, though someone might be willing to die for a person who is especially good. But God showed his great love for us by sending Christ to die for us while we were still sinners" (Romans 5:6–8, NLT).

When we respond to God's love by accepting it, it is planted deep within our hearts and transforms us. Romans 5:5 teaches: "God has poured out his love into our hearts by the Holy Spirit, whom he has given us." The Holy Spirit's presence produces love within our lives. The Bible calls this "the fruit of the Spirit" (Galatians 5:22–23).

Our children share our natures and likenesses. Because of this, they want to imitate us, just as I described my daughter doing. When we are born again, that is "born of the Spirit" (John 3:5–6), the new nature within us bears the spiritual likeness of Christ. Consequently, we are empowered and enabled to love as He loves. The quality and character of our love need to be patterned after our Lord Jesus Christ and stand in contrast with the cheap imitation our culture calls *love*.

Additionally, the character and quality of our speech needs to be distinctively Christian. In contrast to the filthy, trivial chatter of the popular culture, the Christian's conversation should be wholesome and uplifting, characterized by *thanksgiving* (5:4, cf. 4:29). The quality of a believer's daily speech should witness to a changed heart and life.

The love of God expressed within and through us is powerful. Jim Cymbala, pastor of Brooklyn Tabernacle, often tells this moving story:

> One Sunday, in our church service, a woman who sings in our choir, a former drug addict with the HIV virus, told how she came to Christ. She described in raw detail the horrors of her former life. A street person named David stood at the back listening closely.

> The meeting ended, and I was exhausted. After giving and giving, I had just started to unwind when I saw David coming my way. *I'm so tired*, I thought, *Now this guy's going to hit me up for money.*

> When David got close, the smell took my breath away. It was a mixture of urine, sweat, garbage, and alcohol. After a few words, I reached into my pocket and pulled out a couple of dollars for him. I'm sure my posture communicated, "Here's some money. Now get out of here!"

> David looked at me intently, put his finger in my face, and said, "Look, I don't want your money. I'm going to die out there. I want the Jesus this girl talked about."

> I paused, then looked up, closed my eyes, and said, "God, forgive me." For a few moments, I stood with my eyes closed, feeling soiled and cheap. Then a change came over me. I began to feel his pain, to see him as someone Christ had brought into the church for that moment.

> I spread my arms, and we embraced. Holding his head to my chest, I talked to him about his life and about Christ. But they were not just words. I felt them. I loved him. That smell—I do not know how to explain it—it had almost made me sick before, but it became beautiful to me. I reveled in what had been repulsive.

> I felt for him what Paul felt for the Thessalonians: "We were gentle among you, like a mother caring for her little children. We loved you so much that we were delighted to share with you not only the gospel of God but our lives as well, because you had become so dear to us" (1 Thessalonians 2:7–8). God put that kind of love in me.

When you hear the word *love*, what immediately comes to mind? Perhaps our mental image serves as a gauge of just how much our culture has influenced our view of love. Jesus can change how we think about love. He can re-orient our hearts so His concept of love is ours. He demonstrated His love for us when He died for our sins on the Cross. We can experience the marvel of His love. Even more, He stands ready to plant His love in our hearts so it can transform us and flow through us to others. Do you want that? Do you long for that? He stands ready to do it.

Christ Fully Expressed in Our Personal Lives: Part 3 (5:8–21)

Light and darkness are two things that affect people in very different ways. Light represents hope, opportunity, and vision. It is associated with the bright, the beautiful, and the clean. Darkness is usually associated with fear, despondency, and blindness. It represents danger, uncertainty, and crime. Bright sunshine makes us smile and promotes activity; while darkness promotes anxiety and makes us want to find a place of security and safety.

OBJECTIVE

Identify how Paul uses the concepts of light and darkness to compare the life of the nonbeliever to that of a Christian.

OBJECTIVE

Identify ways Paul defines walking in darkness.

9   How does Paul use the concepts of light and dark when teaching about the transformed life of a Christian?

10   In what ways did your life reflect walking in darkness before you found Christ?

Paul uses these two universally recognized symbols to challenge Christians about how they ought to live their lives. He said, "You were once darkness, but now you are light in the Lord. Live as children of light" (5:8). Paul uses the word translated "live" twice in this passage (5:8, 15). He uses it in three other locations as well (4:1, 17; 5:1). Here he tells the Ephesian believers that it was God's will that Christ would be fully expressed in their lives by their living as "children of light."

Those in Christ Must Not Walk in Darkness

What does Paul say to these first-century Christians about how they should live within a pagan culture? How do his words relate to Christians today? Paul identifies five characteristics of *walking in darkness*.

1. The Way They Used to Live

Paul uses the term *darkness* to describe the way Christians once lived—in both moral and spiritual darkness (John 3:19–20; 12.35; 1 John 1:5–7). They had no idea where they were going. Things had changed, however. Light had come into their lives through the Lord Jesus Christ (John 8:12). Now they were children of light (v. 8).

Paul challenges believers to "have nothing to do with" darkness. They are to completely disassociate themselves from that lifestyle. They are to reprove or expose them (v. 11), not so much by their words as by a contrasting way of life. The light of their lives should expose the true nature of the deeds of darkness (Foulkes 1979, 146–147). The "deeds of darkness," according to Paul, are so shameful that to continually make them a topic of conversation might result in their rubbing off on Christians (Wood 1978, 70). His advice? Do not even mention such things.

2. A Fruitless Way of Life

Darkness is a "fruitless" way of life (v. 11). Paul uses this word because the life of darkness produces activities that are dead and sterile (Bruce 1984, 374). The way of darkness leads to an "endless, strenuous, but futile striving" on the part of those who follow it (Foulkes 1979, 146). The futility of the "works of the flesh" is contrasted to the "fruit of the Spirit" in Galatians 5:19–23.

3. Things People Try to Hide

Paul seems to imply that the "deeds of darkness" are things people normally try to hide. He indicates it is shameful to even mention what some people do in secret. We live in a culture that argues that it is our own business what we do in private. Nothing could be further from the truth, biblically. The Bible teaches that a godless culture will ultimately reach the point that "although they know God's righteous decree that those who do such things deserve death, they not only continue to do these very things but also approve of those who practice them" (Romans 1:32). What a tragic and twisted approach to life.

4. Unwise and Foolish Behavior

Rather than their lives expressing values and principles based upon "the fear (or reverence) of God," the lives of those in darkness exhibit no moral compass (Proverbs 1:7). The Book of Proverbs repeatedly warns about this approach to life under the headings of "the fool," "the foolish," or "the wicked." That is why Paul urges, "Be very careful, then how you live—not as the unwise" (v. 15).

5. A Life of Drunkenness and Debauchery

Those living in darkness often exhibit it by drunkenness and a life of moral corruption. Paul warns Christians to avoid drunkenness because it leads to a life of "debauchery" (v. 18). Interestingly, the word Paul uses here is in its adverbial form, and matches the verb used in the story of the prodigal son when it says he "squandered his wealth in wild living" (Luke 15:13) (Wood 1978, 72). A life of alcohol leads to prodigal living. Why would a Christian participate in something that puts him or her at such risk?

When I think about Paul's warning to have "nothing to do with the deeds of darkness," I am reminded of my experiences groping in the dark for a light switch. On more than one occasion, I stubbed my toe, bruised a shin, blackened an eye, and have even fallen down a flight of stairs. The risks of walking in darkness spiritually and morally are much greater.

Those in Christ Must Live as Children of Light

OBJECTIVE
Define what it means to live as children of the light.

11 What is the result of living as children of light?

How much better to live (or walk) as children of light. Jesus claimed, "I am the light of the world. Whoever follows me will never walk in darkness, but will have the light of life" (John 8:12). He said, "Put your trust in the light while you have it, so that you may become sons of light" (John 12:36). God wants His people to live as children of light.

Paul teaches that if we "live as children of the light," positive things result (or are the *fruit*) from that choice:

1. Goodness–Moral excellence combined with a generous spirit (Wood 1978, 69).
2. Righteousness–An approved life after examination or testing (cf. Ephesians 4:24; Philippians 1:11; Hebrews 12:11) (Rienecker 1980, 536).
3. Truth–Genuineness or honesty (Wood 1978, 69).

Paul urges believers to "find out what pleases the Lord" (v. 17). The life of Jesus exemplified this perfectly. On more than one occasion the Father spoke from heaven, saying, "This is my Son, whom I love; with him I am well pleased" (Matthew 3:17; 17:5). Jesus always sought to do what pleased the Father (John 5:30; 8:29). It was also said of Enoch, "He was commended as one who pleased God" (Hebrews 11:5). May this noble quest characterize our lives as children of the light.

Paul sounds a warning for Christians in verse 15. He says, "Be very careful, then, about how you live." Those who are spiritually sleepy need to wake up (5:14). Matthew included this warning: "Watch therefore, for you know neither the day nor the hour in which the Son of Man is coming" (Matthew 25:13, NKJV).

12 What does Paul mean by living as children of light (Ephesians 5:8)?

Especially in these last days, we should live as those who are wise. Paul outlines four things that walking as children of the light involves:

1. Recognizing Life's Principles—"Live as those who are wise" (5:15).

Follow the principles of godly wisdom taught in Scripture, for example in the Book of Proverbs. Live in the light of God's Word (Psalm 119:104–105). Follow Jesus, "the Light of life" and "the Light of the world" (John 8:12).

2. Realizing Our Limited Possibilities—"Make the most of every opportunity" (5:16; cf. Colossians 4:5)

Time is short (1 Corinthians 7:29). In a godless culture, we have only so many God-given opportunities to share the gospel and influence others for Christ. We need to *buy up* or exploit every opportunity while we have them (Bruce 1984, 378–79).

3. Remembering the Lord's Purposes—"Understand what the Lord's will is" (5:17)

We are easily distracted by the responsibilities of this life, issues of all kinds, and even the multitude of good things that beg for our attention. It is easy to be distracted from the best by inferior things (and even the good things). Those who are wise and walk as the children of light will seek to know and do God's will.

4. Revitalizing yourself in the Spirit—"Be filled with the Spirit" (5:18)

Those who are wise and live as the "children of light" recognize how essential it is to be filled with the Spirit. Jesus told His followers, "Apart from me you can do nothing" (John 15:15). Paul's command is one of the most direct imperatives in all Scripture regarding the Spirit-filled life. It is in the imperative mood to emphasize that the infilling of the Spirit is not optional. It is in the present tense, stressing the fact that we need to be continually filled. The verb form *to be filled* is passive, clearly revealing this is not a manufactured experience or something we work up by ourselves. Christ is the One who fills us. Be being filled with the Spirit is the force of the command (Wood 1978, 72).

Paul closes out this passage by giving four key indicators of a person filled with the Spirit (5:19–21). Each is introduced by a participle in the Greek language:

1. They communicate with one another in worship.
2. They personally worship with singing hearts.
3. They have grateful spirits–they are always giving thanks to God.
4. They are teachable—they know how to submit to one another because of their reverence for Christ.

I was driving down the freeway late at night at about seventy miles per hour. I was a bit warm, so I reached down to turn the air conditioning vent toward me. Inadvertently, my hand pushed the control for the headlights, turning them off, and suddenly I was driving blind in the dark. Panic seized me. Where was I on the road, would I wreck, would I die? Feverishly, I tried to find the control for the lights. I finally succeeded. What a relief to once again have light. It is dangerous—yes, even disastrous—to walk in darkness and not live as children of light.

God sent His Son, Jesus, as the Light of the world. God's desire is that we would receive Him, steer clear of anything associated with spiritual and moral darkness, and instead, live as children of light every day of our lives.

Test Yourself

Circle the letter of the *best* answer.

1. What four character qualities contribute to unity based upon Ephesians 4:2?
a) Humility, integrity, purity, and patience
b) Gentleness, integrity, competence, and forbearance
c) Humility, gentleness, patience, and forbearance
d) Patience, competence, gentleness, and humility

2. To prepare believers for works of service, God has appointed
a) presbyters, apostles, prophets, and pastors/teachers.
b) bishops, prophets, presbyters, and apostles.
c) evangelists, presbyters, prophets, and apostles.
d) apostles, prophets, evangelists, and pastors/teachers.

3. Being swayed by every wind of doctrine is a result of
a) immaturity.
b) false teaching.
c) modern culture.
d) television evangelism.

4. In Ephesians 4, what five behaviors are believers instructed to put off?
a) Sorcery, sinful anger, bribery, falsehood, and negative attitudes
b) Sexual immorality, witchcraft, gossip, stealing, and falsehood
c) Bribery, malice, negative attitudes, stealing, and unwholesome speech
d) Lying, sinful anger, stealing, unwholesome speech, and negative attitudes

5. According to Ephesians 5:3, believers are not to possess even a hint of
a) sexual immorality, greed, or impurity.
b) greed, malice, or bitterness.
c) malice, sexual immorality, or bitterness.
d) pride, greed, or sexual immorality.

6. As imitators of God, according to Ephesians 5:2, believers should live a life of
a) peace.
b) joy.
c) love.
d) devotion.

7. In comparing the lives of Christians and unbelievers, Paul uses the analogy of
a) hot and cold.
b) clean and unclean.
c) gold and stubble.
d) light and darkness.

8. According to Ephesians 5, believers who walk in ways that are fruitless, unwise, and foolish are walking in
a) emptiness.
b) darkness.
c) judgment.
d) a desert place.

9. The results of believers living as children of light are
a) salvation, righteousness, and truth.
b) justification, truth, and holiness.
c) salvation, goodness, and truth.
d) goodness, righteousness, and truth.

10. As children of light (Ephesians 5:15–18), believers should
a) make the most of every opportunity, understand the Lord's will, and be filled with the Spirit.
b) be vigilant, endure suffering, and press on in the strength of the Lord.
c) rejoice in the Lord always, understand the Lord's will, and make the most of every opportunity.
d) be filled with the Spirit, rejoice in the Lord always, and press on in the strength of the Lord.

Responses to Interactive Questions

CHAPTER 7

Some of these responses may include information that is supplemental to the IST. These questions are intended to produce reflective thinking beyond the course content and your responses may vary from these examples.

1 What is God's purpose for the church as the body of Christ?

God's wants Christ to be fully expressed through the Church, the body of Christ.

2 How can the church function effectively when people have such differing gifts?

Paul points out that each person is different, uniquely gifted by God. Christ is the One who gifts every believer to help do His work in the world.

3 What is meant by each of the leadership functions Paul identifies in Ephesians 4:11–12?

Apostles declare the gospel and further God's purposes, especially in unreached areas.

Prophets powerfully speak messages from God.

Evangelists proclaim the gospel, both in personal and public contexts.

Pastors and teachers shepherd, disciple, and train Christians.

4 What is the purpose of church leadership?

The task of church leaders is to "prepare God's people for works of service." They were to help them identify their gifts and calling. They were then to train, empower, and release them into ministry.

5 What five behaviors does Paul say Christians should put off?

Paul said believers should put off falsehood, sinful anger, stealing, unwholesome speech, and negative attitudes.

6 How have you changed since believing on Jesus?

Answers will vary.

7 What are believers to put on?

God's people are to put on truthfulness, righteous anger, a good work ethic, wholesome speech, and a positive attitude.

8 How can believers demonstrate the true meaning of love?

Believers show the true meaning of love by imitating Jesus' love and by telling others about the love we have received from God.

9 How does Paul use the concepts of light and dark when teaching about the transformed life of a Christian?

Paul uses light to refer to the kingdom of God and darkness to refer to the world of sin and those lost in sin.

10 In what ways did your life reflect walking in darkness before you found Christ?

Answers will vary.

11 What is the result of living as children of light?

People living as children of the light produce goodness, righteousness, and truth.

12 What does Paul mean by living as children of light (Ephesians 5:8)?

Walking as children of the light involves recognizing life's principles, living as those who are wise, making the most of every opportunity, and remembering God's purposes.

Paul's Appeal and God's Goal: Christ Fully Expressed at Home and at Work (Ephesians 5:21–6:9)

The institution of marriage and the home are facing tremendous challenges today. These time-honored institutions are being assaulted by a secularism (with no acknowledgment of the living God) and an enculturation that rejects biblical principles and substitutes an attitude that says, " I will do it (whatever) my way!" Marriage relationships are also endangered by the mixing of social perceptions and traditions with excerpts from God's Word.

The foundational premise or the crucial principle for a Holy Spirit-directed home life and marriage is clearly established in verse 21. It governs everything that follows in this section of Ephesians (5:21–6:9). It reads, "Submit to one another out of reverence for Christ" (5:21). Submission is to be mutual. It is one of the great *one another* verses of the Bible. Each member of the ancient household of Ephesians: husbands, wives, children, and slaves—had a responsibility to "submit to one another out of reverence for Christ."

The word *submit* is also a link, a transition from the previous passage. It functions as the final, modifying participle describing the Spirit-filled life commanded in verse 18. Spirit-filled Christians speak, sing, give thanks, and submit to one another. Any other understanding of spirituality is a masquerade.

Understanding what is meant by *submission* is crucial. The Greek word used here, *hypotasso*, is in the middle voice. While the active voice would have referred to forced subordination, in this passage *hypotasso* is used in reference to a voluntary act. This subordination is not coerced, but is an attitude marking every Christian in relation to God, to other Christians, to civil authorities, to church leaders, to one's spouse, and to one another (Opperwall 1988, 643–644). This subordination is exemplified by our Savior (Philippians 2:3–8). "It describes a voluntary attitude of giving in, cooperating, assuming responsibility, and carrying a burden" (Barth 1974, 710). In marriage, "each partner subordinates their own interests to their spouse's, the motivation of sacrificial love in which each partner strives to help the other" (Marshall 2005, 204). It is "the use of personal power for another's sake" (May 1969, n.p.)

What is the character of this section of Ephesians (5:21–6:9)? Paul addresses how life in the Spirit transforms the relationships of those within a household—wives and husbands, children and parents, slaves and masters. The technical term for these kinds of lists is the German term *haustafel* or "household code." Although Paul uses lists of duties found in pagan literature, there are important distinctions between theirs and his. New Testament lists emphasize reciprocal responsibilities and the motivation is the practical expression of a vibrant relationship with Jesus Christ.

Paul's instructions to live in mutual love and submission were alien to that culture. Husbands were accustomed to having complete authority over their households, including their wives, children, and slaves. Women were often considered inferior beings and as such had no legal rights or standing. Children and slaves had no rights. The levels of power were so unequal that for Paul to give such instruction without explaining how to carry it out could have led to more abuses than blessings. Therefore, he gives specific examples of how believers, within each social stratum, could express Christ's life in their homes

(Gundry 1980, 95). Such understanding also helps us more accurately apply the principles of living in the Spirit to our lives, centuries later.

- *Read Ephesians 5:21–6:9 before you begin study in this chapter.*

Lesson 8.1   Christ Fully Expressed between Husband and Wife (5:21–33)

Objectives

8.1.1 *Explain how following Paul's teaching on mutual love and submission could transform Christian marriages in his day and ours.*

8.1.2 *Describe Paul's presentation in Ephesians 5:23 regarding the submission of the church to Christ.*

8.1.3 *List and explain the four principles that characterize a Christian husband's love for his wife.*

8.1.4 *List and explain the four characteristics of Christ's love for the church found in Ephesians 5:26–32.*

Lesson 8.2   Christ Fully Expressed between Parents and Children (6:1–4)

Objectives

8.2.1 *Describe how Paul's instructions to Christian children and their parents were different than those that guided the parent-child relationships in ancient Roman culture.*

8.2.2 *Name and define the two key responsibilities that Paul prescribes for Christian children.*

8.2.3 *Describe the two key responsibilities of Christian parents to their children.*

Lesson 8.3   Christ Fully Expressed at Work through Masters and Servants (6:5–9)

Objectives

8.3.1 *Explain why Paul includes instructions to slaves and masters in this list of household duties.*

8.3.2 *List five principles governing how Christian employees should fulfill their responsibilities to their employers.*

8.3.3 *List five principles governing how Christian employers should fulfill their responsibilities to their employees.*

8.1.1
OBJECTIVE

Explain how following Paul's teaching on mutual love and submission could transform Christian marriages in his day and ours.

Christ Fully Expressed between Husband and Wife (5:21–33)

We are watching the erosion, if not the outright destruction, of the family as we know it. Among the many factors contributing to the destruction of the family are immorality, adultery, all forms of sexual promiscuity, homosexuality, abortion, and militant liberation doctrines. The media has been a chief culprit in this erosion: presenting, promoting, and propagandizing these destructive approaches to family life.

The principles of this passage are built on the premise of mutual submission. Paul said, "Submit to one another out of reverence for Christ" (v. 21). This attitude is to be "among yourselves" and was supremely exemplified by our Savior (Philippians 2:3–8). Mutual submission to one another and to Christ is the glue that holds a marriage and home together. Paul is addressing all believers and then turns to the household to explain how these principles play out in daily life. He begins with husbands and wives.

As always, God begins with us where we are. His first purpose is not to bring radical change to society, but radical change to the individual and the way that the individual responds to the life he or she currently leads. Paul does not condone or promote the hierarchical structures which pit humans against one another, but demonstrates that Spirit-filled living renders power structures irrelevant.

As discussed in earlier text in this study, Paul was speaking to a culture quite different from most cultures of today. Since betrothals were arranged, often between individuals who did not know one another, we can assume that husbands and wives did not necessarily love each other. Rather, the man and woman married for financial gain and to produce children to carry on the husband's family line. Into this setting Paul speaks to men and women who may not heretofore have considered their spouses as persons to be loved and valued.

1   How could mutual submission promote love, unity, and harmony in a marital relationship?

Before continuing with this study, note that verse 22 is not a complete verse in the original text. It has no verb; the word *submit* does not appear in this verse. "Literally, the verse reads, 'wives to your own husbands in the Lord'" (Gill and Caveness 2004, 100). Quoting such a verse by itself can lead to misrepresentation of what the author is saying. This verse must be interpreted in light of verse 21, thus setting the pattern for the Christian home as being one of mutual submission. A more literal translation of the Greek text would read: "Submitting yourselves to one another in the fear of Christ, wives to your own husbands as to the Lord in everything" (Gundry 1980, 95). "The words to wives and husbands are to be understood as totally dependent on their being filled with the Spirit. That is, all the words in 5:22–6:9 presuppose a household of believers who are continually being filled with the Spirit of God" (Fee 2002, 4). As they are continually filled, their attitudes and behavior are those of "placing the needs of others above their own" (Brauch 2009, 110). "Husbands and wives are challenged to practice this mutual submission, which at its core is a radical alternative to the culturally prescribed (and one-sided) order of the wife's submission to her husband's authority over her" (Brauch 2009, 198).

Spirit-Filled Wives Submit to Their Husbands (5:21–24, 33)

In Paul's day, Greek wives and husbands did not usually have the close relationship and companionship known in our day. Wives did not need to be told to submit because culture had already dictated their submission, both legally and practically (Gundry 1980, 96). What the Christian wives needed was to know what it meant to submit "in the Spirit" (see verse 18).

Prior to salvation, a woman, the underling of a marriage, had no choice but to submit. She was dependent on her husband for her survival and place in society. Most were married quite young, often in their early teens, to older men. As mentioned earlier, marriage was not the result of romance, but for practical purposes and for producing children to work in the household business and carry on the family line. Their husbands went outside the household to seek pleasure and companionship. Any idea of equality between a husband and wife was nonexistent. (Fee 2002, 6)

In this cultural setting, Paul helps wives "rethink their status in terms of their serving Christ, as they related to the male head of the household" (Fee 2002, 4). In God's kingdom, they were equal, their lives as valuable and valid as that of their husbands. Filled with the Holy Spirit, they would seek the good of their husbands, subordinating their interests and goals to those of their husbands because of their love for and awe of Christ, following His example.

Bonita was a new Christian, having known Christ as Savior for only a short time. She desperately wanted her husband, a successful businessman in our community, to come to Christ. My wife and I encouraged her to let Jesus beautify her character, submit lovingly to her husband, pray for him daily, and prepare herself for the opportunity God would give her. One evening, Jerry said to her, "Hon, I just want you to know, of all the people who call themselves Christian, you are the finest example I know." She told him it was all about Jesus in her life, and a few days later Jerry prayed to receive Christ for himself.

The Church's Submission to Christ

This passage, primarily directed to relationships between husband and wife, also teaches us much about our submission to Christ. It teaches us that it has a foundation.

Submission should be out of reverence.

Life is to be lived in reverence of the Lord. The fear of the Lord is not dread of Him, but our reverence of Him. The Bible teaches much on this subject and Proverbs indicates, "the fear of the Lord is the beginning of knowledge" (Proverbs 1:7; 9:10; 15:33; cf. Psalm 111:10).

Submission should recognize Him as Head and Savior (5:23).

Jesus is worthy of our submission to His person, His will, His plan, and the principles of His Word because He is the "head of His body," the church. He is also our Savior—He offered himself up on our behalf and redeemed us; we are His (1 Corinthians 6:19–20; 1 Peter 1:18–19).

Submission should be complete (5:24).

Knowing the holy, loving character of our Savior, we offer Him our complete submission, without reservation. If we call Him Lord and then fail to submit to His will in everything, that would be a contradiction in terms.

Spirit-Filled Husbands Submit to Their Wives

Does Paul's comparison of the marital relationship with the church's submission to Christ mean husbands have absolute authority over their wives? Are husbands spiritually superior to their wives and in some way their savior? No, Paul "is teaching the Ephesians one truth (the husband-wife relationship) by using another truth (the relationship of Christ and the Church) and the whole teaching concerns living in the Spirit. . . . The 'household of faith is . . . marked by the mutual submission of its members—not anyone or any group being totally *controlled* by another" (Gill and Caveness 2004 164). Only Christ has the power to save and only He is the intermediary between people and God. The mandate is to emulate Christ who used power, not to control, but to serve.

What then does his part of mutual submission mean for a husband filled with the Holy Spirit? A Christian husband's love for his wife is characterized by distinct qualities.

8.1.2
OBJECTIVE
Describe Paul's presentation in Ephesians 5:23 regarding the submission of the church to Christ.

2   How should the church and its members submit to Christ?

List and explain the four principles that characterize a Christian husband's love for his wife.

3   What four principles characterize the love of a Christian husband for his wife?

His love is sacrificial (5:25).

Just as Jesus "gave himself up" on behalf of the church on the Cross, so a Christian husband should express that same quality of love on behalf of his wife. He should exhibit the love of self-sacrifice instead of selfishness. Wives often say, "He does not understand me; he does not care about me; he is insensitive." Christian husbands should put forth an effort to care, to feel, and to understand. First Peter 3:7 emphasizes this truth. It teaches that a husband's sacrificial love is considerate and respectful (or well-mannered), and that he acknowledges that both he and his wife equally share God's grace.

His love has a high and holy purpose (5:26–27).

This means a Christian husband will do everything in his power to sustain her purity. He would never put his wife in a compromising situation. He will not purposefully anger or embitter her. He will exalt and esteem her, doing everything he can to encourage her relationship to God and her spiritual growth as she also does for him.

His love is caring (5:28–30).

The Christian husband is to love his wife as his own body. Many husbands spend a lot of money and effort developing and sustaining their own bodies. They should be just as concerned about the welfare of their wives, not just her physical well-being but her mental, emotional, spiritual, and relational needs as well.

His love is indissoluble (5:31).

Paul's description of marriage is taken from the first marriage, before the Fall. Verse 31 is a direct quote from Genesis 2:24. The husband's commitment to his wife is to be indissoluble or *permanent*, reflecting the absolute oneness of the union, as with the first marriage. It points out to Christian husbands that God's will for marriage is threefold:

1. First it involves leaving the primary relationship of his previous home.
2. Second, it is assumes a primary relationship with a spouse: "The two will become one flesh."
3. Third, it is a spiritual, emotional, and sexual union, binding upon both married partners for life (cf. Matthew 19:3–8).

"This astounding comparison between Christian husbands and Christ has, at its point of comparison, *not* 'lordship language' (in the sense of power and control) *but* sacrificial servant language. The only point at which the husband is called on to identify himself with Christ's behavior or role is the extreme extent of Christ's love for the church" (Brauch 2009, 198).

Christ's Sacrificial Love for the Church

Christ's love for the church in this passage provides the pattern and motivation for the Christian's love for his spouse. It does more, however; it informs us of the character and qualities of Christ's love for His body, the church.

1. Is Sacrificial (5:26)

Christ loved the church selflessly and laid down His life on her behalf (cf. 5:2). His sacrifice made available everything needed for Christian life (Romans 8:31–32; Galatians 1:3–4).

2. Has a High and Holy Purpose (5:26–27)

Jesus died not only to forgive our sins. He gave himself to sanctify His people, cleanse them, and prepare them for the "marriage supper" when they

List and explain the four characteristics of Christ's love for the church found in Ephesians 5:26–32.

4   What are the four characteristics of Christ's love for the church found in this passage? What is the significance of each of them?

will join Christ to enjoy His presence forever (Revelation 19:7–9; 21:2–5,9). His Word has a cleansing effect upon our lives in preparation for that day (John 15:3; 17:15–19) (Foulkes 1979, 158).

3. Cares for His Body (5:29–30)

Christ cares and provides for His church; "We are members of His body." It is unthinkable that the model husband, Jesus Christ, would "give himself up for" the church, His Bride, and then not provide for all her needs (3:16–21). He cares for us (1 Peter 5:7).

4. Is Eternal and Indissoluble (5:32)

The same indissoluble union that characterizes a Christian marriage—*till death alone shall part us*—is now enriched and extended. The language of Genesis 2:24 is applied to Christ and the church. That is why the Bible says, "So will we be with the Lord forever" (1 Thessalonians 4:16–17).

I sat spellbound at Don's funeral. Each of his children and finally his wife got up and sang his praises. This man did not have a lot of money, his financial portfolio was modest, he drove an economy car, his home was economically a middle-class dwelling, but to hear them talk you would have thought he was superman. I was intimidated. I was convicted. I was ashamed to look over at my wife. What was it that Don did? What secret caused his kids, and especially his wife, to go on like this? This man had put love for his wife and family on the front burner of his life, and it worked. It paid off. It will for you and me too.

Verse 33 summarizes this passage: "Each one of you also must love his wife as he loves himself, and the wife must respect her husband." This brings us face to face with two challenges in response to this passage:

1. The challenge of responding biblically as a Christian spouse: Will we submit to one another out of reverence for Christ? Will we demonstrate submission as unto the Lord? Will we love as Christ loved the church? Will we fully express Christ in our marriages?

2. The challenge that faces the church and each of its members: Will we submit to Christ in everything?

Christ Fully Expressed between Parents and Children (6:1–4)

Can you imagine this scene? Paul's letter arrives by courier at the home of a key elder of a house church in or near Ephesus. It is Sunday, the Lord's Day, and everyone is gathered to worship, to hear the Scriptures read and explained from a Christian perspective, to hear the stories of what God is doing, and to give offerings. Entire families are present.

The elder announces, "Dear Christians, we have a letter from Paul." He then reads the epistle to the Ephesians. Young Lukas and Penelope are present. Much in the letter is encouraging. Much is challenging. There is something in the letter for Mom and Dad. And then the elder reads it, "Children, obey your parents in the Lord." Christ has truly brought a new day to all His followers!

What honor and esteem is given to children by the great apostle's addressing children in his letter. How important they must be to the cause of Christ and the church.

In ancient culture, these instructions were revolutionary. In Greek and Roman society, an infant was recognized legally as a person only when the father chose to do so. Culturally, a baby could be abandoned or, if deformed, even killed. Christians and Jews unanimously opposed both abortion and abandonment (Keener 1993, 552). It is therefore abundantly clear that Paul was addressing Christians. Instead of unilateral demands, he defines mutual responsibilities. Instead of ignoring and excluding children, he includes and even directly addresses them.

Our society has created a culture for disaster in the home. The sexual and physical abuse of children is rampant. Children often rule the home or are treated with contempt. Media paints the portrait of a cocky child mouthing off to adults and violating the rules of the home, and viewers merely grin. If there was ever a need for biblical advice on parenting, it is today. It is God's desire that Jesus Christ would be fully expressed in relationships between parents and children.

Spirit-Filled Children Submit to Their Parents

In this passage, children are considered a vital part of the local church. It is clear that Paul believes they can understand, come to know Christ, participate, and contribute. He challenges them with two key responsibilities: obedience and honor to their parents.

1. Obedience

Obedience is an act. The responsibility of obedience on the part of children is general in nature within most cultures. Obedience is taught and expected. In western cultures today, however, it is often questioned. Paul elevated the expectation of obedience of children to a higher level. He appeals to children to obey their parents "in the Lord" (v. 1). In other words, he appeals to them for obedience because they are under the authority of Jesus. The appeal is to their desire to do right and please God. When a parent tells a child to do something, the child has a responsibility to comply unless it is unbiblical, immoral, or unethical. God's law supersedes the authority of the parent. A child who never learns to obey will struggle with the lordship of Jesus.

2. Honor

Honor is an attitude. To obey means to do what another person says. To honor involves respect and love. Children are to obey while they are under their parents' care, though the responsibility to honor continues for life. If we deal with the attitude, we will have fewer problems with the action.

Paul appeals to the fifth commandment (Exodus 20:12). He says it is the first commandment with promise, probably meaning it is first in importance for children and holds a promise that is applicable to them (Barton et al. 1995, 120). The promise is for a long, full life of blessing.

I watched Carissa from the time she was a toddler. She had a delightful personality. She was naturally outgoing and enthusiastic, filled with curiosity (and mischief). She had the uncanny ability to push the limits, get into predicaments, and earn scoldings. But early on, she responded to the gospel story and gave her life to Jesus. Carissa was never one to accept what someone said just because the person said it. But her parents taught her to obey, even when she did not understand or even agree. She learned to obey, and she learned to respect

5   How were Paul's instruction to children and their parents different from common practice in ancient Roman culture?

OBJECTIVE

Name and define the two key responsibilities that Paul prescribes for Christian children.

6   What are the two key responsibilities of children to their parents?

and obey other authority figures as well. She was strong, and could disagree, but she also knew how to submit. I have watched her over the years. She has become a valuable, mature, responsible, and devoted Christian leader, who is balanced in her perspective of submission!

Spirit-Filled Parents Submit to Their Children (6:4)

Paul did not have to establish the father's authority in the ancient world; it was absolute. Instead, he writes to set limits on it and establish responsibilities for parents in keeping with Christian values and teaching. He explains:

1. Do Not Exasperate Your Children.

Children can be challenging. But Paul says to fathers, "Do not exasperate" them (v. 4). The Greek word that Paul uses is literally translated as "to provoke, to anger" and may imply "goading them into resentment." In Colossians the challenge was not to "embitter" them or they "will become discouraged" (lose heart or give up; Colossians 3:21). Do not act like you hate your children. Do not goad them, provoke them, or tease them to the point of anger that results in ill-behavior. Wise parents love and encourage their children while at the same time guiding their behavior.

2. Raise Your Children as Disciples of Jesus.

Two responsibilities are implied by the words "bring them up in the training and instruction of the Lord" (v. 4). The first is the parents' responsibility to mold their children's lives. The second is to provide instruction in the things of the Lord. Effective Christian parents will teach children the Bible, emphasize the example of Jesus, guide their friendships, and keep a watchful eye on the heroes their children choose. They will seek to provide a model of godliness and consistent Christian living. Discipline will be consistent and administered for the purpose of instructing and training, not for revenge or an outlet for anger and frustration. They will seek to fill their home with love and grace. Their local church will become an extended family. All of this is involved in "bringing them up in the training and instruction of the Lord."

I was standing in the checkout line at a store when I noticed a mother with two small children ahead of me, acting as though she would rather be anywhere but here with these children. She was obviously frustrated and acted as if both children were a terrible bother to her. They could do nothing right. Nothing less than perfect stillness would have pleased her. Her remarks were cutting, her voice harsh, her language vulgar. I wonder if they will grow up to love and respect her.

Do you want a Christian home where Christ is the focus? Do you long to live where the Bible is treasured and taught, where love is given and received, where mutual respect is shared, where peace and contentment dominate, and where prayer and problems meet? It is not too late. You can begin now. God needs children who will say, "I want to do my part" and parents who will accept their responsibility. Is Jesus Lord in your home? Is He Lord in your heart?

8.2.3
OBJECTIVE

Describe two key responsibilities of Christian parents to their children.

7 What two responsibilities do parents have for their children?

8 How would Paul's words apply to parents of the church today?

8.3.1
OBJECTIVE

Explain why Paul includes instructions to slaves and masters in this list of household duties.

9   Why does Paul include instructions to slaves and masters in his list of household duties?

Christ Fully Expressed at Work through Masters and Servants (6:5–9)

Paul turns to the final group on his list of household duties (*haustafel*). He addresses the responsibilities of slaves and masters. Slaves are included in his list because they were considered part of the household (Bruce 1984, 161).

Slaves were an integral part of ancient Roman culture. The entire Roman economy depended upon the slave system. Some estimates of the slave population within Roman culture run as high as fifty percent. People became slaves by birth, as punishment, by being kidnapped by a slave trader as a result of war, or being sold into slavery by their parents to pay off a debt. Slaves had no civil rights. The treatment of slaves varied widely. Some were cruelly treated. Others were treated with esteem and dignity. Many held positions of responsibility within the home and society. Many slaves and owners became Christians and worshiped together. They were treated equally in the church. But what was the responsibility of Christian slaves and Christian masters in the marketplace (Barton et al. 1995, 123–124)?

This is Paul's last example of Spirit-filled relationships addressed in Ephesians. We have no exact counterpart to this relationship in our culture. The closest we can come for application is the relationship between an employee and employer. A successful relationship in the marketplace depends upon a biblical understanding of the principles of authority and submission.

In our day the struggle between employers and employees has reached monumental proportions. There is mistrust, selfishness, and insensitivity. Labor and management are continually at odds. In most cases, the conflict is fueled by greed or misunderstanding. God's desire is that both Christian employers and Christian employees demonstrate the lordship of Jesus. Paul gives instruction for how this can be done.

List five principles governing how Christian employees should fulfill their responsibilities to their employers.

10   What are five principles for Christian employees?

Spirit-Filled Slaves/Employees Submit to Their Masters/Employers (6:5–8)

Paul instructs Christian employees to obey their employers. Interestingly, he uses the same Greek word here that he used of children obeying their parents. The only exception would be if they were instructed to do something wrong. The course of action in such instances would be a respectful appeal to their authority (cf. Daniel 1) and then refusal to comply (1 Peter 4:15–16,19).

Slave/Employees Were to Have the Proper Perspective (6:5)

Notice how Paul qualifies *masters* with the word *earthly*. Paul purposefully emphasizes that while masters are the acknowledged authority, it is only an earthly, temporal relationship, yet the submissive relationship is important and is to be respected. If you are chafing under your job right now, remember it will not last forever. The way you do your job now, however, has eternal consequences (cf. 6:8).

Slaves/Employees Were to Have the Right Attitude (6:5)

Christian employees must have an attitude of respect and fear. Here we are not talking about cowering and being afraid, but an attitude of honor and respect for their employer's position. We may not agree with that person and may feel he or she is unworthy of our respect, but as Christians we must give it (Romans 13:7). Who is ultimately the source of authority, anyway? Who led you to where you are? If God did that, then it is your responsibility, under God, to submit to that individual. You may say, "I can just quit my job!" You can, but while you are there and until God opens another door, you are to submit. Failure to do this will not only affect you in your job; it will affect your walk with God. Attitudes are key.

Christian Employees Must Serve from the Heart (6:5)

God wants us to submit; yet it is possible for us to do His will but not to do it His way. We can carry out the letter of the law and not fulfill the spirit of it. So Paul tells us to obey, sincerely honoring our employer God can give us a heart to do these things for the right reasons: love for God and our employer.

Christian Employees Must Have the Right Motives (6:5)

It is essential for us to do our jobs for Christ. Notice how the phrases add up in this passage: "just as you would Christ," "like slaves of Christ," and "as if you were serving the Lord." If that is not your motivation, do you know what will happen? When you do not get the promotion or raise, you will find yourself struggling with your attitude. What is worse, you will lose your eternal reward. You will just get whatever you can down here. But if your motivation is right and you do what you do for Christ, whether that is serving in a pulpit or a production line—God will honor and reward you. Ask yourself, "For whom am I working? For what am I working?" Ultimately, we should be serving the Lord.

Christian Employees Must Have Good Work Habits (6:6–8)

Believers in the workplace should not do only the minimum or work only when people are watching. You work to the best of your ability because you know that ultimately you are working for the Lord's approval (Colossians 3:23). "The Lord will reward everyone for whatever good he or she does, whether as "a slave or free" (6:8). Your employer may not appreciate the extra hours. He or she may not notice your attention to detail. But God does and ultimately He is the one you are serving. Nothing you ever do will escape His notice, His reward, or His blessing.

Leaving full-time ministry seemed like such a defeat at first for Tom. But what was he going to do? Try as he might, no door of opportunity seemed to be opening. He finally took a secular job for a while. He decided, "I will just keep my mouth shut about being a pastor and do the best job I can for the Lord." He worked hard, went above and beyond the call of duty, and shared his love for Jesus whenever he had an opportunity. He told me about an ethical crisis that arose while he was on the job and how he handled it. The Lord began to open doors to minister to fellow workers—even his boss. He led some to the Lord and prayed with others about their needs. Someone found out he had been a preacher. His colleagues jokingly began calling him *Preach*. His boss told him one day, "Tom you don't need a church—you've got us." What a testimony!

OBJECTIVE

List five principles governing how Christian employers should fulfill their responsibilities to their employees.

Spirit-Filled Masters/Employers Submit to Their Employees (6:9)

You may be saying to yourself, "What about employers? Are there not responsibilities for Christian employers also?" Paul provides an interesting answer. Verse 9 begins, "Masters, treat your slaves in the same way." To quote a popular cliché, "What is good for the goose is good for the gander" or "The principles that I have laid down for labor also apply to management."

Christian Employers Must Have the Proper Perspective

11 What are five principles for Christian employers?

Christian employers need to be aware that their authority is temporary and only applies to the here and now. Things may be different later (Matthew 19:30; 20:16; Mark 10:31; Luke 13:30).

Christian Employers Must Have a Right Attitude

Christian employers are responsible to treat their employees with respect. They must remember what it was like when the shoe was on the other foot and apply the "golden rule" (Matthew 7:12). They should not be unreasonable or harsh.

Christian Employers Must Manage with a Right Heart

A sincere heart does not say one thing to an employee while thinking another. A sincere heart does not tell them they are doing a great job and then put them down to others.

Christian Employers Must Have the Right Motives

Paul says, "He who is both their Master and yours is in heaven and there is no favoritism with Him" (6:9). Remember that you, too, are serving Christ. Just as your employees will give an accounting for their work, you also will give an account for how you used your authority (2 Corinthians 10:8; 13:10).

Christian Employers Must Have Good Management Habits

Resist the temptation to give in to lazy leadership or shifting blame. Do not give in to shoddy management practices. Do not resort to *motivation-by-volume* or the *whoever-produces-the-most* theories. Can you imagine the impact that following the advice "do not threaten them" (Ephesians 6:9) would have on management practices and morale in the workplace?

The late Truett Cathy, founder of the Chick-fil-A restaurant chain was not only well-known as a businessman but also as one whose faith had a direct impact on how he chose to lead his company, leverage his influence, and utilize the resources at his disposal.

The following serve as examples: (1) Cathy chose to close all his restaurants on Sunday as a means of showing respect for the Lord's day. Given the popularity of Chick-fil-A, this decision has meant the loss of revenue totaling in the millions of dollars. (2) In 1948, in the midst of the segregated south, Cathy made the decision to hire a 12-year old African-American boy named Eddie White. (3) Mr. Cathy became a mentor to Woody Faulk when Faulk was just 13. At the time of this writing, Faulk is an executive with Chick-fil-A, serving as vice president of innovation and design. (4) Cathy, through his WinShape Foudation, has been responsible for the establishment of scholarship programs and a network of foster homes that have been instrumental in influencing children and young people for Christ and have helped them to reach their God-given potential.

Woody Faulk said of Cathy, "He's the personification of James 1:22: 'Do not merely listen to the word, and so deceive yourselves. Do what it says.' I sincerely owe my life to that man." (Neven 2000).

Our model in all of this, whether we are employee or employer, is Jesus Christ. He "who, being in very nature God" took upon himself "the very nature of a servant." In the difficult task of redemption, He "became obedient to death— even death on a cross" (Philippians 2:6–8). He finished the task, too. From the Cross He proclaimed, "It is finished" (John 19:30).

If you are an employee, will you choose to make Jesus Lord of your life, fulfilling your work responsibilities for His honor and glory? If you are an employer, will you acknowledge His lordship in your life, make Him CEO of your company, and treat your employees as you would Him? It will make a difference in the workplace!

Test Yourself

Circle the letter of the *best* answer.

1. The IST defines submission as a/an
a) voluntary act.
b) forced act.
c) obligatory act.
d) sacrificial act.

2. A Spirit-filled wife submits to her husband by
a) resisting her husband's unreasonable demands.
b) obeying her husband's demands without question.
c) loving, respecting, and yielding in support of her husband.
d) playing a servant's role in her marriage.

3. The submission of the church to Christ should be out of
a) fear.
b) reverence.
c) obedience.
d) obligation.

4. A Spirit-filled husband submits to his wife by
a) allowing her to have her way in all things.
b) providing her with a lavish and extravagant lifestyle.
c) demonstrating sacrificial, caring, and indissoluble love.
d) seeing that she maintains a submissive attitude at all times.

5. What is meant when we say that a husband's love for his wife is indissoluble?
a) His commitment is permanent.
b) His commitment is conditional.
c) His vows are dissolvable.
d) His vows are important.

6. In Ephesians 5, Paul instructs husbands to love their wives and for wives to
a) obey their husbands.
b) serve their husbands.
c) cherish their husbands.
d) respect their husbands.

7. Children are instructed to
a) honor and respect their parents.
b) respect and admire their parents.
c) fear and obey their parents.
d) obey and honor their parents.

8. Instead of exasperating their children (Ephesians 6:4), fathers should
a) respect them and love them for who they are in Christ.
b) discipline them in a loving manner.
c) love them and overlook their shortcomings.
d) train them and instruct them in the Lord.

9. Each Christian employee must have a proper perspective, a right attitude, right motives, good work habits, and a
a) servant's heart.
b) joyful heart.
c) grateful heart.
d) generous heart.

10. Christian employers must have a proper perspective, right motives, good management habits, their employees' respect, and a
a) servant's heart.
b) joyful heart.
c) right heart.
d) grateful heart.

Responses to Interactive Questions

CHAPTER 8

Some of these responses may include information that is supplemental to the IST. These questions are intended to produce reflective thinking beyond the course content and your responses may vary from these examples.

1   How could mutual submission promote love, unity, and harmony in a marital relationship?

When each partner is motivated to meet the needs of the other, the needs of each are met. Removing control of one spouse by the other ends any thoughts of defensiveness. Neither needs to feel threatened by the other, but both will draw joy and pleasure from serving the other. Such an arrangement would lead to love, unity, and harmony.

2   How should the church and its members submit to Christ?

The church can joyfully throw herself onto the grace and mercy of Jesus. No fear can skew our relationship because we can totally trust the One to whom we submit. Our submission is a letting go of attitudes and behaviors that destroy relationships and taking on attitudes that promote love and unity. We will reverently acknowledge that Jesus is the only One who gets relationships right. By completely surrendering our will to His, we leave behind the broken ways of relating to others. We rest in Jesus, who as our Head, leads us into joyful, loving unity with our brothers and sisters in Christ.

3   What four principles characterize the love of a Christian husband for his wife?

A man full of the Holy Spirit will love his wife sacrificially, with holy purpose. He will care for her as he cares for his own body. He will be committed to her for life.

4   What are the four characteristics of Christ's love for the church found in this passage? What is the significance of each of them?

Christ's love for the church is sacrificial. He willingly laid down His life to make salvation available to all who believe. Jesus gave himself to sanctify His people, cleanse them, and prepare them eternity in His presence. Christ cares for His body, the church, providing for all its needs. His commitment to the church is eternal.

5   How were Paul's instructions to children and their parents different from common practice in ancient Roman culture?

In ancient culture, an infant was recognized legally as a person only when the father chose to do so. A baby could be abandoned or even killed. The people of God value a child from conception. Paul is careful to remind parents that the way they treat their children can impact the lives of those children. In return, children respond to their parents with respect and obedience.

6   What are the two key responsibilities of children to their parents?

Children are considered a vital part of the local church. Paul challenged them with two key responsibilities. First, was obedience to their parents in the Lord. Second was honoring their parents. To obey means to do what another person says. To honor involves respect and love. Children are to obey while they are under their parents' care. The responsibility to honor continues for life.

7   What two responsibilities do parents have for their children?

Parents demonstrate the lordship of Christ in their lives through their treatment of and nurture of their children. Paul set limits on their power over their children and established responsibilities for them in keeping with Christian values and teaching. They were not to exasperate their children or goad them into resentment. Do not act like you hate your children. Do not goad them, provoke them, or tease them to the point of anger.

Second, parents were to raise their children to follow Jesus. Wise parents love and encourage their children while at the same time guiding their behavior. Parents were to mold their children's lives and provide instruction in the things of the Lord.

8 How would Paul's words apply to parents within the church today?

The same principles apply to today's parents that applied in Paul's day. Godly parents will provide instruction in the things of the Lord. They will teach their children the Bible, emphasize the example of Jesus, guide their friendships, and keep a watchful eye on the heroes their children choose. They will provide a model of godliness and consistent Christian living. Discipline will be consistent and administered for the purpose of instructing and training, not for revenge or an outlet for anger and frustration. They will seek to fill their home with love and grace. Their local church will become an extended family. All of this is involved in "bringing them up in the training and instruction of the Lord."

9 Why does Paul include instructions to slaves and masters in his list of household duties?

Slaves were an integral part of ancient Roman culture. The entire Roman economy depended upon the slave system. Some estimates of the slave population within Roman culture run as high as fifty percent. Many slaves and owners became Christians and worshiped together. They were treated equally in the church. But they needed to know their responsibilities in the marketplace.

10 What are five principles for Christian employees?

Christian employees must have the proper perspective. They should remember that their current situation is temporary, but the way they do that job has eternal consequences. Christian employees must have right attitudes. Their attitude should be one of honor and respect for their employer's position. These employees should serve with sincerity and with right motives. If they do everything as to the Lord, God will honor and reward them. Finally, Christian employees must have good work habits. They should work to the best of their ability, again as unto the Lord.

11 What are five principles for Christian employers?

Christian employers demonstrate the lordship of Christ in their lives by how they treat their employees. They must have the proper perspective. Their authority is temporary and only applies to the here and now. They must have a right attitude. They are responsible to treat their employees with respect. They should not be unreasonable or harsh. Christian employers must manage with a right heart. They will be sincere and honest in dealing with those who work for them. They will have right motives and good management habits.

A Final Charge to Those Who Are in Christ (Ephesians 6:10–24)

The situation Paul addressed in his letter to the Ephesians is best determined by examining its sister epistle, Colossians. (See Chapter 1, "Introduction to Colossians"). The churches in the Lycus Valley, in and around Ephesus, had been influenced by teaching that fed pride and minimized the sufficiency of Christ. Individuals were developing spiritual pride that threatened to divide the church. Before they had come to Christ they had been involved in paganism and had been tyrannized by evil spiritual forces. They needed encouragement and practical instruction to face these challenges and satanic attack.

Paul's answer to this, in the first part of the letter (chapters 1–3), was to emphasize who they were and what they had in Christ. God had abundantly blessed His people with everything they would ever need to live victoriously in Christ Jesus. At the end of this section of his letter, he erupts in praise. "To him who is able to do immeasurably more than all we ask or imagine, according to His power that is at work within us, to him be glory in the church and in Christ Jesus throughout all generations, for ever and ever. Amen" (3:20–21).

In the second part of this letter Paul emphasizes the practical. His message was, "Be who you are in Christ." Let Christ be fully expressed in every dimension of your lives. First, let Him be expressed in and through the church (4:1–16). Then, express Him in your personal lives and interpersonal relationships (4:17–5:21). Finally, express Christ in your homes and in the workplace (5:21–6:9).

They were in a spiritual battle and Paul knew it. In this final section Paul prepares them for spiritual warfare. He emphasizes the spiritual armor they need to put on, and he stresses the importance of prayer.

• *Read Ephesians 6:10–24 before you begin study in this chapter.*

Lesson 9.1   The Fully Outfitted Christian Warrior (6:10–17)

Objectives

9.1.1   *Compare ancient warfare to warfare today, and describe how this relates to the battles Christians face today.*

9.1.2   *Explain the two challenges the Christian warrior faces in the spiritual conflict.*

9.1.3   *List and briefly describe the importance of each piece of spiritual armor.*

Lesson 9.2   The Praying Christian (6:18–24)

Objective

9.2.1   *Describe the prayer life of a godly person.*

LESSON
9.1

The Fully Outfitted Christian Warrior (6:10–17)

The Christian life is not ten days on a Carnival Cruise to the Bahamas. It is not a skiing vacation in the Colorado Rockies. The Christian life is not even a weekend retreat for several power-packed days at an old-fashioned camp meeting. Paul describes it in this passage as warfare—spiritual warfare.

If you have never experienced a spiritual attack, never felt under siege by your *spiritual adversary*, something is wrong. The Christian life is a battle. If you do not have a sense of being in a battle, it does not mean there is not one. It may mean you just have not shown up for duty. If so, you are spiritually AWOL. Satan is a spiritual terrorist. The Bible calls him "your enemy" (1 Peter 5:8). He is out to rob, kill, and destroy every believer he can.

Paul is writing to first century Christians living in Asia Minor in and around Ephesus. They had been delivered from the dark spiritual forces that had once bound them. They were under attack from the devil for trying to work for the Lord. Often they experienced ridicule and belittling from their old pagan friends. For them, persecution was not imaginary. Temptation to compromise or even return to their old sinful lifestyle was real. They were sometimes bewildered by the multitude of religious and philosophical options of the day. Even fellow believers, who saw themselves as some kind of super-saints because of their experiences, were trying to make them feel inferior. Living the Christian life in Ephesus was a battle and it is a battle in our world today.

Paul has tried to encourage, instruct, and warn these believers. He has systematically pumped into their spiritual psyche who they are and what they have *in Christ*. He has reminded them of all Christ has accomplished on their behalf. He has given specific instructions about how to live victorious for Christ in a pagan culture. Now Paul, this great field general for the Lord, gives his troops their charge for the spiritual warfare they face. The point is, Christians are involved in a real spiritual battle and need to make use of everything the Lord provides in order to be victorious.

The Christian Warrior Is Engaged in a Real Battle with a Real Enemy (6:12)

The first thing to remember as you read this passage is that this is not a modern battle scene. Soldiers are not located hundreds of yards or miles apart taking pot-shots at their enemy. This warfare is not waged by dropping bombs on a faceless enemy. What is envisioned here is hand-to-hand combat—to the death!

The battle being waged is not natural. This is a spiritual battle, but very real nonetheless. This is a war against spiritual forces using spiritual weapons (cf. 2 Corinthians 10:3–6). It is a perpetual, unceasing battle. It is not limited by space or time. It can be waged in a cathedral or a bar, in a car or at a place of business. An attack can come any time of day or night. This battle is ongoing. Even when there seems to be no direct assault, the enemy can be preparing another attack.

It is a battle for survival—for "life or death." Scripture says, "The thief comes to rob, kill and destroy" (John 10:10). Satan is out to destroy the effectiveness and reputation of every believer. He would snuff out the spiritual life and even the physical life of those who follow Christ.

We are not playing a game. Following Jesus is not an interesting hobby. We have a real enemy, but he is not human. At times we may think our enemy is, but he is not. Ephesians 6:12 teaches that our struggle is "not against flesh and blood." It is a spiritual battle against spiritual forces; it is "against the rulers, against the authorities, against the powers of this dark world and against the spiritual forces of evil in the heavenly realms."

9.1.1
OBJECTIVE

Compare ancient warfare to warfare today, and describe how this relates to the battles Christians face today.

1 How did ancient warfare differ from warfare today? How does this relate to spiritual battles we face?

In this battle we do not put on an electronic mask, put a DVD into a machine, set a dial or two, press play, and then begin feverishly mashing buttons on a handheld console in a game of virtual warfare. This is the real thing. It is spiritual to be sure, but it is more real than the war on terrorism that our allies wage around the world every day.

Christ's Warriors Must Be Strong and Stand Firm (6:10–14)

The first need we have in this battle is strength. That is why the passage opens with these words, "be strong in the Lord and in his mighty power" (6:10). In ancient warfare a warrior's armor could weigh over a hundred pounds. Couple this with hours of travel on foot and the physical exertion of hand-to-hand combat and it becomes clear how important physical conditioning and strength was. In spiritual warfare strength is no less needed. We need the Lord's strength. We need the mighty power He provides. The command of verse 10 is in the imperative mood: Paul implores them, "Be strong!" This strength is essential, not optional. It is in the passive voice: Human strength is not needed, it is a matter of yielding over to the strength and power God readily and fully provides. The verb is in the present tense: The need for empowerment is continual, "be being strengthened" (Foulkes 1979, 170–171).

The next challenge we face in this battle is the need to "stand firm" (v. 14). *Stand* is a military term. It means "hold your position" (Wood 1987, 86). Any military person will tell you that you must be able to hold your position before you can mount an offensive. Do this so that when things are at their worst, you will still be standing (Wood 1987, 87). Do not give in or give up; you do not have to. You may be staggering and tired. Your spiritual legs may feel like gelatin, your spiritual arms like lead, your body bruised, bloody, aching—but fight on. Christ will empower you (Philippians 4:12–13; Colossians 1:28–29).

I run a periodic marathon. I train long and hard for each one, hardening my body and legs to the stress of the road. I remember running White Rock Marathon several years ago in Dallas. At about twenty-two miles of a 26.2-mile race, I hit what runners call, the wall. An old leg injury began to make trouble for me. I felt I just could not go on. It was at that point, I took control. I began to talk to my body. I commanded my mind, I yelled at my weakness, I pressed on; I defeated *the wall* and finished the race at a sprint. Some Christians are just too soft. They think the Christian life is a simulated heavenly vacation. Harden your resolve, but keep a tender spirit.

Christ's Warriors Must Be Fully Outfitted (6:11, 13–17)

Most people hearing this letter read had seen Roman soldiers many times. They could immediately relate the picture Paul painted to their daily experiences. The soldier was fully outfitted: he had a *panoplia*, "full armor." Paul does not list every piece of armor a Roman soldier wore in this passage, but lists those that best serve the point he is making. Although there is significance in the pieces of armor he describes, the emphasis is placed upon the importance of building into our spiritual life the qualities he names (Keener 1993, 553–554). The point is this: To keep from being a victim, listed as missing in action, a prisoner of war, or a spiritual casualty in the spiritual battles we face, build these things into your life. Put on all your spiritual armor:

9.1.2
OBJECTIVE

Explain the two challenges the Christian warrior faces in the spiritual conflict.

2   Why was strength so important to the ancient warrior?

9.1.3
OBJECTIVE

List and briefly describe the importance of each piece of spiritual armor.

3   What is the significance to you of the words "Be strong in the Lord" (Ephesians 6:10)?

4 How did Paul use the example of the armor of a Roman soldier to help believers understand how to be ready for spiritual battle?

1. The belt of truth

   We need to allow God's truth to mold our life and thinking. We need to let it renew and protect our minds (Romans 12:1–2). Be a person of truth.

2. The breastplate of righteousness

   The Lord imparts righteousness to those who trust Him. But we also have a responsibility to practice righteousness, that is, to be righteous in our thoughts, attitudes, and actions. Be, in a practical way, what you are positionally in Christ.

5 What are the various items of spiritual armor Paul identified, and what is their importance to your spiritual life?

3. Feet fitted with readiness that comes from the gospel of peace

   Do you know the gospel? Do you know how to share it with a lost person? We are involved in spiritual warfare, seeking to rescue those for whom Jesus has provided redemption from the power of the enemy. Every Christian has a responsibility to be continually prepared to share the good news (1 Peter 3:15).

4. The shield of faith

   The shield of faith (v. 16) is protective armor for believers. It protects their hearts—their lives. Faith, for a Christian, is a growing, firm, vibrant confidence in God that neutralizes satanic attacks or the fiery darts of temptation, discouragement, and pressure to compromise.

5. The helmet of salvation

   The helmet of salvation (v. 17) protects against satanic attack by providing assurance of salvation. It is produced by the Spirit and is accompanied by an inner witness that we are God's children (Romans 8:15–16; Galatians 4:4–7; 2 Timothy 1:12).

6. The sword of the Spirit—the Word of God

   The Bible, the Word of God, is both an offensive and defensive weapon (Psalm 119:9,11; 2 Timothy 3:14–17; Hebrews 4:12). Consider the example of Jesus when He was tempted by Satan. Over and over He quoted Scripture saying, "It is written" (Matthew 4:1–11; Luke 4:1–13). How well do you know the Word? Do you have a working knowledge of the Bible?

6 What is the significance of prayer as part of the believer's spiritual armor?

7. Prayer

   Although prayer is not directly related as a piece of armor in this passage, Paul stresses its value (18–20). Any casual reader of the Bible knows its importance. Additionally, any victorious Christian will testify about how important prayer is to them both defensively and offensively in the Christian life. We will amplify what Paul has to say about this theme in the next lesson.

Listen, are you going to get involved in this conflict or simply sit in your living room, tuned to your local news station, watching as an interested observer? Enlist. Prepare yourself. Get into basic training. Get to know your Bible. Commit yourself to the conflict. If there ever was a *just* war, it is this one. If you have been in a spiritual battle or two, do not just retire from action, reminiscing about the battles of the past. Be like Caleb; have a *different* spirit, proclaiming, "Give me this mountain" (Joshua 14:7–8, 10–14).

The Praying Christian (6:18–24)

Although Paul's prayer emphasis in Ephesians 6 is not directly identified with a piece of armor, it is closely tied to the concept grammatically and conceptually. What is more, any casual reader of Scripture will quickly note the importance it places on prayer. Prayer is necessary; both defensively and offensively, in the Christian life.

7 How is prayer a ministry, rather than simply a devotional experience?

Prayer must be more than simply a devotional habit in the Christian's life. It must be a ministry, both in the lives of individual Christians and within the life of the local church. Prayer nourishes the believer. It deepens his or her relationship with God, brings perspective, refreshes, provides guidance, lifts cares, and results in God's meeting each believer's daily needs. But prayer is more than that. Paul pleads for prayer as ministry. He cries for prayer in the Spirit, prayer on all kinds of occasions: prayer for fellow believers and prayer for key spiritual leaders. All kinds of prayer are needed for victory in the Christian life.

Prayer in the Spirit Is Effective (6:18)

8 What does praying in the Spirit include?

People who have been filled with the Spirit, those whom we refer to as being *baptized in the Holy Spirit* (Acts 1:4–5; cf. Mark 1:7–8), rightfully think of prayer *in other tongues* when they read Paul's words here (1 Corinthians 14:2–3, 14). It is that, but it is more. Praying in the Spirit also includes prayer in a known language, enabled by the Holy Spirit (cf. 1 Corinthians 14:15). Both aspects of prayer in the Spirit are included in what Paul talks about in Romans 8:26–27. "The Spirit himself intercedes for us with groans that words cannot express." In fact, there are times in Spirit intercession when words are not possible, just a deep inner "groaning in the Spirit" (Fee 1994, 730–732; Barton et al. 1995, 136–137).

9 Can you identify times you have prayed in the Spirit? What was the value of those experiences?

I had just finished teaching on the subject of prayer, in a message titled *Turning Your Groaning Into a Prayer*," based on Romans 8:18–27, at a camp meeting. In conclusion, I invited those who were going through a difficult situation—one that produced a groaning within them—to allow the Holy Spirit to give it a voice through them in prayer. A Hispanic pastor came forward and began to engage in intercession. I noticed him and the deep intensity of his prayer. I do not know that I have ever seen anyone travail in prayer more fervently. I observed his wife watching him pray and spoke to her. She verified that what we were seeing was unusual. I do not know the details of what transpired in the heavenlies that morning, but I can tell you something remarkable happened as that man prayed. "The prayer of a righteous man is powerful and effective" (James 5:16).

Occasions for Prayer Are Everywhere (6:18)

Paul encourages believers to pray "on all occasions with all kinds of prayers and requests" (v. 18). He urges them to be alert for opportunities to pray.

10 What occasions for prayer do you have as a Christian?

First, we are told to pray on all occasions. We should pray for personal needs and the needs of others. We are to ask for help in trouble and temptation. We are allowed to express our concerns and feelings in prayer. We can pray for guidance and direction. We should pray when we need to calm down and gain perspective. Prayer is the way to receive salvation, the baptism in the Holy Spirit, healing, deliverance from habits, demonic attack, or oppression. We should pray when we have sinned to ask for forgiveness, cleansing, and restoration. It is proper to pray for renewal and revival. Thanksgiving should be offered for God's blessings—this too is lifting up our prayers. All kinds of occasions can and should prompt prayer.

11 What did Paul mean by "all kinds of prayer" (Ephesians 6:18)?

We are also challenged to utilize all kinds of prayer. A great danger for Christians is to become comfortable with just one kind of prayer, to get into a spiritual rut. The Bible uses words like *petitions*, *requests*, *supplication*, and *entreaty* to describe the variety of prayer available to us. We should learn to listen to God when we pray and meditate prayerfully on His Word. We can pray Scripture, intercede (earnestly praying for others), praise, and worship. Thanksgiving, rejoicing, and exultation in God's goodness are appropriate.

We must not forget confession of sin and contrition. Fasting (whether going without food and/or drink for purposes of prayer) is important. There is a place for militant, assertive prayer, but prayers of submission are just as necessary. Persistent, prevailing prayer always has power.

12 Can you identify opportunities for you to pray?

In addition, we need to learn to pray in all kinds of settings: personal or private, in busy noisy places or quiet locations, with or without music. We need to know how to lead in prayer, participate in a concert of prayer, or lead out spontaneously in a circle of prayer. We need to get used to praying with people from other denominations.

I was parked at a railroad crossing, waiting, not so patiently, for a long train to pass. I began to fret about challenges we were facing in the church I was pastoring. A particular person came to mind whose recent behavior deeply troubled me. I thought about the trouble he was stirring up and his independent, uncooperative spirit. The more I mulled over these things, the more upset I became. The train was almost gone now. The arms of the crossing were about to lift. And there on the other side of the crossing in his car . . . . You guessed it! It was the man I had been fussing about. In that moment, God spoke to me as clearly as I can ever remember. He said, "Son, in the future, when I bring a name to your mind, I want you to assume it is for the purpose of prayer." What a rebuke. What an opportunity. I learned a marvelous lesson from the Lord that day. A lesson that has expanded my prayer ministry in directions and depths multiplied over and over. Opportunities for prayer are everywhere.

Intercessory Prayer Helps Fellow Christians and Spreads the Gospel (6:18–20)

13 What part does intercession play in the lives of believers and the spread of the gospel?

Paul knew the power of Holy Spirit enabled intercession. In this passage to Christians in Asia he told them to keep on praying for all the saints and for him also—that he would be enabled to continue to proclaim the gospel fearlessly and effectively (vv. 18–19). As incredible as it may seem, Paul did not ask fellow believers to pray for his release from prison. Rather he asked them to pray for the continued spread of the gospel. We really have no idea of the challenges faced by fellow believers in our communities and around the world. Those who lead the church and guide nations need our prayers. It is God's will that we pray for them (cf. 1 Timothy 2:1–4). Our selfless intercession helps fellow Christians and spreads the gospel around the world.

I teach in a university where each class is opened with prayer for a different nation of the world. A prayer guide is used to focus our prayer. Participating in this practice every day has helped form an intercessor's heart in many lives. At the time of this writing, I continue to observe students pouring out their hearts in fervent prayer for AIDS victims in South Africa and for the mobilization of the church to minister to their needs and reach them with the gospel. Assemblies of God World Missions and U.S. Missions can provide tools to help make systematic prayer for other nations, fields of service, various ministries, missionaries, and leaders a reality in your life.

A Benediction (6:21–24)

The closing remarks of this letter are similar to those in Colossians, revealing the close relationship between the two letters (cf. Colossians 4:7–9). Tychicus was Paul's faithful and trusted ministry associate. On several occasions, he willingly tackled difficult assignments for the apostle (Acts 20:1–5; 2 Timothy 4:12; Titus 3:12). In this case, Paul assigns him the task of carrying this letter, Colossians, and probably the letter to Philemon to the churches in Asia Minor. Tychicus was to bring news about Paul's situation and encourage their hearts in the Lord. He was not a complainer; he just faithfully served the Lord and Paul, his leader. May God give the church more people like Tychicus.

Paul closes with a benediction upon the believers and churches in and around Ephesus. He ends the letter as he began it with peace, love with faith, and grace as his focus (cf. Ephesians 1:1–19). Paul's final words emphasize the importance of our love for the Lord as a wellspring from which all other blessings flow. May we love our Lord Jesus Christ with an undying love!

Any military strategist will tell you that, while ground troops are essential in winning a war, air superiority gives an overwhelming and often decisive advantage. Paul description of the use of prayer and its effectiveness is a graphic picture of the Christian's air support. Remember, God's army prevails on its knees (Barton et al. 1995, 137). Will you pray? Will you pray daily? Will you pray continually? Will you watch for situations and needs that call for your prayer? Will you pray for fellow believers who are facing incredible challenges? Will you pray for those who lead the church and the nations? Paul's closing exhortation is needed today as much as it was then: Pray. Pray. Pray.

Test Yourself

Circle the letter of the *best* answer.

1. The battle Christians face is against
a) flesh and blood.
b) unbelievers.
c) evil spiritual forces and authorities in the heavenly realms.
d) governments and politicians.

2. Based upon Ephesians 6, when in the midst of spiritual warfare, a Christian must
a) be strong and stand firm.
b) fight until the end.
c) retreat and take refuge in God.
d) declare his or her fear to others.

3. *Stand* is a military term meaning "to
a) do nothing."
b) be encouraged."
c) hold one's position."
d) harden one's resolve."

4. The piece of armor that provides the inner witness that an individual is a child of God is called the
a) belt of truth.
b) breastplate of righteousness.
c) shield of faith.
d) helmet of salvation.

5. Which piece of armor is needed to mold a believer's thinking?
a) The belt of truth
b) The helmet of salvation
c) The breastplate of righteousness
d) The shield of faith

6. The piece of armor that protects a Christian's heart and life from the fiery darts of the enemy is the
a) shield of faith.
b) belt of truth.
c) sword of the Spirit.
d) breastplate of righteousness.

7. What piece of armor is both an offensive and defensive weapon?
a) The belt of truth
b) The shield of faith
c) The breastplate of righteousness
d) The sword of the Spirit

8. What is not listed directly as a piece of armor in Ephesians 6, but is emphasized by Paul as being essential in spiritual warfare?
a) Singing choruses and hymns to God
b) Praying in the Spirit
c) Reading the Word of God
d) Thanksgiving

9. The piece of armor that is linked to sharing the good news is
a) a shield.
b) a sword.
c) a pair of shoes.
d) a helmet.

10. How do Pentecostals interpret Paul's words to *pray in the Spirit*?
a) To pray in other tongues
b) To pray in a known language, enabled by the Holy Spirit
c) To pray with groans that words cannot express
d) It can include all of the above.

Responses to Interactive Questions
CHAPTER 9

Some of these responses may include information that is supplemental to the IST. These questions are intended to produce reflective thinking beyond the course content and your responses may vary from these examples.

1 How did ancient warfare differ from warfare today? How does this relate to spiritual battles we face?

Ancient warfare involved hand-to-hand combat. Today, attacks can be launched at an enemy miles away. The believer's battle is spiritual, and the enemy uses spiritual weapons. This battle is continual, without letup. It is not limited by time or space. Believers need to always be on guard and stay fully armed at all times.

2 Why was strength so important to the ancient warrior?

In ancient warfare a warrior's armor could weigh over a hundred pounds. Soldiers often had to travel on foot for hours, then engage in hand-to-hand combat. Physical training and stamina were a must for survival.

3 What is the significance to you of the words "Be strong in the Lord" (Ephesians 6:10)?

Answers will vary.

4 How did Paul use the armor of a Roman to help the believers understand how to be ready for spiritual battle?

The people hearing this letter read were familiar with Roman soldiers, their armor, and their weapons. They could immediately relate the picture Paul painted to their daily experiences.

5 What are the various items of spiritual armor Paul identified and what is their importance to your spiritual life?

The belt of truth: We need God's truth to mold our lives and our thought patterns. His truth will renew and protect our minds.

The breastplate of righteousness: The Lord imparts righteousness to believers. Believers seek His help in practicing righteousness.

Feet fitted with readiness that comes from the gospel of peace: Believers are in spiritual warfare, seeking to rescue those Jesus has redeemed from the power of the enemy. Every Christian should be continually prepared to share the good news.

The shield of faith: This is protective armor for believers. It protects their hearts and their lives. Faith is a growing, firm, vibrant confidence in God that neutralizes satanic attacks of temptation, discouragement, and pressure to compromise.

The helmet of salvation: This protects against satanic attack by providing assurance of salvation.

The sword of the Spirit—the Word of God: The Bible is both an offensive and defensive weapon to be used to defeat Satan.

6 What is the significance of prayer as part of the believer's spiritual armor?

Prayer is a powerful weapon to be used both defensively and offensively in the Christian life.

7 How is prayer a ministry rather than simply a devotional experience?

Prayer nourishes the believer. It deepens his or her relationship with God, brings perspective, refreshes, provides guidance, lifts care, and results in God's meeting his or her daily needs. Prayer is also a ministry. One can pray in the Spirit on all kinds of occasions, for fellow believers, and for key spiritual leaders. All kinds of prayer are needed for victory in the Christian life.

8 What does praying in the Spirit include?

Praying in the Spirit includes speaking in other tongues as well as in a known language, enabled by the Holy Spirit. The Holy Spirit intercedes for us, at times without words.

9 Can you identify times you have prayed in the Spirit? What was the value of those experiences?

Answers will vary.

10 What occasions for prayer do you have as a Christian?

Answers may include: We can be alert for opportunities to pray. We should pray for personal needs and the needs of others. We are to ask for help in trouble and temptation. We are allowed to express our concerns and feelings in prayer. We can pray for guidance and direction. We should pray when we need to calm down and gain perspective. Prayer is the way to receive salvation, the baptism in the Holy Spirit, healing, deliverance from habits, demonic attack, or oppression. We should pray when we have sinned to ask for forgiveness, cleansing, and restoration. It is proper to pray for renewal and revival. Thanksgiving should be offered for God's blessings. All kinds of occasions can and should prompt prayer.

11 What did Paul mean by "all kinds of prayer" (Ephesians 6:18)?

The Bible uses words like petitions, requests, supplication, and entreaty to describe the variety of prayer available to us. We should learn to listen to God when we pray and meditate prayerfully on His word. We can pray Scripture, intercede (i.e. pray for others), praise, and worship. Thanksgiving, rejoicing, and exultation in God's goodness are appropriate. We must not forget confession of sin and contrition. Fasting (i.e. going without food and/or drink for purposes of prayer) is important. There is a place for militant, assertive prayer, but prayers of submission are also important. Persistent, prevailing prayer always has power.

12 Can you identify opportunities for you to pray?

Answers will vary.

13 What part does intercession play in the lives of believers and the spread of the gospel?

Paul asked for fellow believers to pray for the continued spread of the gospel. We have no idea of the challenges faced by fellow believers in our communities and around the world. Those who lead the church and guide nations need our prayers. It is God's will that we pray for them. Our selfless intercession helps fellow Christians and spreads the gospel around the world.

UNIT PROGRESS EVALUATION 2

Now that you have finished Unit 2, review the lessons in preparation for Unit Progress Evaluation 2. You will find it in the Essential Course Materials section at the back of this IST. Answer all of the questions without referring to your course materials, Bible, or notes. When you have completed the UPE, check your answers with the answer key provided in the Essential Course Materials section, and review any items you may have answered incorrectly. Then you may proceed with your study of Unit 3. (Although UPE scores do not count as part of your final course grade, they indicate how well you learned the material and how well you may perform on the closed-book final examination.)

Philippians

How amazing and inspiring it is to observe committed Christians who face pressure, problems and persecution with grace, dignity, patience, and joy! When others who are facing similar situations observe their vibrant, victorious Christianity they take heart. It encourages them to draw on the strength of the Lord, view their problems from a Christian perspective, and "rejoice in the Lord!" This is really the message of Paul's great epistle to the Philippians.

Philippi was a prosperous and influential Roman colony located in ancient Macedonia. It was a special church to Paul and his memories of its planting and the people who made it up were warm and rich. Paul's imprisonment made it impossible for him to visit them. So he writes an apostolic letter to them that radiates love, friendship, and concern for their welfare.

The congregation in Philippi was facing challenges within and without. There was pressure and persecution. A competitive, self-seeking atmosphere poisoned the fellowship. Disagreements and petty bickering troubled their fellowship. In this letter Paul draws upon his own experience and situation in prison to encourage the believers in Philippi to sustain or regain their perspective. He points to Jesus as the model of the servant leadership needed in their situation. Paul's passion is that the progress of the gospel not be hindered by the actions and attitudes of professing Christians in Philippi. Yet in all of the pastoral concern Paul exhibits in the letter, an atmosphere of radiant, overcoming rejoicing dominates.

What an appropriate message for Christians in the modern world who face the daily pressures of living for Christ. Problems and pressures can rob us of the divine perspective on our lives. Interpersonal issues can damage the fellowship among believers. Disagreements can explode into conflicts that hinder the progress of the gospel. Joy evaporates, complaining increases, the church is damaged and the lost are disillusioned. The answer presented in Philippians is for us to keep our eyes upon Jesus, follow His example of servanthood, put Him first in our lives, pray about everything, and rejoice in the Lord.

Chapter 12   **Encouragement, Exhortation, and Evaluation (Philippians 2:19–4:1)**

Lessons
12.1   Deep Appreciation for Two Quality People (2:19–30)
12.2   An Appeal and Warning From a Concerned Christian Friend (3:1–3, 17–19)
12.3   An Appeal Supported by Paul's Personal Testimony (3:4–16; 3:20–4:1)

Chapter 13   **Concluding Exhortations, Thanks, and Greeting (Philippians 4:2–23)**

Lessons
13.1   Exhortations: To Unity, Reconciliation, Rejoicing, and Generosity (4:2–5)
13.2   Exhortations: To Prayer and Positive Participation in Culture (4:6–9)
13.3   Thanksgiving and Final Greetings (4:10–23)

Introducing Philippians (Philippians 1:1–11)

Perspective is important. Perspective makes a difference in our ability to see things accurately, in evaluating their true roles. The story is told of a group of blindfolded children trying to describe an elephant. All they had to go on was their sense of touch. One described the elephant like the trunk of a tree. Another said after taking hold of its tail, "It seems to me like a rope." Another was sure the elephant was like a big curved pipe because of its trunk. None had the total picture. None saw the elephant in proper perspective.

Losing perspective can be dangerous. It causes us to panic when there is no reason to panic. We do dangerous and silly things when we see things improperly. We act in inappropriate ways because we think things are different from how they really are. It is essential for Christians to maintain proper perspective.

Although we find Paul in prison at the writing of this epistle and the believers in Philippi are struggling, his message to them is this: having Christ in your life brings perspective to difficult situations and produces unquenchable joy within.

• *Read Philippians 1:1–11 before you begin study in this chapter.*

Lesson 10.1   Introductory Matters (1:1–11)

Objectives
10.1.1 Summarize the issues of authorship and the integrity of Philippians.
10.1.2 Explain the importance of Philippi in the ancient world and to Paul personally.
10.1.3 Summarize Paul's reasons for writing to the church at Philippi.
10.1.4 Identify two major themes of Philippians.

Lesson 10.2   Deep Feelings and Prayer for Fellow Christians (1:1–11)

Objectives

10.2.1 Describe how Paul opened his letter to the church at Philippi.

10.2.2 Explain why Paul gave thanks each time the church in Philippi came to mind.

10.2.3 Describe the confidence Paul had in the church at Philippi.

10.2.4 Explain the importance of expressing concern and love for people in your life.

10.2.5 List and explain four outcomes Paul sought in prayer for the Philippian believers.

10.1.1
OBJECTIVE

Summarize the issues of authorship and the integrity of Philippians.

1   How can Paul's use of the word *finally* in Philippians 3:1 be explained?

10.1.2
OBJECTIVE

Explain the importance of Philippi in the ancient world and to Paul personally.

2   How important was Philippi in the ancient world?

3   What made Philippi special to Paul?

Introductory Matters (1:1–11)

This commentary is written with the conviction that Paul authored this letter (1:1). The integrity of Philippians as a complete document is assumed. Although Paul uses the words "Finally, my brothers" at 3:1 and does not immediately finish the letter, this can be explained in other ways than the adding of a separate document by a different author. Paul may have been prompted by the Holy Spirit to address another issue or additional information may have come to his attention after he had prepared to close the letter (Kent 1978, 96–97). As many know well (who have heard numerous sermons that included two or three endings, all prefaced with *finally*), the end of a message does not come until the preacher has said all that the occasion permits his or her heart to express! Philippians is Paul's record of this practice.

The Importance of Philippi to Paul

Philippi was a key city in the ancient Roman world (Acts 16:12). It was a thriving, Gentile city located in northeastern Greece, on the Egnatian Way, an important highway linking the Aegean and Adriatic Seas. It was the gateway to the east, Greek in culture and proud of its status as a Roman colony. Politically, it was like Rome in every way—Roman laws, Roman citizenship for its residents, immunity from taxation—all the rights and privileges of Rome. Religiously, it reflected the pagan diversity of its population.

Paul visited Philippi on his second missionary journey, about ten years before the writing of this letter. Paul and his team had been traveling through ancient Phrygia and Galatia, preaching the gospel. They attempted to go into Asia, but the Holy Spirit prevented them from doing so. Then they tried to enter Bithynia, but again the Spirit would not allow it. One night in Troas, Paul saw a vision of a Macedonian man standing and imploring him, "Come over to Macedonia and help us" (Acts 16:9). That settled God's will for Paul. He headed for Macedonia. When he arrived at Philippi, it was largely Gentile in its population. The fact that there was no synagogue in the city indicates there were probably few Jews living there.

Acts 16 tells of three remarkable conversion experiences that gave birth to the church in Philippi: First, the Lord "opened the heart" (v. 14) of Lydia, a successful businesswoman, and her entire family found the Lord. Next was the deliverance of a demon-possessed girl who was a fortune teller. Her conversion resulted in a beating and imprisonment for Paul and Silas. But God's miraculous deliverance of them from prison led to the conversion of the third person, their jailer and his family. Clement, Euodia, and Syntyche, who are mentioned in this letter, may also have been converted at this time.

The congregation of believers in Philippi was special to Paul. Luke, Paul's personal physician and chief member of his missionary team, appears to have been left there to carry on the ministry for several years (Luke stops using the word *we* in Acts at 16:17 and does not resume using it again until 20:5) (O'Brien 1993, 8). Paul maintained special interest in and friendly contact with this church over the intervening years. They sent monetary gifts to him on several occasions (cf. 1:3–5; 2:25–30; 4:10–20). Paul even boasted about their generosity to other churches (2 Corinthians 8:1–5). This congregation went so far as to send Epaphroditus, their personal representative, to minister to Paul's needs while he was in prison. This letter breathes the warmth of an ongoing friendship. In fact, a close examination of its contents and form reveals that Philippians has many similarities to other letters of friendship in the ancient Roman world (Fee 1995, 2–14).

The Circumstances Behind Philippians

10.1.3
OBJECTIVE

Summarize Paul's reasons for writing to the church at Philippi.

Paul is in prison in chains (1:7, 13–14, 17), most likely in Rome (Fee 1995, 34–37). Because of his close ties to the church in Philippi, his heart is filled with appreciation, confidence, and love for the believers there. They were godly people, but needed more love and discernment to live righteous, fruitful lives (1:9–11). He has not heard from them in a while, but knows they have been concerned about him (1:12; 4:10). He confesses that he misses them (1:3–8) and looks forward to receiving reports about them and eventually seeing them (2:19–24). Although he is in chains and faces personal adversaries and attacks, he has been busy taking advantage of the opportunities he has to share Christ with those around him. He may be facing death, but he is confident, optimistic about the future, and filled with resolve (1:12–26).

4   Based on the clues within the letter to the Philippians, how would you describe the situation within the church?

Paul was concerned about the reports he had heard about the state of mind of the believers in Philippi. He was also concerned about certain attitudes that existed within the church (1:27–28; 2:1–2). The church was being divided by disunity, selfishness, differences of opinion, and pride (2:1–5). Complaining and arguing had set in (2:14–16). Paul's concern extended to their attitude toward Epaphroditus (2:25–30). His heart is filled with concern, even indignation over those troubling the body of Christ. In particular, he is troubled by the disagreements between two long-standing members of the church (4:2–3). The church was losing perspective, forgetting what they had been taught (4:4–9). This situation prompted Paul to write to the church. After dealing with the issues of concern, he closes the letter with deep appreciation, warm friendship, and contentment in Christ (4:10–19).

The Purpose of Philippians

5   What purposes are given for the writing of Philippians?

A careful examination of Paul's letter to the church at Philippi gives a clear picture of his purpose for writing.

Restoring Perspective

Paul wanted to help the believers get their circumstances and his in proper perspective. They found it difficult to understand why Paul was in prison. After all, he was God's faithful servant and apostle. And their circumstances only complicated matters. They were trying to live for God, so why were they experiencing persecution and difficulties? Their loss of perspective was beginning to show in petty disagreements and discontentment. Paul knew that remembering their relationship with Christ would bring perspective to the situations they faced and bring them joy within.

An Encouraging Report

Paul wanted to update the believers regarding his circumstances. He was again the object of their concern. Was it going badly for him? He wanted them to know the true state of affairs: God was using his circumstances to spread the gospel.

He also wanted them to know what had happened to Epaphroditus. The church had sent Epaphroditus to Paul with money, but he had not returned. Paul wrote to let them know what had happened to this brother and to encourage them to receive him back with honor.

A Warning

Paul felt the need to warn these believers about destructive influences both within and without the congregation, which if left unattended, could destroy the congregation or render it ineffective.

Emphasizing Unity

Resistance to the gospel was coming from the outside. Disagreements and wrong attitudes were dividing the church. Paul wrote to encourage them to stand firm and present a united front against the attacks they faced.

Expressing Appreciation

Finally, Paul wanted the believers to know how much he appreciated their loving concern for his welfare which they had expressed by their sacrificial gift delivered by Epaphroditus.

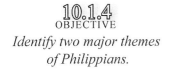

10.1.4
OBJECTIVE

Identify two major themes of Philippians.

6   What are the two key themes of Philippians?

7   How does each of the two key themes of Philippians apply to your life?

The Key Themes of Philippians

Two key themes dominate Philippians:

1. Joy—Rejoicing in the Lord

Although restoring perspective in the face of difficult circumstances appears to be Paul's purpose, the major theme of his letter is joy "in the Lord." This theme is emphasized at least sixteen times by use of various forms of the words *joy* or *rejoice* (cf. 1:4, 18, 25–26; 2:2, 17–18, 28–29; 3:1; 4:1, 4, 10). Joy is how believers respond to trying circumstances. Paul is not afraid to use himself as a case study. This joy is not simply a feeling; it is an activity flowing from an inner reality. Paul says, "Rejoice in the Lord!" "Rejoice in the Lord always." (3:1; 4:4). Whatever else the Christian life is, it is to be a life of joy. Regardless of the circumstances or trials we face, our joy is found in the Lord (Barton et al. 1995, 8–9).

2. The Advancement of the Gospel

Paul's ultimate concern is that the gospel be preached, regardless of the challenges facing the church. He was grateful for the believers' participation in the gospel over the years (1:5; 4:15). His concern is for their testimony and its impact on the effectiveness of the gospel (Fee 1995, 47).

Paul saw his own imprisonment as an opportunity for the "defense and confirmation of the gospel" (1:7, 17; 1:12). He was determined to go on preaching the gospel, regardless of what happened to him (1:18–20). Jesus Christ was central to his life, and Paul considered anything of this world as "loss" in comparison to knowing Him fully (3:7–10).

How passionately are you committed to the advancement of the gospel? How do you see your present circumstances in light of furthering the gospel? What would you be willing to do personally, and in partnership with others, to spread its message and safeguard its influence?

The Outline of Philippians

I.   Christian Greetings (1:1–2)

II. Thanksgiving and Prayer for the Philippian Believers (1:3–11)

III. Paul: A Model of Positive Perspective in Difficult Circumstances (1:12–27)

IV. Paul Shares What Would Make His Joy Complete (1:27–2:18)

    A. If they would live a life worthy of the gospel (1:27–30)

    B. If they would follow the servant attitude of Jesus (2:1–18)

V.   Appreciation for Two Quality People (2:19–30)

    A. Timothy: Paul's personal representative to them (2:19–24)

    B. Epaphroditus: Their representative to him (2:25–30)

VI. An Appeal from a Friend for Regained Perspective (3:1–4:1)

    A. An exhortation to rejoice (3:1)

    B. A warning regarding the perspective of false teachers (3:2–3)

    C. Paul: A case study in regained perspective (3:4–14)

    D. Warnings and exhortations continued (3:15–20)

    E. A summary: "This is how you should stand firm in the Lord." (4:1)

VII. Concluding Exhortations (4:2–9)

VIII. Appreciation for Their Gift (4:10–21)

IX. Final Greetings (4:21–23)

Deep Feelings and Prayer for Fellow Christians (1:1–11).

Philippi was a Roman colony and the leading city of Macedonia. Paul had been called, by a soverign act of God, to minister in the city (Acts 16:6–10). It had been a challenging and gratifying place of ministry for Paul. Remarkable miracles and wonderful *stories of grace* had taken place from the first day he and his team set foot in Philippi.

Although Paul wrote the epistle to Philippi while chained to guards, a joyful spirit dominates the letter. It is a personal letter of friendship and love to a church that holds a special place in his heart.

Paul Begins the Letter in a Characteristically Pauline Fashion

10.2.1
OBJECTIVE
Describe how Paul opened his letter to the church at Philippi.

Paul begins his letter to the Philippians in typical Pauline style. Paul greets the Philippians by stating, "To all the saints in Christ Jesus who are in Philippi." By addressing his audience in this manner, he establishes their status as "saints" associated with Christ, instead of with any other local pagan gods or deities perpetuated by the Hellenistic Greek culture of Philippi.

Paul identifies Timothy and himself as "fellow-servants of Jesus Christ," thus modeling the servant-leadership mindset he emphasizes throughout the letter (cf. 2:3–11). He does not refer to his apostleship as he does in other letters. He is not stressing his authority, but basing his appeal on mutual friendship.

Then he says, "Grace and peace to you from God our Father and the Lord Jesus Christ" (1:2). This is a typical secular greeting adapted to the values of Christianity. These two blessings summarize everything found *in Christ* (Kent 1978, 103–114).

After greeting these dear friends in this affectionate way, he expresses his thanks for their partnership in ministry and his confidence in what God is doing in their lives. He lets them know how much he cares for them and finishes with a prayer on their behalf.

Here is a point to remember: Great Christian leaders care deeply about fellow Christians and want God's best for them. They do at least four of the things Paul did in this passage:

Give Thanks for Partners in Ministry (1:3–5)

10.2.2
OBJECTIVE

Explain why Paul gave thanks each time the church in Philippi came to mind.

Paul said he thanked God for the believers in Philippi "every time I remember you . . . from the first day" (v. 3) he had preached to them ten years before. No doubt he remembered the Sabbath day he and his colleagues went to the river and found some women at their place of prayer. The Lord opened the heart of a woman named Lydia to the gospel. He also would have remembered the slave girl from whom he cast out demons. He would have thought back to the jailer who had locked him in stocks after beating him, then was saved, along with his family. Then there were the financial gifts the Philippian church had sent on more than one occasion (4:9–10; cf. 2 Corinthians 8:1–5). He would have remembered how they sent not only money but Epaphroditus, a person who worked himself almost to death for Paul. And with each memory came thanksgiving and prayer. What a wonderful personal guideline this is for us to use regarding those we know and love in the Lord—continual thanksgiving and joyful prayer.

8 What things about those in Philippi would have prompted Paul to give thanks?

Partnership (*koinonia* in the Greek) in the Lord's work brings an intimate bond between people (Gingrich 1983, 118). When we pray together, plan together, give together, and serve together, an unusually close bond is created. These were people who had sustained their friendship and partnership "from the first day until now" (v. 5). The Bible teaches "A friend loves at all times, and a brother is born for adversity" (Proverbs 17:17).

9 How does partnership in ministry affect the church?

The names of so many people flood my mind from the years of serving as a pastor: people I have worked with, prayed with, and faced challenges with, people who are dear to me in the Lord's work. Whenever they come to mind, I give thanks for them. I remember with sweetness their contribution.

Who enters your mind right now? Start rehearsing the names. Lift your heart to God in thanks for them.

Express Confidence in What God Is Doing in Their Lives (1:6)

10.2.3
OBJECTIVE

Describe the confidence Paul had in the church at Philippi.

God had been the source that had brought these believers into the knowledge of himself, through His Son Jesus. This had been their starting point, being *in Christ*. Paul assures them that God would complete what He had begun in them, through His Son Jesus. At the Cross, Jesus proclaimed "It is finished" regarding redemption (John 19:30). Hebrews 12:2 (KJV) asserts that He is "the author and finisher of our faith." The confidence of every believer should be placed in Jesus.

Those of us oriented by Western culture tend to see such words of assurance as applying primarily to our personal salvation. We easily overlook the contextual clues that make the primary application God's work within a corporate body of believers, for example, His work of completion within a church or ministry (O'Brien 1993, 63–64).

We do well to remember that the confidence Paul expressed in this passage was not foremost a confidence in the believers, but rather a confidence in God. He did have confidence in the believers, but he also knew their weaknesses and problems. His confidence was ultimately in Almighty God. Praise God for the assurances of 1 Thessalonians 5:23 and 2 Corinthians 3:18 that remind us of God's awesome ability to keep and transform us.

I had the privilege of pastoring a great and thriving church. But it was not always like that. God gave a vision. Then wonderful people came alongside to share it with me. We began small. We prayed and sought God together. We worked hard. God worked marvelous miracles. We faced seemingly overwhelming challenges. Satan resisted us in so many ways. Yet I had a deep-seated confidence, based upon verse 6 of this passage: "He who began a work in you will carry it on to completion until the day of Christ Jesus." Praise the Lord!

Let Others Know How Much You Care about Them (1:7–8)

We need to let other people know how much we love and care about them. Paul claimed the Philippian believers were in his heart all the time—in all kinds of situations and circumstances. Why? Because they had partnered with him in spreading the gospel (1:5), drawing on God's grace (1:7). God's grace had provided what they needed to handle these things victoriously. In fact, regardless of what Paul had been through (absent or present) the believers had taken part in it with him.

First Corinthians 12:21–26 declares we need each other. Each of us is indispensable to the other, and thus we rejoice or suffer together.

Paul could truthfully say, "I long for all of you with the affection of Christ Jesus" (1:8). The word translated "affection" here is a strong one. The term is *splagchnon* which literally means intestines, inner parts, bowels, or kidneys and is used of those deep inner feelings we have when we are moved to tears (Kent 1978, 106–107). Those we labor with and share God's grace with come to mean much to us. Paul could truthfully say, "I have the same deep love for you that Jesus has for His own" (cf. 4:1; John 17). Paul claims, "It is right" to feel that way about fellow servants of the Lord, brothers and sisters in Christ.

Expressing deep feelings is not easy for many of us. We find it difficult to look someone we care for in the eye and say what we feel. I remember a woman sharing her feelings for my wife and me when we left the church we were pastoring. She put it off until the last minute, but she did it. She looked us right in the eye and told us how much it had meant to her to serve as our children's pastor, how we had contributed to her growth in the Lord, how we had helped her and her husband through trials, and how much they loved us. I will never forget it as long as I live. It even moves me to tears again as I think of it now.

Pray Fervently for Their Spiritual Well-Being (1:9–11)

Paul prayed for fellow Christians continually. He prayed for specific things to increase in their lives, both personally and collectively:

- Their love for each other and the Lord. This, the core of his prayer, was critical. Out of it all else would flow (cf. Matthew 22:36–40; Romans 13:8–10).

- He prayed their love would grow in knowledge and depth of insight. The word for knowledge here *(epignosis)* means a deep, personal knowledge of the Lord and a firm convictions that would guide their relationships with one another and their world. Depth of insight *(aisthesi)* is moral and

---

10.2.4
OBJECTIVE

Explain the importance of expressing concern and love for people in your life.

10 To what fellow Christians will you express your love and concern?

10.2.5
OBJECTIVE

List and explain four outcomes Paul sought in prayer for the Philippian believers.

11 What did Paul pray would happen in the lives of the Philippian believers?

spiritual perception, for example, being spiritually wise and discerning (O'Brien 1993, 76–77).

The four-fold purpose or outcome of all of this would be

1. that they might be able to discern what is best (not simply good).

2. that they might be morally and spiritually prepared for the Lord's return.

3. that they would live lives that were heavy with the fruit of righteousness.

4. and ultimately, that everything would be for God's glory and praise.

I purchased a sapling pear tree for a home we owned and planted it in the backyard. I carefully watered and fertilized it, and it began to grow. It reached maturity and began to produce pears. In all my years, I have never seen a little tree grow like this one. It produced so many pears it alarmed me. Its branches bent, heavy with fruit. The branches were so loaded that I would have to prop them up so they would not break. We would harvest wheelbarrows of delicious fruit from that tree. That kind of fruitfulness is what God wants from our lives. That kind of fruitfulness is what real Christian leaders pray for in the lives of those they serve. That is the kind of fruitfulness for which we all should long.

The Four-Fold Purpose
Philippians 1:9–11

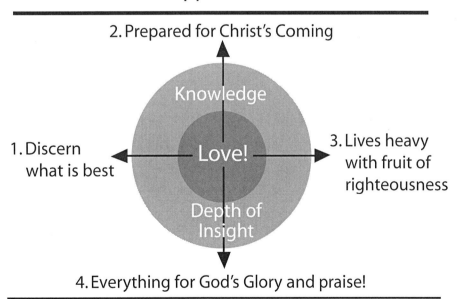

2. Prepared for Christ's Coming

Knowledge

1. Discern what is best — Love! — 3. Lives heavy with fruit of righteousness

Depth of Insight

4. Everything for God's Glory and praise!

Test Yourself

Circle the letter of the *best* answer.

1. Which verse of Philippians causes debate concerning the integrity and authorship of this letter?
a) 1:3
b) 2:1
c) 3:1
d) 4:3

2. Philippi was the leading city in the Roman province of
a) Asia.
b) Macedonia.
c) Galatia.
d) Thracia.

3. It is believed that Philippi was largely Gentile in population because
a) those mentioned in Acts all had Greek names.
b) the city had no synagogue.
c) Jews were not welcome in Philippi.
d) Paul mentions this in his opening comment to the Philippians.

4. Which was NOT one of Paul's express purposes in writing to the church at Philippi?
a) To rebuke
b) To emphasize unity
c) To express appreciation
d) To restore perspective.

5. The two major themes that dominate the letter to the Philippians are the
a) supremacy of Christ and the advancement of the gospel.
b) joy of the Lord and the supremacy of Christ.
c) second coming of Christ and the joy of the Lord.
d) joy of the Lord and the advancement of the gospel.

6. Paul is thankful for the church in Philippi because of their
a) persistence in midst of suffering.
b) partnership in ministry.
c) faith in Christ.
d) effectiveness in spreading the gospel.

7. How is the Greek word *koinonia* translated in Philippians 1:5?
a) "Affection"
b) "Courageous"
c) "Partnership"
d) "Thankfulness"

8. The Greek word *epignōsis* as used in Philippians 1:9 means
a) "affection."
b) "partnership."
c) "a deep, personal knowledge of Christ."
d) "moral and spiritual perception."

9. In Philippians 1:8, the Greek word for affection literally means
a) "intestines, bowels, or kidneys."
b) "heart or chest area."
c) "kindred spirit."
d) "a longing of heart."

10. In Paul's prayer for the believers in Philippi (1:9–11), what four things does he pray for?
a) That they may discern what is best, be morally and spiritually ready for Christ's return, be filled with fruit of righteousness, and give glory and praise to God for everything
b) That they may be thankful in all circumstances, be morally and spiritually ready for Christ's return, be filled with fruit of righteousness, and give glory and praise to God for everything
c) That they may give glory and praise to God for everything, pray for all the saints, be morally and spiritually ready for Christ's return, and be filled with fruit of righteousness
d) That they may know the joy of the Lord, discern what is best, be morally and spiritually ready for Christ's return, and be filled with fruit of righteousness

Responses to Interactive Questions
CHAPTER 10

Some of these responses may include information that is supplemental to the IST. These questions are intended to produce reflective thinking beyond the course content and your responses may vary from these examples.

1 How can Paul's use of the word *finally* in Philippians 3:1 be explained?

Paul may have been prompted by the Holy Spirit to address another issue or additional information may have come to his attention after he had prepared to close the letter. As we all know, the words finally or in conclusion do not necessarily mean the end of a sermon.

2 How important was Philippi in the ancient world?

Philippi was a thriving, Gentile city located in northeastern Greece, on the Egnatian Way, a key highway linking the Aegean and Adriatic Seas. It was the gateway to the east.

3 What made Philippi special to Paul?

Paul visited Philippi on his second missionary journey, after Paul saw a vision of a Macedonian man imploring, "Come over to Macedonia and help us." Three conversions gave birth to the church in Philippi: Lydia, a successful businesswoman, and her entire family; a demon-possessed girl who was a fortune teller; and a jailer and his family. Clement, Euodia, and Syntyche, who are mentioned in this letter, may also have been converted at this time.

The congregation of believers in Philippi was special to Paul. Luke, Paul's personal physician and a valuable member of his missionary team, appears to have been left there in his hometown to carry on the ministry for several years. Paul maintained contact with this church. They sent monetary gifts to him and went so far as to send Epaphroditus, their personal representative, to minister to Paul's needs while he was in prison.

4 Based on the clues within the letter to the Philippians, how would you describe the situation within the church?

The church was being divided by disunity, selfishness, differences of opinion, and pride. Complaining and arguing had set in. The church was losing perspective, forgetting what they had been taught.

5 What purposes are given for the writing of Philippians?

Paul wrote to the church to help restore perspective, to update them on his personal condition, to warn them of destructive influences both within and without the congregation, to encourage them to stand firm and present a united front against the attacks they faced. Finally, Paul wanted the believers to know how much he appreciated their loving concern for his welfare.

6 What are the two key themes of Philippians?

The two themes that dominate Philippians are joy (rejoicing in the Lord) and the advancement of the gospel. Joy is how believers respond to trying circumstances. It is not simply a feeling; it is an activity flowing from an inner reality. Paul's ultimate concern is that the gospel be preached, regardless of the challenges facing the church.

7 How does each of the two key themes of Philippians apply to your life?

Answers will vary.

8 What things about those in Philippi would have prompted Paul to give thanks?

Paul would have remembered how Lydia accepted the gospel. He also would have remembered the slave girl from whom he cast out demons. He would have thought back to the jailer who was saved with his family. Then there were the financial gifts the Philippian church had sent on more than one occasion. They sent not only money, but Epaphroditus, a person who worked for Paul.

9 How does partnership in ministry affect the church?

Fellowship in the Lord's work brings an intimate bond between people. When we pray together, plan together, give together, and serve together, an unusually close bond is created.

10 To what fellow Christians will you express your love and concern?

Answers will vary.

11 What did Paul pray would happen in the lives of the Philippian believers?

Paul prayed for their love for each other and the Lord. He prayed their love would grow in knowledge and depth of insight. This knowledge would guide their relationships with one another and their world. The result would be that they would be able to discern what was best, they would be morally and spiritually prepared for the Lord's return, they would live lives that were heavy with the fruit of righteousness, and that everything would be for God's glory and praise.

Christ's Example and Christian Responsibility (Philippians 1:12–2:18)

This part of Paul's epistle to the church in Philippi is one of the most theologically profound, yet practical sections of the Bible. The believers in Philippi were facing challenges both within and outside of the church. They were in danger of losing a godly perspective in their circumstances and falling prey to attitudes and actions that could render them ineffective, neutralizing their witness and leading to the ruin of their congregation.

How can people maintain a positive perspective in difficult circumstances? In Philippians 1:12–26, Paul himself becomes an example to follow. How can we live overcoming Christian lives in a pagan world? Paul teaches us how in Philippians 1:27–30. What brings joy to the heart of God and true Christian leaders? Paul says it is unity and Christ-likeness in Philippians 2:1–11. How can congregations deal with the periodic challenges they face? Paul provides advice in 2:12–18.

In all of this, Paul emphasizes the importance of a godly perspective, unity in the Spirit, Christ-like character, and a consistent Christian lifestyle. What wonderful advice for individual Christians and congregations who seek to positively impact a godless culture.

• *Read Philippians 1:12–2:18 before you begin study in this chapter.*

Lesson 11.1   Maintaining a Positive Perspective in Difficult Circumstances (1:12–26)

Objectives
11.1.1 Describe how Paul's view of his imprisonment demonstrated a Christ-centered life.
11.1.2 Describe how Paul's response to unfair criticism demonstrated his inner joy.
11.1.3 List and explain five anchors that sustained Paul in the face of an uncertain future.

Lesson 11.2   Living as Christians in a Pagan World (1:27–30)

Objectives
11.2.1 Explain how Paul's analogy of Roman citizenship could help the believers at Philippi.
11.2.2 Identify the strategies Paul gave the Philippian believers for victory in the face of opposition.
11.2.3 Describe the church's main source of victory.
11.2.4 Describe Paul's attitude toward suffering.

Lesson 11.3   Making a Leader's Joy Complete (2:1–11)

Objectives
11.3.1 List and explain four godly motives for maintaining unity in the church.
11.3.2 List six behaviors that lead to unity in a church.
11.3.3 Describe what it means to be Christ-like.

Lesson 11.4   Living as God's Children (2:12–18)

Objectives

11.4.1 Explain the relationship between Paul's command "to work out your salvation with fear and trembling" and believers' responsibility to safeguard the work of God in the body of Christ.

11.4.2 Describe how living pure and blameless lives can impact a depraved generation for Christ.

11.4.3 Explain Paul's use of the imagery of the Old Testament sacrificial system.

Maintaining a Positive Perspective in Difficult Circumstances (1:12–26)

Today's culture is on feverish quest for pleasure and happiness. People try everything imaginable to achieve it—wealth, possessions, power, leisure, thrills, alcohol, drugs, sex, etc. The list could go on and on. Yet real joy remains elusive. Others, however, have discovered that a life centered in Jesus Christ makes joy possible in any situation, whether good or bad.

We Can Rejoice in Unfavorable Circumstances (1:12–14)

11.1.1
OBJECTIVE
Describe how Paul's view of his imprisonment demonstrated a Christ-centered life.

The Circumstances Paul Faced

Paul writes this letter of joy from prison in Rome, the place he had longed for years to visit (Romans 1:10; 15:28–29). Now he is in Rome, but not under pleasant circumstances. His journey has been marked by hardship, riots, shipwreck, and imprisonment (cf. Acts 21–28). This ordeal has gone on for four years.

One might think that because Paul was in chains he would be saying, "Woe is me." Instead, he tells the Philippians just the opposite is true. God had an even better plan for him. His circumstances had actually served to advance the gospel" (1:12). The word *advance* used here has the idea of moving forward in spite of obstacles. It is used in secular literature to describe armies moving forward under fire (Keener 1993, 558; Kent 1978, 110; Muller 1995, 48). Opposition does not stop the spread of the gospel.

1 What was Paul's attitude toward his prison experience?

The Gospel Advanced Outside the Church

While in prison, Paul was bound twenty-four hours a day to various Roman soldiers who rotated shifts. Escape was impossible, privacy nonexistent. Can you imagine being a sinner chained to Paul six hours a day? What was the result? Caesar's entire palace guard—one thousand handpicked troops—was reached with the gospel (1:13).

The Gospel Advanced Inside the Church

Verse 14 implies that some believers were afraid to tell others about Christ. That is understandable due to the growing hostility toward Christians. But as these fellow believers saw Paul's courage, they were inspired to be bold and speak the Word of God more courageously and fearlessly (v. 14).

Paul's joy was unrelated to his circumstances. If you tie your joy to your circumstances, you will lose your joy when things go wrong. Enduring joy comes through "advancing the gospel" (v. 12).

John Bunyan, author of the Christian classic *The Pilgrim's Progress*, was thrown into Bedford Jail in England to silence his preaching. But he continued to preach at the top of his lungs. His voice carried over the prison walls, and crowds gathered to listen. Authorities then threw him into the inner part of the prison where he could not be heard. From that cell he wrote his marvelously inspiring classic that has touched the lives of millions over the centuries. He had genuine joy in spite of his circumstances.

We Can Rejoice in the Face of Unfair Criticism (1:15–18)

11.1.2
OBJECTIVE

Describe how Paul's response to unfair criticism demonstrated his inner joy.

Paul had his share of critics: people who accused him, assaulted his reputation, and questioned his character. Who where they? They were people Paul had ministered to and encouraged; they were not heretics or idol worshipers. They were not angry Jews or enemies outside the church; these were people who preached Christ. This was not a doctrinal problem. It was a personal problem. They were jealous and motivated by rivalry. This can happen in today's church. When it does, it is ugly.

2   How did Paul respond to unfair criticism?

On the other hand, many believers were loving. They prayed for Paul, and continued preaching the gospel out of love, understanding the reason for his imprisonment. Paul said they knew he had been "put here for the defense of the gospel" (v. 16). The words *put here* reflect military terminology and are used about soldiers under orders and on duty. Paul saw himself in prison under assignment by his heavenly Commander (O'Brien 1993, 101). He was in prison, not because he was out of God's will, but because he was in God's will.

Did suffering steal Paul's joy? No. Do you want to know what Paul's attitude was? Read verse 18. He says, "What does it matter? Christ is preached. And because of this I rejoice" (paraphrased). All Paul cared about was the gospel. That was his passion. That is what he lived for. He was not in the ministry to be appreciated by people, he was not living for accolades, and he was not looking for status. He lived to reach lost people with the gospel.

What is your passion? If it is to be well-thought-of by people, then their criticism will steal your joy. But if your passion is to spread the gospel, you will evaluate everything in light of the kingdom of God.

One of the sad realities of war is that some soldiers die as a result of what has been called *friendly fire*. No enemy bullet kills them. They die at the hand of a fellow soldier. I wish I could tell you that friendly fire is limited to the battlefields of our world. But it is not. It happens in churches; it happens in religious organizations. Unfortunately, among professing Christians, friendly fire is usually not the result of an innocent mistake, but rather a malicious spirit. It takes a person with divine perspective and a big heart to be hurt by friendly fire and avoid becoming embittered. Paul was such a person. "What does it matter?" he said, "The important thing is, Christ is preached."

We Can Rejoice in the Midst of an Uncertain Future (1:18–26)

11.1.3
OBJECTIVE

List and explain five anchors that sustained Paul in the face of an uncertain future.

Some versions of the Bible introduce this section with the last clause of verse 18: "Yes, and I will continue to rejoice." It sets the tone for this entire section emphasizing Paul's decision to rejoice, even in the face of an uncertain future. Paul knew his imprisonment could end in death. But he did not lose his joy. He could not care less what happened to him, what people said about him, or whether he lived or died. All he wanted was for Christ to be glorified in his life (Acts 20:24). He drew upon five anchors when facing an uncertain future:

3   What sustained Paul in the face of an uncertain future?

1. Paul Had Confidence in the Faithfulness of God and His Word

Paul believed in a principle taught over and over in Scripture: circumstances are temporary, God is faithful, and He will bring good out of bad situations. Paul almost directly quotes Job 13:16. He identified with Job's struggles. Job was righteous. Paul knew that although Job was tried severely, in the end, God delivered him. So he says, "We know that in all things God works for the good of those who love Him, who have been called according to His purpose" (Romans 8:28).

2. Paul Was Confident in the Prayers of God's People

Paul knew God answered prayer. He regularly asked people to pray for him (Romans 15:30; Ephesians 6:19; 1 Thessalonians 5:25). He had a deep conviction that God works powerfully through the prayers of His people. That is why you need to ask people to pray when you are going through a difficult situation. And do not just ask them to pray, have the confidence Paul had and believe those prayers will make a difference.

3. Paul Was Confident in the Help of the Holy Spirit

Paul believed everything would work out because he had confidence in "the help given by the Spirit of Jesus Christ" (1:19). He believed the Holy Spirit would come alongside and provide the strength, grace, hope, and assistance he needed. We can be confident because the Holy Spirit is working on our behalf as well.

4. Paul Was Confident He Would Not Be Put to Shame

When we are going through a trial or difficult time, we are often afraid we will fail. We are afraid God will not come through. Paul lived with the expectation that he would never be put to shame, not before the world, not before Caesar, not before God (Psalm 25:1–3; Isaiah 49:23).

5. Paul Had Confidence in God's Plan and Purposes

Paul reaches the climax of everything he is saying to the believers at Philippi. He does not know if he will live or die. He is torn between wanting to build the church and wanting to be with Christ. He prefers to die and be with the Lord, but knew the Lord might let him live because of their needs. He was saying, "Either way, God. Whatever you want. I just want whatever brings You glory." He affirmed, "Christ will be exalted in my body, whether by life or by death" (v. 20). That is the key to joy—to abandon yourself to the will of God. He sums up the issues in verse 21 when he affirms the supreme purpose of a devoted follower of Jesus: "For me to live is Christ and to die is gain." The purpose of Paul's life was Christ. Christ *was* his life: Christ and His will in everything.

Early on a Monday morning sirens wailed in our small town. An ambulance was making a run, and somehow I felt that someone in our church was involved. A few moments later, the telephone rang. It was the hospital. Carl, a young businessman from our community had died unexpectedly. I arrived at the hospital to meet his wife who now faced an uncertain future. She had one small child and was expecting another. She said to me, "Pastor, I cannot explain the peace and joy I feel. I'm just going to trust Jesus." And she did. With grace and dignity she faced the coming months. God sustained her, provided for her, and helped her through. Today, she is happily married again. She kept the joy of the Lord and a sweet spirit. She proved we *can* rejoice in the face of an uncertain future.

What a way to live. What a way to deal with an uncertain future. Put your present and your future in God's hands. Determine that regardless of the outcome of events, God will be glorified. The purpose of life is not to make money, not to settle into comfortable existence, not to make names for ourselves. Our purpose is to serve Christ. "To live is Christ" (v. 21).

Living as Christians in a Pagan World (1:27–30)

Family dynamics are interesting to observe. Some families, when facing a crisis, disintegrate. Suddenly, it is every family member for himself or herself. Squabbling sets in, accusations fly, voices raise, and members may even come to blows. The family literally comes apart at the seams.

Other families in a crisis are awesome to watch. They unite. What affects one, impacts all. Do not get me wrong, these families have challenges, even petty disagreements, but when they are attacked, they stand together. They stand by one another and help one another. There is an unwritten code of honor binding them together.

4   Why was Paul concerned about the Philippian church?

Paul was concerned about the lack of unity among the believers at Philippi. Opposition was coming both from within and outside the church. Feelings of fear and intimidation were real. Christians were struggling with a loss of perspective. Their joy in the Lord was slipping away. Would they come together as the family of God and the body of Christ? Or would their differences degenerate into petty infighting and a self-survival mentality?

Paul begins verse 27 with the words *whatever happens*. This is easily translated "only" (Martin 1959, 82–83). It is placed first in the sentence to emphasize the point Paul is making. Paul wants one thing: for the church to unite and "conduct themselves in a manner worthy of the gospel of Christ." Church bodies today face similar challenges. Will they allow challenges to distract, divide, and destroy the body? Or will they purpose to live as worthy citizens of the kingdom of heaven in an alien culture?

Live Worthy Lives in an Alien Culture (1:27)

11.2.1
OBJECTIVE
Explain how Paul's analogy of Roman citizenship could help the believers at Philippi.

The word translated *conduct* literally means to "behave or conduct oneself as a citizen" (Rienecker 1980, 548). The Greek word is *politeuomai* and is derived from the noun, *polis*, which is used of a city. You can see the word carried over into the names of some North American cities, such as Minneapolis or Indianapolis. The words *police* and *politics* are also derivatives. The use of this word would have had special significance for those living in Philippi, a colony of Rome. They were in every way Roman citizens, although they lived in the frontier of ancient Macedonia or today's modern Greece. They had Roman citizenship, lived by Roman laws, enjoyed Roman benefits, and celebrated Roman values and customs. Paul uses this analogy to remind the believers of their nobler citizenship. Theirs was a citizenship brought about by their responding to the gospel of Christ, a citizenship in the "kingdom of heaven" (Fee 1995, 161–62).

5   What analogy did Paul use to help the Philippian believers know how to live in their present culture?

The challenge the church in Philippi faced was to live "worthy of the gospel of Christ" in the face of opposition, that is, to behave as citizens of heaven. The word *worthy* gives the idea of balancing scales so that what is on one side equals the weight on the other side. Paul's point is that their behavior should match their beliefs and values. They should live as people transformed by the gospel whose temporary residence was within an alien culture.

6   How can our lives either help or hinder the impact of the gospel in our culture?

When Christians within a congregation fall apart in times of crisis, it negatively impacts the work of the gospel. A wrong signal is sent to the world when the family of God behave in ways that contradict the values of the heavenly kingdom. The challenge for members of a local church is to behave like Christians—like citizens of the kingdom of heaven—worthy of the gospel they claim transformed their lives.

I know of a church that faced a serious challenge. There were disagreements, arguments, charges, and counter-charges. Finally, the opposing sides filed suits against one another. Word of their dispute made it to the local newspapers. During a heated exchange early in the deliberations, the judge overseeing the case called both parties to the bench. He delivered a stinging rebuke, telling them they had a responsibility to the community to behave in keeping with their Christian values. He urged them to go home and work things out as a family of faith.

Stand Firm under Attack (1:27–28)

11.2.2
OBJECTIVE

Identify the strategies Paul gave the Philippian believers for victory in the face of opposition.

Paul fully understood that these believers were engaged in a spiritual battle. He realized the challenges they faced. He was facing some of his own. Paul would have liked to have been with them in person to help resolve these problems, but that was not possible. He urged them, in his presence or absence, to demonstrate the following characteristics of fearless Christian soldiers:

Unity in the Spirit

7   How did Paul encourage the church to face opposition?

The words translated *Holy Spirit* are interpreted by some to mean simply spirit. But Greek usage in pagan literature, grammar, context (cf. 2:1–4), and Paul's use of this language in another epistle (Ephesians 2:18; cf. 1 Corinthians 12:13) indicate he means the Holy Spirit is the source of their unity (Fee 1995, 164–166).

Camaraderie in Ministry

Paul wanted to know the believers were "contending as one man" for the truth of the gospel. This Greek term conveys the idea of players on an athletic team, working side-by-side against an opposing force. The context is definitely influenced by the idea of conflict (Fee 1995, 166–67). In the challenges they faced, these believers needed to act as a team. They needed to plan together, pray together, and serve together.

Fearlessness in the Face of Opposition

Paul adds how the believers should face opposition: "Without being frightened in any way." The word translated *frightened* was sometimes used in ancient Greek literature in relation to spooking horses. It conveys the idea of not allowing the opposition to intimidate them, frighten, or throw them into consternation (Fee 1995, 168).

The local church needs to stand firm and unified in the face of opposition. Instead of falling apart we come together. Instead of letting the enemy divide us, we stand as one. Instead of fighting, we are united.

I am a fan of American football. Few things are more intimidating than a defensive or offensive line of skilled, determined 250-pound players working together under expert coaching. May each local church see itself as a similarly equipped team, empowered by the Holy Spirit, and guided by their great coach Jesus Christ, heading to victory against the forces of darkness.

Rest Assured that God Will Defend You (1:28)

11.2.3
OBJECTIVE

Describe the church's main source of victory.

Paul assures the congregation in Philippi that if the qualities of unity, cooperation, and resolve are present among them, the enemy faces defeat. Such unity in the Spirit, solidarity in service, and fearlessness in battle strikes fear in the heart of the opposition. It points toward the ultimate destruction of the enemy and the salvation of the believers (Kent 1978, 119). Victory does not depend solely upon us. Our strength and strategies are inadequate. God is the One who sees to it that both goals, the destruction of the enemy and the salvation of the church, are realized.

In athletic competition, a fighting song or rallying cry can lift the spirits of the competitors, infuse them with new strength, intimidate the opposition, and provide the edge necessary to win a victory. A unified body of believers, serving together fearlessly under the banner of the Cross and in the power of the Holy Spirit, has the same effect on our spiritual enemy.

Rejoice in the Privilege of Suffering for Him (1:29–30)

11.2.4
OBJECTIVE
Describe Paul's attitude toward suffering.

Paul gives a final reminder designed to put things in perspective for the congregation in Philippi. "It has been granted to you on behalf of Christ not only to believe on him, but also to suffer for him" (v. 29). The impact of this reminder is strengthened by the fact that it comes from the heart of a faithful servant of the Lord in prison (a comparison Paul draws upon in verse 30). Paul did not view his imprisonment as a burden. Rather, he sees it as a privilege or a gracious gift (*echaristhe*) equivalent to "believing on" Christ (Kent 1978, 119). What an incredible comparison. How this flies in the face of much modern theology and self-serving Christianity. The ancient church viewed suffering for Christ as an honor and privilege (1 Peter 4:12–16). So should we.

Francois de Fenelon, a priest who lived during the Huguenot conflicts of the seventeenth century, wrote the following words of encouragement to a struggling fellow-priest:

> I am sorry to hear of your troubles, but I am sure you realize that you must carry the Cross with Christ in this life. Soon enough there will come a time when you will no longer suffer. You will reign with God and He will wipe away your tears with His own hand. In His presence, pain and sighing will forever flee away.
>
> So while you have the opportunity to experience difficult trials, do not lose the slightest opportunity to embrace the Cross. Learn to suffer with simplicity and a heart full of love. If you do, you will not only be happy in spite of the Cross, but because of it. Love is pleased to suffer for the Well-Beloved. (Fenelon 1992)

Making a Leader's Joy Complete (2:1–11)

When Paul had heard the report about the Christian community in Philippi, he was concerned that rather than presenting a united front, the believers would scatter. One thing, and only one, would make Paul's joy complete: for the lives of these beloved Christians to exemplify the servant spirit of their Savior, Jesus Christ.

11.3.1
OBJECTIVE
List and explain four godly motives for maintaining unity in the church.

8   What better translation might be made of the word *if* in Philippians 2:1?

Christ's Blessings Are Foundational for Joy (2:1)

Paul directs our attention to four motives for maintaining unity in the church. Each starts with the word *if.* The meaning of the word *if* would be better translated, "Since there exists" or "Because you have" (Fee 1995, 177).

Since you receive encouragement from Christ

The context (1:29–30) indicates Paul is saying that since they share in suffering for Christ, they also share in the comfort He provides (cf. 2 Corinthians 1:5).

Since you receive comfort from His love

Here Paul is probably referring to their common experience of the Father's love being poured upon them and shed abroad in their hearts by the Holy Spirit (Romans 5:5).

Since you have fellowship in the Spirit

Here Paul refers to what he has just said (1:27) about unity in the Spirit, in whom and by whom they "contend for the faith of the gospel."

Since you have tenderness and compassion

Having just appealed to each member of the Trinity, Paul now appeals to each member of this congregation to demonstrate the deep feelings they share with one another (Fee 1995, 179–182).

The attitudes and motives that generate authentic spiritual unity within the body of Christ always produce joy within the heart of Christian leaders and the body of Christ.

11.3.2
OBJECTIVE
List six behaviors that lead to unity in a church.

9   What six behaviors lead to unity in a church?

Unity among Believers Contributes to Joy (2:2–4)

Having reminded the believers of what Christ was providing them, Paul says, "Make my joy complete" by doing the following things that lead to unity:

1. "Be like-minded."

    Show unity of thought and will. Agree with each other. This is an attitude of harmony.

2. "Have the same love."

    Love each other; love as you are loved by Christ (Ephesians 5:1–2).

3. "Be one in spirit and purpose."

    Be united in spirit, "working together with one heart and purpose" (NLT).

4. "Do nothing from selfish ambition or vain conceit."

    Do not have a me-first attitude. Do not do anything motivated by self-seeking attitude or pretentiousness. "Do not try to make a good impression on others" (NLT).

5. "In humility consider others better than yourselves."

    Do not be high and mighty. Be willing to associate with the lowly. "Give more honor to others than to yourselves" (NCV).

6. "Look not only to your own interests, but also to the interests of others."

    Do not think only of yourself. Be concerned about others. Show interest in what interests others (O'Brien 1991, 178–183).

Authentic unity can be illustrated by comparing a number of marbles held in a bag to some metal shavings dropped on a magnet. The marbles are held together only by a flimsy bag, but a strong, attractive force, stimulated by the magnet, draws the metal shavings together. The same is to be true of the church. We are not held together by a denominational label, but by Jesus Christ in us and the unifying power of the Holy Spirit.

Paul's six commands set a high standard, but it is the only way to unity. Without unity the church loses its stability, its authoritative voice, and its influence within a culture. On the other hand, by meeting this standard, the potential for the competitiveness and self-seeking is removed.

11.3.3
OBJECTIVE
Describe what it means to be Christ-like.

Following Christ's Attitude and Example Produces Ultimate Joy (2:6–11)

Who can we look to as a model of the attitudes and lifestyle Paul describes? Paul points to Jesus as the example to follow. Christ-like attitudes in our relationships with others will bring joy to our leaders, the church body, and our individual lives. Paul lists five characteristics of being Christ-like.

10 What does being Christ-like mean for you?

1. Being Christ-like Means We Are Willing to Relinquish Our Place

Jesus is God. Before He came to earth, He was God with all that implies. He was not a sub-god, a semi-god, or a lesser-god. Colossians 1:15–17 tells us just how far He had to stoop to save us. He relinquished His place in heavenly glory and stooped to become a man to serve humanity. He did this, not for His own benefit, but for ours. What does it mean to be Christ-like? It means we are willing to step down from our position, our place of significance, for the benefit of someone else.

11 What attitudes enabled Jesus to come to earth and give himself on the Cross?

2. Being Christ-like Means We Are Willing to Give Up Our Privileges

We live in a society that is conscious of rights. Jesus Christ was equal to God in every way—He was God. But He did not regard that position as something to be grasped. He did not cling to it or hold on to His position. He separated himself from His privileges. He gave up His rights. What does it mean to be Christ-like? It means we willingly give up our privileges, our rights for the sake of fulfilling God's plan for our lives.

3. Being Christ-like Means that We Are Willing to Step Down from Our Position

Human nature craves for position. It craves to be at the top. Jesus was "in very nature God" (v. 6), but "took the very nature of a servant" (v. 7). He said, "I am among you as One who serves" (Luke 22:27). "The Son of man did not come to be served, but to serve, and to give life as a ransom for many" (Matthew 20:28). He became a servant to the point of death on a Cross. Most people did not realize who He was. In fact, many thought Him a mere man. He was like us in every way, but without sin. That is why He can sympathize with us (Hebrews 4:15). Being Christ-like means serving. It does not mean putting out effort to get our names on plaques. It does not mean winning the volunteer-of-the-year award and receiving public mention or the compliments of others. It means we are willing to renounce our position and serve others without notoriety or applause.

4. Being Christ-like Means We Understand Our Purpose

What was Jesus' purpose? To die on a Cross, giving His life for others. God's holiness required a sacrifice for sin and Jesus became that sacrifice. He experienced separation from God on behalf of sinners who neither cared nor desired the salvation He was providing. He understood His eternal purpose (John 3:16). What does it mean to be Christ-like? It means we know our purpose as expressed by Jesus: "If anyone would come after me, he must deny himself and take up his cross and follow me" (Mark 8:34).

5. Being Christ-like Means We Are Willing to Rest in His Promise of Reward and Future Glory

A key principle of God's word is, "humble yourselves, therefore, under God's mighty hand, that he may lift you up in due time" (1 Peter 5:6). The Christian life ends in victory and reward. Read about the outcome of Christ's humble self-sacrifice in verses 9–11. Jesus humbled himself and God exalted Him to the highest place, gave Him a name above every name, and will ultimately cause every knee to bow before Him. You do not have to fight, kick, and claw for your rights, for power, or for position. Being Christ-like means you humble yourself, relinquish your place, refuse to cling to your privileges, renounce your position, realize your purpose, and willingly rest in His promises. He will reward you.

Peter expressed a key principle for Christians to live by: "To this you were called, because Christ suffered for you, leaving you an example, that you should follow in his steps" (1 Peter 2:21).

Former General Superintendent of the Assemblies of God, the late G. Raymond Carlson, was one of the finest examples of "the attitude of Christ Jesus" I know. Stories abound of his self-effacing, humble, servant leadership. While serving as general superintendent he could regularly be found handing out bulletins and assisting guests when at his home church.

My wife and I were young pastors in the Dakotas and were traveling home, feeling alone and intimidated after a large ministers' gathering. We felt like nobodies around all those important people. We stopped at a restaurant for a bite to eat along the freeway. Brother and Sister Carlson arrived just as we were leaving. They recognized us from the meeting we had just attended, and walked all the way across a parking lot to greet and encourage us. "Let this mind be in you, which was also in Christ Jesus" (Philippians 2:5, KJV).

Living as God's Children (2:12–18)

If you had asked Paul, "What do you think of the church at Philippi?" His answer would have been firm and enthusiastic. "Philippi is a good church!"

Philippi was most certainly a good church. The congregation was dear to Paul. But even the best of churches face periodic challenges. I am certain the church you are a part of has had to contend with a problem or two over the years.

Even in good churches Christians sometimes forget who they are in Christ and what God has done for them. Stress and trials come and people lose perspective. When we face these kinds of challenges our joy sometimes evaporates into petty arguments and disagreements. The unity of the body suffers. If problems continue unresolved, they can grow until the testimony of the church is neutralized or even destroyed.

This was the very thing Paul feared would happen in Philippi. Paul dealt with the problems early and decisively. He appealed to the believers to follow his advice. His appeal was based on his past and present relationships with them. They had followed Paul's instructions over the years of their association with him. "Therefore, my dear friends, as you have always obeyed—not only in my presence, but now much more in my absence . . . " (2:12).

Christians today cannot afford to behave as though all that mattered was their own blessing and welfare. The Christian way is not self-centered. We cannot act as if ignoring spiritual problems will make them go away. The truth is, those who are truly the children of God sincerely care for the welfare of the church, just as Paul did.

We Must Be Concerned about the Church's Welfare (2:12–13)

11.4.1
OBJECTIVE

Explain the relationship between Paul's command to "work out your salvation with fear and trembling" and believers' responsibility to safeguard the work of God in the body of Christ.

Paul's appeal was first for the sake of the church's welfare and survival. His command to the congregation in Philippi was, "Work out your salvation" (2:12). In our tendency, as Western evangelical Protestants, to individualize the message of the epistles, we have applied this passage to personal salvation. We too often fail to recognize the epistles were written first and foremost to congregations. Within such a context, it is clear that Paul is dealing with the need for unity and a servant spirit among God's people (2:1–11). He is concerned with how believers live out their salvation as the church of Jesus Christ in the world. He wants them to "become blameless and pure, children of God without fault in a crooked and depraved generation" (2:15). His concern is that their disagreements, opinionated attitudes, and self-seeking will destroy the body of Christ in Philippi. As redeemed people, they need to live out their salvation with unity of the Spirit and devotion of heart to one another and the Lord (Fee 1995, 234–36; O'Brien 1991, 277–78).

12   What did Paul mean when he said, "Work out your salvation with fear and trembling"?

The attitude that should motivate this obedience is "fear and trembling," not a frightened dread or anxious alarm. Rather, with a holy awe of God and a reverence for His presence among them, they are to be diligent about seeking the welfare of the body of Christ.

The concern of a mother for her child is beautiful to observe. The slightest sound in the night, the paleness of a cheek, the faintest cry elicits an immediate and concerned response. She guards the welfare of her child.

How concerned are you for the welfare and spiritual health of your church? Paul assures us that when Christians give attention to this, God will work powerfully. He will work within and among them (both ideas are supported by the Greek preposition; Fee 1995, 238). He will produce in His people the desire to fulfill His purposes and the power and ability to carry them out. God wants to work powerfully in your congregation to fulfill His purposes. What a wonderful promise!

11.4.2
OBJECTIVE

Describe how living pure and blameless lives can impact a depraved generation for Christ.

We Need to Be Concerned about Our Testimony (2:14–16)

Paul's second appeal was his concern for the church's testimony within Philippi. He urges the believers to "do everything without complaining or arguing" (14). A complaining spirit has plagued the people of God down through the centuries. It expressed itself through the children of Israel over and over. It finally led to God's judgment. Nothing has changed. Murmuring and complaining have not ceased. They are typical church problems.

13   How can our testimonies influence our culture for Jesus?

The purpose of Paul's command was simple. He wanted them to impact their culture by being different. He wanted them to "become blameless and pure, children of God without fault in a crooked and depraved generation" (15). They were to be what they were, the children of God. Both their outward conduct ("blameless") and their inner motivation ("pure") needed to reflect their relationship with the Lord. Their lives were to shine like stars in the spiritual darkness of a crooked and depraved culture. They were to be a lighthouse (light bearers) for God where they lived and worked. They were to share the hope of the gospel in their community ("as you hold out the word of life").

God wants our lives and congregations to have this kind of impact on our culture. Never has moral darkness been deeper. Never has there been a greater need for the church to truly be the light within its culture.

One of the finest compliments I have ever received came from a rough-living, foul-mouthed woman who was a supervisor where a friend of mine and I worked. She continually griped and complained. She was never satisfied with anything. The smallest inconvenience or mistake could set her off. One day, in a reflective moment, she asked me, "What makes you and your friend different? You do not gripe about everything. You do your job. You are kind and helpful. When everyone else is complaining about management, you guys keep your mouth shut. You're just nice to be around." God had opened a door for the gospel. Our lifestyle had opened a way to share with our supervisor that Jesus made the difference in our lives.

11.4.3
OBJECTIVE

Explain Paul's use of the imagery of the Old Testament sacrificial system.

We Need to Be Concerned for One Another's Spiritual Welfare (2:17–18)

Finally, Paul wanted his efforts and their service to result in mutual self-sacrifice and rejoicing. The imagery of these verses is drawn from the Old Testament sacrificial system (Numbers 28:1–8). After offering an animal sacrifice and while the animal was still on the altar, the worshiper would pour wine or water on the ground or on top of the sacrifice. Paul pictured the Philippian Christians offering a sacrifice that issued from their faith. He saw himself topping off or completing their sacrifice by pouring himself out as a drink offering on their behalf and for the Lord (Hawthorne 1983, 105–106). This probably refers back to their mutual suffering for the Lord he had discussed in Philippians 1:29–30 (Fee 1995, 255). He was saying we should not feel unfairly treated when we suffer for the Lord. Rather we should rejoice with each other in the privilege of suffering for the gospel.

In February, 1941, Father Maximilian Kolbe was arrested by the Gestapo and sent to Auschwitz. Eventually, he was assigned to Barracks 14 where he continued to minister to his fellow prisoners. Because Christ's cross had triumphed over its enemies in every age, he believed, in the end, even in these darkest days in Poland, the Cross would triumph over the swastika. He prayed that he would be faithful to that end.

Then one night a man escaped from Barracks 14. The next morning, Commandant Fritsch ordered the men in Barracks 14 to stand in the hot sun until the prisoner was found. By evening, the fugitive had not been found. "Ten of you will die for him in the starvation bunker," he screamed.

After the ten were chosen, a cry rang out from one of the men chosen, "My poor children. My wife. What will they do?" Suddenly, there was commotion in the ranks. A prisoner had broken out of ranks and volunteered to take this crying man's place. It was Father Kolbe. The commandant ordered it done.

Franciszek Gajowniczek was the prisoner whose life was spared. He survived Auschwitz and for fifty-three years, until his death at age ninety-five, he joyously told everyone about the man who had died in his place (Colson and Vaughan 1978, 6–8).

Test Yourself

CHAPTER
11

Circle the letter of the *best* answer.

1. Joy in the life of the believer is tied to
a) circumstances.
b) personality.
c) his or her relationship with Christ.
d) his or her relationships with other people.

2. What are five anchors that sustained Paul in the face of an uncertain future?
a) Confidence in God's faithfulness, the prayers of God's people, the help of the Holy Spirit, God's plans and purposes, and that he would not be put to shame
b) Confidence in the Roman judicial system, the prayers of God's people, the help of the Holy Spirit, God's plans and purposes, and that he would not be put to shame
c) Confidence in the prayers of God's people, the help of the Holy Spirit, God's plans and purposes, the goodness of the Caesar, and that he would not be put to shame
d) Confidence in the goodness of the Caesar, the Roman judicial system, the prayers of God's people, the help of the Holy Spirit, and God's plans and purposes

3. In Philippians 1, Paul responded to jealous, contentious, fellow preachers by
a) praying for protection.
b) confronting ungodliness.
c) warning the church.
d) thanking God that Christ was exalted.

4. The Greek word for *conduct yourselves* used in Philippians 1:27 literally means to
a) "be organized and in order."
b) "behave or conduct oneself as a citizen."
c) "live in harmony with others."
d) "take responsibility for one's actions."

5. In Philippians 1:27–28, Paul encourages believers to be fearless in the face of opposition, unified in Spirit, and to
a) live in harmony with their society.
b) work as a team.
c) lay down their lives for the cause of Christ.
d) pray daily for each other.

6. What are two godly motives for maintaining unity in the church?
a) Having fellowship with other believers, and experiencing God's tenderness and compassion
b) Receiving encouragement from other believers and comfort from God
c) Having fellowship in the Spirit and encouragement from other believers
d) Receiving encouragement from Christ and comfort from His love

7. According to Philippians 2:2–4, what are some behaviors that would make Paul's joy complete?
a) Being like-minded, humble, and unselfish
b) Being generous, humble, and one in spirit and purpose
c) Being self-controlled, unselfish, and generous
d) Being like-minded, generous, and self-controlled

8. Based upon Philippians 2, being Christlike means being willing to
a) relinquish position, give up privileges, and rest in God's promise of future reward and glory.
b) give up, relinquish position, and accept God's plan for one's life.
c) fight to the end, hold on to God's promises, and never give up.
d) give up and rest in God's promise of future reward and glory.

9. Paul's command in Philippians 2:12 is to work out one's salvation with
a) wisdom.
b) fear and trembling.
c) guidance from the Holy Spirit.
d) love and patience.

10. Paul wanted his life and the service of the Philippian believers to result in mutual
a) self-sacrifice and satisfaction.
b) satisfaction and rejoicing.
c) rejoicing and sorrow.
d) self-sacrifice and rejoicing.

Responses to Interactive Questions
CHAPTER 11

Some of these responses may include information that is supplemental to the IST. These questions are intended to produce reflective thinking beyond the course content and your responses may vary from these examples.

1 What was Paul's attitude toward his prison experience?

Paul recognized that his circumstances had actually helped to spread the gospel. He shared the gospel inside the prison with soldiers chained to him and people who visited. His imprisonment helped spread the gospel outside the prison because Christians who had been afraid to share the gospel gained courage by watching his example.

2 How did Paul respond to unfair criticism?

Paul said, "What does it matter? The important thing is . . . that Christ is preached. And because of this I rejoice." All Paul cared about was the gospel. That was his passion. That is what he lived for. He was not in the ministry to be appreciated by people, he was not living for accolades, he was not looking for status. He lived to reach lost people with the gospel.

3 What sustained Paul in the face of an uncertain future?

Paul remained strong because had confidence in the faithfulness of God and His Word, his was confident in the prayers of God's people, he was confident in the help of the Holy Spirit, he was confident he would not be put to shame, and he had confidence in God's plan and purposes.

4 Why was Paul concerned about the Philippian church?

Paul was concerned about the lack of unity among the believers at Philippi. Opposition was coming both from within and outside the church. Feelings of fear and intimidation were real. Christians were struggling with a loss of perspective. Their joy in the Lord was slipping away.

5 What analogy did Paul use to help the Philippian believers know how to live in their present culture?

The congregation at Philippi had Roman citizenship, lived by Roman laws, enjoyed Roman benefits, and celebrated Roman values and customs. Paul used this analogy to remind them of their citizenship in the kingdom of heaven. He challenged them to live lives "worthy of the gospel of Christ" in the face of opposition, to behave as citizens of heaven. Paul's point was that their behavior should match their beliefs and values. They should live as people transformed by the gospel whose temporary residence was within an alien culture.

6 How can our lives either help or hinder the impact of the gospel in our culture?

When Christians within a congregation fall apart in times of crisis, it negatively impacts the work of the gospel. A wrong signal is sent to the world when the family of God behaves in ways that contradict the values of the heavenly kingdom.

7 How did Paul encourage the church to face opposition?

Paul urged them to demonstrate the characteristics of fearless Christian soldiers: Unity in the Spirit, camaraderie in ministry, and fearlessness in the face of opposition.

8 What better translation might be made of the word *if* in Philippians 2:1?

The meaning of the word *if* would be better translated, "Since there exists" or "Because you have" benefits from God.

9 What six behaviors lead to unity in a church?

The behaviors that lead to unity in a church are being like-minded, having the same love, being one in spirit and purpose, doing nothing out of selfish ambition or vain conceit, humbly considering others to be better than ourselves, and looking out for the interests of others, not just our own.

10 What does being Christlike mean for you?

Being Christlike means we are willing to relinquish our place, we are willing to give up our privileges, we are willing to step down from our position, we understand our purpose, and we are willing to rest in His promise of reward and future glory.

11 What attitudes enabled Jesus to come to earth and give himself on the Cross?

Jesus Christ was equal to God in every way—He was God. But He did not regard that position as something to be grasped. He did not cling to it or hold on to His position. He separated himself from His privileges. He gave up His rights in order to bring us salvation.

12 What did Paul mean when he said, "Work out your salvation with fear and trembling"?

Paul is not addressing individual salvation in this passage. He is dealing with the need for unity and a servant spirit among God's people. He is concerned with how believers live out their salvation as the church of Jesus Christ in the world. His concern is that their disagreements, opinionated attitudes, and self-seeking will destroy the body of Christ in Philippi. As redeemed people, they need to live out their salvation with unity of the Spirit and devotion of heart to one another and the Lord.

13 How can our testimonies influence our culture for Jesus?

Paul wanted believers to impact their culture by being different. He wanted us to "become blameless and pure, children of God without fault in a crooked and depraved generation." Both our outward conduct and inner motivation need to reflect our relationship with the Lord. Our lives should shine like stars in the spiritual darkness of a depraved culture. We are to be lighthouses for God where we live and work. We are to share the hope of the gospel in our communities.

Encouragement, Exhortation, and Evaluation (Philippians 2:19–4:1)

Timothy and Epaphroditus brought great encouragement to Paul in prison. Timothy was a faithful and capable "son" in the Lord (1 Timothy 1:2). Paul had depended on him many times. Epaphroditus had come to Paul as the personal representative of the church in Philippi. He brought a valuable report, much needed money, and most of all, encouragement and help. Paul loved him and the church in Philippi.

Paul had planned to finish his letter to the church, but the report from Epaphroditus and others prompted him to write further exhortations and warnings. Apparently, legalism had made inroads into the church as well as teaching that corrupted the church's understanding of God's grace. In dealing with this situation, Paul testifies to God's working in his own life to bring about a marvelous transformation of his personal priorities.

> • *Read Philippians 2:19–4:1 before you begin study in this chapter.*

Lesson 12.1   Deep Appreciation for Two Quality People (2:19–30)

Objectives

12.1.1   Describe how Timothy fits the description of a servant leader.

12.1.2   Describe the characteristics of Epaphroditus that caused the church in Philippi to select him and caused Paul to commend him as a servant leader.

Lesson 12.2   An Appeal and Warning from a Concerned Christian Friend (3:1–3, 17–19)

Objectives

12.2.1   Identify Paul's reason for emphasizing joy throughout his letter to the Philippians.

12.2.2   Explain why legalism is a danger to authentic Christianity.

12.2.3   Describe what Paul meant by lawlessness.

Lesson 12.3   An Appeal Supported by Paul's Personal Testimony (3:4–16; 3:20–4:1)

Objectives

12.3.1   Explain how Paul's position and privilege in the past might have given him a reason for confidence in the flesh.

12.3.2   Describe how to live in victory.

12.3.3   Explain how Paul used the analogy of citizenship to explain how Christians should view their time on earth.

Deep Appreciation for Two Quality People (2:19–30)

Models crafted for future manufactured items are valuable. I have a childhood friend who is very talented in this area. When he was in high school, he got involved in several contests developing models for new car manufacturers. His challenge was to devise clay models of car designs and submit them to the manufacturer as possible designs for their new vehicles. Several of his prototypes were selected and appeared on showroom floors. He received generous awards for these models. High prices are paid for prototypes.

Models are also helpful. Students assigned to new projects appreciate having a model to follow. A model gives them access to a completed assignment that is just what the professor wants. Being able to see a model that received a perfect score and then being able to pattern your work after it can make the difference between an excellent grade or a mediocre grade. Models help students know what to do.

Models are powerful. We are inspired when an individual shows us how to live with purpose and productivity. We are encouraged to greater things when we see how others solve problems successfully, make their marriages work, and carry out family responsibilities. How gratifying to observe a person fulfilling obligations at work, responding positively to provocation or pressure, and dealing with difficulties and discouragement. To see a real Christian up close every day is a great discipling tool and exerts a powerful influence on others. That is why mentoring relationships are so influential in Christian living.

Paul expresses deep appreciation for two quality individuals—models, if you please, of what servant leadership looks like. Each was important in his own way to the Christians in Philippi.

Authentic, devoted, servant leaders are no less valuable in the church today. Timothy and Epaphroditus are symbolic of faithful servant leaders in the church today who share Christ's priorities and give their lives for His cause. They model the actions and attitudes Paul presented in Philippians 2:1–11.

OBJECTIVE

Describe how Timothy fits the description of a servant leader.

1   What qualified Timothy for the task Paul had given him?

Timothy as a Model: Servant Leaders Seek the Things of Christ (2:19–24)

Timothy was the man Paul selected as his representative to the church in Philippi. Timothy was a native of Derbe or Lystra in Galatia. His father was Greek and his mother was Jewish. He had come to Christ through the influence of his mother and grandmother, and Paul had personally mentored him. Paul took Timothy with him almost everywhere he went. He had served as Paul's personal representative on several occasions. Timothy had been with Paul on his second missionary journey when the church at Philippi was planted. Consequently, the Philippian believers knew Timothy well. Timothy was now with Paul in Rome, and had been an encouragement to Paul. Because Paul could not go himself, Timothy was the perfect choice to send to Philippi.

The Motive of a Servant Leader

True servant leaders are more concerned about those they serve than they are about themselves. Paul's primary concern is not to inform the church about his own condition, but to learn how they are doing. He sends Timothy, "That I may also be cheered when I receive news about you" (v. 19).

The Character of a Servant Leader

2   What was Paul's twofold mission for Timothy in Philippi?

Paul points out several character traits of this servant-leader he had grown to love and trust. First he points out that Timothy shared his own pastoral concern for the church at Philippi. He said Timothy "takes a genuine interest in your welfare" (20). The words "no one like him" could be better translated, *no one else who feels about you as I do*, that is, who is "of equal soul" (Kent 1978, 132). Not only that, Paul points out that Timothy is a person with Christ's interests at heart. And Paul is willing to personally vouch for his character because he has shared a mentoring relationship with Timothy. They have shared a father–son relationship in the Lord's work.

The Mission of a Servant Leader

The mission Paul gave Timothy was twofold. Paul wanted Timothy to give the church reliable information about his welfare. But more than that, he anxiously awaited a positive report about their spiritual welfare. He knew that Timothy, servant leader that he was, shared his concern.

3   How many people can you identify by name who have Timothy's character qualities?

Believe me, servant leaders with these qualities are rare indeed. They were rare even within Paul's circles of ministry. To care more about others than you care about yourself, to take a genuine interest in the welfare others, to have a passion for the cause of Christ, all of these are marks of a true servant leader. The same Jesus who took the role of an ordinary slave and washed His disciples feet challenges us all: "I have set you an example that you should do as I have done for you" (John 13:15).

Basketball fans recognize the name of David Robinson. Now retired, Robinson played center for the San Antonio Spurs and is regarded as one of the premier players of his era; however, the respect given to him goes beyond his on-court abilities. Robinson and his wife Valerie were part of the founding, and in a large part the funding, of the George Washington Carver Academy. This private school serves inner city children in San Antonio, most of whom are African-Americans or Latinos. The former NBA player's involvement with the school goes beyond helping from a distance, he has personally invested time in the students.

Prior to Robinson's retirement, Spurs Coach Gregg Popovich, speculated that Robinson's future plans would not likely focus on basketball. The coach said, "He's got much more sense than to stay involved in basketball. He's got a lot of interests that actually have an impact on the world and have some value, unlike the rest of us. He's way to committed to real life to do something as silly as basketball for the rest of his life" (Sheridan 2009).

OBJECTIVE

Describe the characteristics of Epaphroditus that caused the church in Philippi to select him and caused Paul to commend him as a servant leader.

Epaphroditus as a Model: Servant Leaders Faithfully Serve in Spite of the Risks (2:25–30)

The church at Philippi had chosen Epaphroditus, one of their own, to find out about Paul and take care of his needs. We do not know a lot about his background. He is mentioned only in Philippians. We do not know who his parents were or how long he had been a Christian. We do know that when the church wanted to find a reliable person to do what they could not do—visit Paul and minister to his needs—they chose Epaphroditus. Epaphroditus may have been an elder in Philippi (2:25–30; 4:18).

4   Who was Epaphroditus and what had the Philippian church chosen him to do?

The Mission of a Servant Leader

Paul wants Epaphroditus to deliver his letter. He was the faithful servant the church had sent to deliver their monetary gift and minister to Paul's needs. They were deeply concerned about him. Paul wants to bring relief and rejoicing to their hearts. What was Paul's message to the church in Philippi regarding Epaphroditus? Mission accomplished.

The Character of a Servant Leader

5   What was Epaphroditus like?

Paul praises Epaphroditus in this letter. He refers to him as "my brother," a "fellow worker," and a "fellow soldier" (v. 25). Over the months Paul has come to appreciate the close bond they shared as members of the same spiritual family, the hours they labored together in the Lord's work, and the spiritual battles they fought together.

Not only does Paul refer to Epaphroditus as their messenger (*apostolon,* a term meaning "special emissary") to care for his needs, he identifies him as a faithful servant of the church. Epaphroditus was deeply concerned for others. Paul said Epaphroditus deeply longed for the church in Philippi, using the term *epipoîtheō,* an intensified Greek word for "longing." He was also *distressed* when he heard they knew he was ill. The word *distressed* (v. 26) is used of the Lord's emotions in Gethsemane (Matthew 26:37; Mark 14:33) (Kent 1978, 135).

As a servant leader, Epaphroditus was caring and compassionate. He "risked his life" for the Lord's work (v. 27). In other words, he embodied the spirit of Paul when the apostle said, "I consider my life worth nothing to me, if only I may finish the race and complete the task the Lord Jesus has given me" (Acts 20:24). He also exemplified the attitude of Jesus, "The author and perfecter of our faith, who for the joy set before him endured the cross, scorning its shame" (Hebrews 12:2).

The Proper Treatment of a Servant Leader

6   What three things did Paul instruct the congregation at Philippi to do for Epaphroditus?

Paul instructs this congregation about the appropriate treatment for such a person. He says *welcome* people like this, in the Lord; *show great joy* at their presence; *honor* them.

A church I pastored had a magnificent custom. Whenever faithful missionaries came to our congregation to report their service and vision to reach and disciple the lost of the world, the church gave them a standing ovation. Hundreds of people stood to their feet and with sustained applause, honored those who faithfully served with a servant's heart. You could feel the presence and power of God.

Do you know of people in your church who are servant leaders? Are there those who give evidence of the attitude of Christ described in Philippians 2:1–11? This would be a great time to identify them and devise a way to welcome them in the Lord, show great joy at their presence, and honor them in a way that appropriately expresses your esteem for them as a church body.

An Appeal and Warning from a Concerned Christian Friend (3:1–3, 17–19)

It is easy to lose perspective as a Christian and to begin to see things through spiritually distorted eyes. Sunglasses protect our eyes from the dangerous rays of the sun. But if left on all of the time, they keep us from seeing the splendor of a sunny day, darken our perspective, and make us think a day is dreary and perhaps about to storm. Looking in a distorted mirror can be discouraging, making a person feel dismayed at what, at least, appears to be his or her reflection. We need a proper perspective—a godly, biblical perspective—about things.

As Paul begins chapter 3 of the epistle, it appears that he is about to bring the letter to a close, thus he writes, "Finally, my brothers (and sisters)."

This part of the letter can be puzzling since it does not end immediately, especially after these closing words. Paul may have intended to bring the letter to a close at this point or he may have meant *furthermore,* as a result of a report brought to him or something he remembers that moves him to a point of concern (Kent 1978, 138; O'Brien 1991, 348). But we do have a continuation where he addresses two additional issues that had the potential of robbing the Philippian believers of their joy. The issues: their adoption of legalism and the attempt to substitute a lawlessness that would preempt the sufficiency of being in Christ. Legalism was the tendency to reduce the Christian life to a list of rules. Lawlessness placed so much emphasis on God's grace as to promote the idea that anything goes. Both are distortions of the truth. Christians still need to be reminded to keep their joy in the Lord and beware of the dangers of legalism and lawlessness.

An Appeal: We Need Reminders to Rejoice in the Lord (3:1)

12.2.1
OBJECTIVE

Identify Paul's reason for emphasizing joy throughout his letter to the Philippians.

7   How can the joy of the Lord, or the lack of it, indicate one's spiritual state?

The tone of Philippians is consistently joyful. This theme is emphasized at least sixteen times in this short epistle by the use of various forms of the words "joy" or "rejoice" (cf. 1:4, 18, 25–26; 2:2, 17–18, 28–29; 3:1; 4:1, 4, 10). As Paul prepares to write his final word to the believers in Philippi he feels compelled to affirm their need to keep rejoicing.

True joy comes from knowing and trusting the Lord. It lasts. We can have joy in spite of deep trials and trouble. It enables us to overcome difficult circumstances. It sustains us. It enables us to walk through adversity without sinking into despondency. Joy protects us from surging to unrealistic highs when circumstances are good. It comes from a consistent relationship with the Lord. But we must beware; joy is one of the first things to go when we slip into a sinful lifestyle, lose sight of our Savior, are deceived by the enemy, or slip back into self-reliance. The presence or absence of the joy of the Lord is a good indicator of how things are going with us spiritually (Barton et al. 1995, 81–83).

As a result, Paul does not apologize for repeatedly emphasizing the need for rejoicing. He is concerned that some of the error that he will shortly discuss with them, if left unattended, could rob them of their joy. Thus, his repeated emphasis on joy is a safeguard for them.

Most of us have watched with amusement or dismay the highs and lows of an athletic team. Joy and elation one moment, utter despair and frustration the next. Quality coaches understand consistency. They train their team in the basics of the game so that when they encounter the uncertainties and the inconsistencies of the other team, they can sustain effort and maintain a consistent pattern of play. That is how victory comes. That is also how joy comes. Paul says it again, "Rejoice in the Lord."

A Warning: Beware of Legalism (3:2–3)

12.2.2
OBJECTIVE

Explain why legalism is a danger to authentic Christianity.

8   How does Paul describe the Judaizers in the church at Philippi?

Paul's first warning is about the persistent problem of legalism that dogged the first century church. The Jerusalem church was called on to deal with this issue early in its life (Acts 15). It was also the problem that plagued the church in Galatia and caused Paul to write a terse, straightforward letter. It was a problem that Paul had to deal with over and over again as any casual reading of Paul's epistles will reveal.

Three times Paul repeats the word *beware* in the Greek text of verse 2. This is a strong warning delivered with force (Fee 1995, 293–294). Its equivalent in English would be *watch out for* or *be on your guard against* (O'Brien 1991, 352–353). Then Paul characterizes the true nature of the false teachers, Judaizers, who taught that Gentile believers must be circumcised and keep the Mosaic law in order to be saved. Paul says of the Judaizers, "Watch out for those dogs." They prided themselves on being righteous, but Paul says they are "evil workers." They prided themselves on being circumcised. Paul characterizes them as "mutilators of the flesh," the same language he had used for them in Galatians (5:7–12; Kent 1978, 139).

9 What are the dangers of legalism?

The problem with legalism is that it attempts to add requirements for obtaining salvation (Ephesians 2:8–9). Legalism distorts the gospel and detracts from Christ as our adequate sacrifice for sin (Romans 6:10; Hebrews 7:26–28; 9:11–12, 25–28; 10:8–10; 1 Peter 3:18). Legalism does nothing but feed pride and self-sufficiency (Ephesians 2:8–9). It brings people into bondage and back into sin (Matthew 23:15). It reduces the dynamic of "living according to the Spirit" and nurtures "walking according to the flesh" or "law" (Romans 8:1–17; Galatians 5:16–18).

10 Are you affected by legalism? If so, what will you do to change this focus?

Paul says to the believers, "It is we who are the circumcision, we who worship by the Spirit of God, who glory in Christ Jesus, and who put no confidence in the flesh" (3:3; cf. Romans 2:28–29). What a wonderful description of authentic Christianity based upon the gospel: salvation by faith, spiritual worship, rejoicing in Christ, not depending on our own righteousness or works.

Two young men stood outside my door. Their sincerity and zeal were impressive. There was no doubt they were well-dressed and devoted to their cause. When we began an exchange, I listened to them for awhile and then asked them this probing question: "How would you tell me I could experience salvation and be ready to go to heaven?" Then the error of their doctrine began to surface. Their message could be summarized like this: "Works, works, works, works." Legalism can come in many shapes and forms, some bizarre and some appealing. This error can surface in evangelical garb, cultish clothes, or the flowing robes of ancient and esoteric religions. It makes no difference. Legalism is dangerous; watch out for it!

12.2.3
OBJECTIVE
Describe what Paul meant by lawlessness.

A Warning: Beware of Lawlessness (3:17–19)

The second major warning in this passage is against lawlessness, namely, using the grace of God as an excuse for sinful living. Another name given to this error is antinomianism. Those who subscribe to this error believe that once a person has been saved, what they do in their bodies is no one's concern. They throw aside morality and self-restraint, believing that nothing done in their already-redeemed souls matters (Barton et al. 1995, 104). It is a perverted form of **eternal security**. This issue is addressed in several locations in the New Testament (1 Corinthians 8:9; 1 Peter 2:16; 2 Peter 2:17–22; Jude 4). Paul indicates that tragically, "there are many who walk along the Christian road who are really enemies of the cross of Christ" (3:18, TLB). He highlights four characteristics of this kind of person.

11 What four characteristics did Paul list to describe the state of a person living in lawlessness?

1. **Their ultimate destiny**: These individuals may think they are going to heaven. They may hope for eternal life, but "their destiny is destruction" (3:19; 1 Corinthians 6:9–10; Galatians 5:19–21; 6:7–8).

2. **Their preference for pleasure**: These are individuals whose whole goal in life is the satisfaction of their physical and sexual desires (3:19; cf. Ephesians 2:1–3; 5:3–7).

3. **Their objects of admiration**: These people admire those who are defiant, sensual, conniving, crafty, and coercive. "They are proud of what they should be ashamed of" (3:19, TLB; cf. Romans 1:32).

4. **Their orientation to life**: Their focus is upon the here and now, the physical and material interests (Romans 8:5–8; Colossians 3:2, 5–6). They stand in stark contrast to those described in the following verse whose "citizenship is in heaven" (3:20).

What a tragedy to meet someone who professes Christianity, yet whose lifestyle and values are counter to Christ's will. These individuals are like evil yeast or a toxic seasoning in the life of the church. Can you imagine preparing a succulent roast for dinner and discovering to your dismay, after it has been served, that it is rotten meat? Can you picture the crisis such a discovery would create? Lawlessness—grace used as an excuse to sin—has the same deadly effect.

Paul confronted the same problem in his letter to the Romans. In chapter 6 he begins with an anticipated question, after his discussion of the grace of God, "Shall we go on sinning so that grace may increase?" Is it any wonder he responds in the following verse with an emphatic, "God forbid"? The literal translation of the Greek is, "May it never be!" (v. 2). This error is dangerous; watch out for it.

Look deep within and examine your heart. Do you still have your joy in the Lord? If not, what happened to it? What caused it to evaporate? Are you trapped by a performance orientation to living for God, a legalism that reduces everything in the Christian life to a list of rules? Or has someone duped you and convinced you that you can participate in sinful activities, adopt the world's value system, or do whatever you please and still make it to heaven? Do not be deceived—that is incredibly dangerous teaching. What is the solution? Repent. Turn from your sin. Embrace the Cross. Trust Christ alone to forgive, cleanse, and restore you. You can depend on it. He will restore your joy.

An Appeal Supported by Paul's Personal Testimony (3:4–16; 3:20–4:1)

Paul had reminded the believers in Philippi to go on rejoicing in the Lord. He told them not to let anyone or anything steal their joy (3:1). He had warned them about the dangers of legalism, about those who would reduce the Christian life to a list of rules, those who would try to make it to heaven by their own efforts (3:2–3). He also warned them about the lawlessness of an *anything-goes-for-I-have-the-grace-of-God attitude* (3:17–19).

The need for these appeals and warnings has not diminished over the centuries. Some who call themselves Christian are still trying to reach heaven by keeping a list of rules or by being good enough to get in. Others think the grace of God gives them the right and protection to live however they please.

Now Paul continues his arguments by sharing his personal testimony. He strongly proclaims that he has discovered that knowing Christ, having Christ, and serving Christ are all that matter in life.

Confidence in Self Leads Nowhere and Should Be Renounced (3:4–6)

Before he met Jesus, Paul had depended upon religious ceremonies and rituals by which he had become a "child of the covenant." He was a Jew and proud of his national heritage. He was not just any Jew. He had lived in the strictest

12.3.1
OBJECTIVE

Explain how Paul's position and privilege in the past might have given him a reason for confidence in the flesh.

adherence to the Jewish law. He was a "Hebrew of Hebrews; in regard to the law, a Pharisee." Zealous? In his zeal he had done what he believed was right by persecuting Christians (Acts 8:3; 9:1–2; 22:3–5; 26:9–11).

But Paul came to realize there was no future in the flesh, not even in his driving religious acts of righteousness. All deeds and acknowledgments acquired in his past and anything else that he once considered gain or advantage, he now considered loss. They were abandoned or forgotten refuse. They were foul smelling street garbage. He had left it all for the surpassing worth of knowing Christ Jesus as Lord (Fee 1995, 304, 319).

Most incompetent people do not know they are incompetent. In fact, researcher Dr. David A. Dunning, of Cornell University, reports that people who are incompetent are more confident of their abilities than competent people. That is the way we are spiritually without Christ, and Paul came to realize it. Our sin not only separates us from God, it blinds us to our predicament (Kruger and Dunning 1999, 1121–1134).

Knowing and Serving Christ Are Supreme (3:7–16)

Paul now shares what really matters to him now that he has come to know Christ. Notice the progression in the phrases that he uses to describe his relationship with and to the Lord: "knowing Christ . . . gaining Christ . . . being found in him . . . having his righteousness" and, finally—fully identifying with and conforming to both Christ's suffering and His resurrection. What a lofty aspiration! The focus of Paul's life had now become knowing and serving Christ. Having Christ's righteousness (granted by faith, not earned by works) was what he aspired to.

What does Paul say had become his life's goal? He was no longer satisfied with his present level of attainment or past successes. His ultimate goal was attaining what Christ had in store for him in the future. This involved God's purposes and activity in his life at the present. It involved his personal, wholehearted effort and cooperation with what God was doing in his life. But it also embraced the future heavenly goal, the heavenward call he sensed.

Paul gives us five elements that will help us walk in victory.

1. If We Are Going to Walk in Victory, We Must Face Our Deficiencies (3:12–13)

Paul starts with the admission that he has not already arrived. What an amazing observation from the mouth of this great apostle. Here is a man who has seen the glorified Christ—a man who is a powerful communicator of the gospel. He has done amazing miracles. Yet he knows he has not arrived. If we have come to the place where we feel spiritually satisfied, we are in a dangerous position (cf. Revelation 3:17). Spiritual growth and victory begin with the awareness that we have not arrived and a longing to be different.

2. If We Are Going to Walk in Victory, We Must Focus on the Prize (3:12)

This is terminology a distance runner would identify with. What is the prize you are running for? Are you running to just make it to heaven, to have a life free of problems, to build a business, or to have a perfect marriage? All of these things are good, but they were not the ultimate goal for Paul. He was running "to take hold of that for which Christ Jesus took hold of me." Why did God take hold of you? Why did He save you? He wants to make you like His Son. You see, the goal of every Christian is, and always ought to be, to be like Christ (cf. Galatians 4:19; Ephesians 4:13; Colossians 1:28). Paul does not say, "I press on to get out of

---

12 What things in Paul's life before the lordship of Christ might have tempted him to be self-reliant?

13 What are believers today tempted to rely on?

12.3.2
OBJECTIVE
Describe how to live in victory.

14 What are some of the phrases that Paul uses to describe his relationship or position in Christ Jesus?

15 Using Paul's testimony as a guide, how can we walk in victory?

prison." He says, "I want to be like Christ." The most important thing you can do is become like Christ. If we succeed at that, God will take care of the other things—we'll be better husbands and wives, better parents, better employees, and better students.

3. If We Are Going to Walk in Victory, We Must Forget the Past (3:13)

You will need to forget a few things if you want to live in victory. You cannot always be looking back. Roger Bannister and John Landy were racing in Canada. Landy was ahead until he looked back. Bannister passed by him on the right side and set a new world record—the first sub-four minute mile. Do not look back. Do not look back on your successes, as wonderful as they may have been. Forget your failures, the disasters, the disappointments. Forget the excuses. Learn from them and move on.

4. If We Are Going to Walk in Victory, We Must Forge Ahead (3:13–14)

To "strain toward what is ahead" is to press toward the goal, regardless of fatigue or pain, to lean with the whole body toward the finish line (Barton et al. 1995, 100). It is giving everything you have got to the race. As a runner would say, "Leave it on the pavement." Go for it!

5. If We Are Going to Walk in Victory, We Must Forgo Comparisons (3:15)

Many people never know victory because they are so busy looking at everyone else, they lose sight of the objective. Mature people understand victory is not automatic—you have to work at it. They know some will try to make excuses for themselves. They will compare themselves with others. Paul says we should leave others to God. God will speak to their hearts. We cannot force someone to grow. We cannot force them to walk in victory. We cannot make them accept instruction or teaching. We can tell them the truth in love, show them the standard, but then leave them to God.

Of what was Paul convinced? That everyone who follows Christ needs to take this Christ-centered view (3:15). He was convinced that Christ had made available to us all we needed to live up "to what we had already attained" (3:16). He also believed he and others had set a reliable example (3:17).

12.3.3
OBJECTIVE

Explain how Paul used the analogy of citizenship to explain how Christians should view their time on earth.

16   How oriented would you say your life really is to your heavenly citizenship?

Our Heavenly Citizenship Is Our Hope (3:20–4:1)

Paul draws a parallel to the Philippians' Roman citizenship for the second time in this letter (cf. 1:27). They were, indeed, earthly citizens of Rome, but the greater reality for them was that they were citizens of heaven. They were waiting expectantly for the full realization of that reality. But until that was fully realized, they were to live by the values, principles, and dynamics of their heavenly kingdom here in the present world.

Philippi, although located in the far-off province of Macedonia, was a Roman colony. Its citizens lived under the values, laws, and benefits of Rome. In the same manner, the believers at Philippi, as citizens of heaven, were to function as a colony of heaven. This world was not their home. Although they lived in Philippi, these Christians eagerly awaited a Savior from *there* (i.e. heaven). The term *Savior* was commonly used for Caesar, the Roman emperor. However, it was an even more significant term for Christians. This term was frequently used in the Old Testament to refer to God. This Savior was the Lord Jesus Christ. A day was coming when Christ would return for His own and transfer their existences to heaven (1 Corinthians 15:42–57). This was their confident hope; this was their motivating expectation (Fee 1995, 377–381).

A Sunday school teacher asked the children to raise their hands if they wanted to go to heaven. Every child raised a hand except one. "You do not want to go to heaven?" asked the surprised teacher. "No," came the almost tearful reply, "I want to go home!"

Tragically, that is how some Christians respond. They have not yet grasped the fact that heaven is their home. They have not reached the place where they feel more at home with their heavenly citizenship then in their temporary abode here are earth. May we come to truly believe and live by the truth, "Our citizenship is in heaven. And we eagerly await a Savior from there" (3:20).

Is heaven your home? Have you renounced your citizenship in the kingdom of darkness and asked God to transfer you into the kingdom of His dear Son (Colossians 1:13–14)?

Test Yourself

Circle the letter of the *best* answer.

1. Two servant leaders who assisted Paul and are mentioned in Philippians are
a) Luke and Timothy.
b) Tychicus and Epaphroditus.
c) Epaphras and Timothy.
d) Timothy and Epaphroditus.

2. With whom did Paul have a father-son relationship?
a) Epaphras
b) Tychicus
c) Timothy
d) Epaphroditus

3. Marks of a servant leader are having a genuine interest in the welfare of others and a
a) charisma to lead people.
b) passion for the cause of Christ.
c) determination to complete a project that has been started.
d) passion to work hard.

4. Who delivered the letter of Philippians to the church in Philippi?
a) Epaphras
b) Tychicus
c) Epaphroditus
d) Timothy

5. How many times does Paul mention the concept of joy or rejoicing in Philippians?
a) 12
b) 16
c) 20
d) 23

6. What does Paul call the Judaizers in Philippians 3?
a) Evil workers, dogs, and mutilators of the flesh
b) Rats, scoundrels, and mutilators of the flesh
c) False teachers, rats, and scoundrels
d) False teachers, scoundrels, and dogs

7. Lawlessness is also called
a) heathenism.
b) hedonism.
c) antinomianism.
d) atheism.

8. Paul was of the tribe of
a) Judah.
b) Benjamin.
c) Manasseh.
d) Ephraim.

9. According to the IST, if believers want to walk in victory they must
a) face their future, focus on the things of this world, forget the past, forge ahead, and forgo comparisons.
b) face their enemies, focus on the future, forget the past, forge ahead, and forgo comparisons.
c) face their deficiencies, focus on the prize, forget the past, forge ahead, and forgo comparisons.
d) face their fears, focus on the prize, forget the past, be comfortable, and forgo comparisons.

10. For Paul, what type of citizenship was most important?
a) Heavenly
b) Roman
c) Jewish
d) Earthly

Responses to Interactive Questions
CHAPTER 12

Some of these responses may include information that is supplemental to the IST. These questions are intended to produce reflective thinking beyond the course content and your responses may vary from these examples.

1 What qualified Timothy for the task Paul had given him?

Timothy had come to Christ through the influence of his mother and grandmother, and Paul had personally mentored him. He had served as Paul's personal representative on several occasions. Timothy had been with Paul on his second missionary journey when the church at Philippi was planted. Consequently, the Philippian believers knew Timothy well. Timothy was now with Paul in Rome, and had been an encouragement to Paul.

2 What was Paul's twofold mission for Timothy in Philippi?

The mission Paul gave Timothy was twofold. Paul wanted Timothy to give the church reliable information about his welfare. He also wanted to receive a positive report about the church's spiritual welfare.

3 How many people can you identify by name who have Timothy's character qualities?

Answers will vary.

4 Who was Epaphroditus and what had the Philippian church chosen him to do?

We do not know a lot about his background. He is mentioned only in Philippians. We do not know who his parents were or how long he had been a Christian. We do know that when the church wanted to find a reliable person to do what they could not do—visit Paul and minister to his needs—they chose Epaphroditus. Epaphroditus may have been an elder in Philippi.

5 What was Epaphroditus like?

Paul refers to Epaphroditus as "my brother," a "fellow worker," a "fellow soldier, " and the church's messenger to care for Paul's needs. Paul also identifies him as a faithful servant of the church. Epaphroditus was deeply concerned for others. Epaphroditus longed for the church in Philippi and was also "distressed" when he heard they knew he was ill. As a servant leader, Epaphroditus was caring and compassionate. He "risked his life" for the Lord's work. He embodied the spirit of Paul and the attitude of Jesus.

6 What three things did Paul instruct the congregation at Philippi to do for Epaphroditus?

Paul instructs this congregation about the appropriate treatment for such a person. He instructs them to welcome people like this in the Lord, to show great joy at their presence, and to honor them.

7 How can the joy of the Lord, or the lack of it, indicate one's spiritual state?

True joy comes from knowing and trusting the Lord. It lasts. We can have joy in spite of deep trials and trouble. It enables us to overcome difficult circumstances. It sustains us. It enables us to walk through adversity without sinking into despondency. It protects us from surging to unrealistic highs when circumstances are good. It comes from a consistent relationship with the Lord. But joy is one of the first things to go when we slip into a sinful lifestyle, lose sight of our Savior, are deceived by the enemy, or slip back into self-reliance.

8 How does Paul describe the Judaizers in the church at Philippi?

Paul characterized the true nature of the false teachers when he said, "Watch out for those dogs." Paul said they were "evil workers." Paul characterizes them as "mutilators of the flesh."

9 What are the dangers of legalism?

Legalism attempts to add requirements for obtaining salvation. It distorts the gospel and detracts from Christ as our adequate sacrifice for sin. Legalism feeds pride and self-sufficiency, bringing people into bondage and sin. It reduces living in the Spirit to obey a list of human-made rules.

10 Are you affected by legalism? If so, what will you do to change?

Answers will vary.

11 What four characteristics did Paul list to describe the state of a person living in lawlessness?

These individuals only think they are going to heaven. They hope for eternal life, but "their destiny is destruction." Their life's goal is the satisfaction of their physical and sexual desires. They admire those who are defiant, sensual, conniving, crafty, and coercive. Their focus is on the here and now—physical and material interests.

12 What things in Paul's life before the lordship of Christ might have tempted him to be self-reliant?

Paul had depended upon religious ceremonies and rituals to please God. He was a Jew and proud of his national heritage. He was not just any Jew. He had lived in the strictest adherence to the Jewish law. He was a "Hebrew of Hebrews; in regard to the law, a Pharisee." In his zeal he had done what he believed was right by persecuting Christians.

13 What are believers today tempted to rely on?

Believers today may be tempted to rely on doing good works, attending church, being better than others, giving to charities or ministries, or a host of other good acts. They may also be tempted to believe that their knowledge of the Bible and the church guarantees them a place in God's kingdom. They may rely on personal skills and abilities instead of on the power of God to try to do God's work.

14 What are some of the phrases Paul uses to describe his relationship or position in Christ Jesus?

Paul uses the following phrases: "Knowing Christ;" "Gaining Christ;" "Being found in him;" and "Having his righteousness."

15 Using Paul's testimony as a guide, how can we walk in victory?

Paul gives us five elements that will help us walk in victory. We must face our deficiencies, focus on the prize, forget the past, forge ahead, and forgo compromise.

16 How oriented would you say your life really is to your heavenly citizenship?

Answers will vary.

Concluding Exhortations, Thanks, and Greeting (Philippians 4:2–23)

Christians have a personal adversary, the devil; his plan is our defeat (1 Peter 5:8). One of our greatest fears is that of failure. Yet, if we are going to have victory ultimately, we will need the Lord's help. Our danger is that we will lose perspective. Satan tried to get Paul to lose perspective in Rome, but he stood firm. Satan was trying to cause believers in Philippi to lose perspective. Paul wants them to stand firm.

At the beginning of Philippians, Paul said, "Whatever happens, conduct yourselves in a manner worthy of the gospel of Christ. Then, whether I come and see you or only hear about you in my absence, I will know that you stand firm" (1:27). Paul continued his letter, with this theme reappearing near the end of the epistle where he says, "Therefore, my brothers, you whom I love and long for, my joy and crown, that is how you should stand firm in the Lord, dear friends" (4:1). It appears that "standing firm" is important to Paul. It is also important to these believers. Looking back, the entire epistle has been an encouragement to keep perspective and stand firm. His concluding exhortations stress at least six ways for this to be accomplished. He then closes his epistle with a gracious, final greeting.

* *Read Philippians 4:2–23 before you begin study in this chapter.*

Lesson 13.1   Exhortations: To Unity, Reconciliation, Rejoicing, and Generosity (4:2–5)

Objectives

13.1.1 Explain the problem that threatened the unity and stability of the church in Philippi.

13.1.2 Identify Paul's reasons for emphasizing rejoicing.

13.1.3 Compare the response of the unbeliever to the gentleness with which Paul instructs each believer to respond to all people.

Lesson 13.2   Exhortations: To Prayer and Positive Participation in Culture (4:6–9)

Objectives

13.2.1 Explain God's antidote for anxiety.

13.2.2 Explain how Paul recommends we influence our culture rather than letting it influence us in harmful ways.

13.2.3 Explain the relationship between obedience and peace.

Lesson 13.3   Thanksgiving and Final Greetings (4:10–23)

Objectives

13.3.1 Describe how giving can impact people in need.

13.3.2 Describe Paul's attitude toward money and possessions.

13.3.3 Explain how giving is partnering with others in ministry.

13.3.4 Explain how giving can be both a sacrifice and an investment.

13.3.5 Explain how Philippians 4:19 has been improperly applied and how it can be properly applied.

Exhortations to Unity, Reconciliation, Rejoicing, and Generosity (4:2–5)

Stability gives a sense of security. We admire people who stand firm: people who remain stable under pressure, people who are unwavering, individuals who cannot be bought, bribed, or intimidated. Is their strength the result of genetics or personality? Paul contended that it was a spiritual issue and emphasized that there were certain principles that contributed to a person's or church's stability. He claims that a forgiving, rejoicing, and generous spirit is essential for personal stability and for unity within the church.

Agreement Is Essential for Unity (4:2–3)

I am convinced the pursuit of spiritual stability is dependent on the character of our relationships within the church. Fellowship is a huge factor in maintaining stability. The church is a place of relationship, a place where lives intertwine with one another in the Lord. Here is a reliable spiritual principle: a high level of conflict within a church will generate instability in the personal lives of members of the congregation. This was the difficulty in Philippi.

The Tragedy: A Significant Disagreement

Two key church leaders, Euodia and Syntyche, had a significant disagreement. These ladies were probably *charter members* (as we would call it today) of this congregation. They had worked with Paul, probably in the founding of the church. But something had come between them. An issue had gotten so big they could not agree with each other, even in the Lord. It was apparently not a doctrinal issue that divided them (which, were it so, I believe Paul would have addressed directly and clearly so that all others would avoid the same problem); but, rather, a personal one. Today it might have been any one of the petty issues Satan capitalizes on to divide congregations: a position in the church, a decorating choice, a construction issue, perceived favoritism with children, an overlooked invitation. You name it; Satan uses it.

The Tone: An Urgent Appeal

Paul does not make an arbitrary demand. He makes a personal appeal. He uses the Greek word *parakaleo,* used here to mean beg, implore, entreat, or beseech. The fact that the Greek word is used twice emphasizes that both women were being appealed to directly and personally (O'Brien, 477–478).

The Proposed Solution: Reconciliation in the Lord

Only one solution was adequate. These two ladies needed to be reconciled to each other. Paul first appeals to their mutual relationship to Christ, "Agree," he says, "in the Lord" (v. 2). Then he asks a third, well-known and mutually respected, person in the church to serve as peacemaker to help bring them together. Some scholars believe the word translated "loyal yokefellow" (*syzygus*) is actually a proper name (Kent 1978, 150). Without help, their continued disagreement and malice toward each other would have a destructive impact on the body of Christ. Can you picture this graphic event? The letter is read to the congregation at Philippi. Euodia and Syntyche are present. Syzygus goes to each one, takes them by the hand, and there, in the healing context of the body of believers, reconciliation begins.

This passage suggests several principles that can be used to solve severe, interpersonal problems within the local church:

1. Appeal directly to the parties involved.
2. Do not be afraid to reveal your deep feelings about the situation.

13.1.1
OBJECTIVE
Explain the problem that threatened the unity and stability of the church in Philippi.

1 How does conflict between believers affect the church?

2 What suggestions did Paul recommend for ending the conflict between Euodia and Syntyche?

3 What principles can be drawn from this passage for solving interpersonal problems within a church?

3. Never take sides.

4. Realize the parties involved probably cannot resolve the issue without help.

5. A spiritual person that both parties respect needs to help them or be a *syzygus* to them.

6. Try to reconcile them within the redemptive atmosphere of the body.

I was party to a misunderstanding. Another Christian brother felt I had wronged him. I felt he had abused others and tried to destroy a ministry. We separated. We did not talk to each other. Time did not solve the problem—it never does. One day my telephone rang. It was a respected mutual friend. He appealed to me to make a phone call seeking healing to the relationship. I made the call, forgiveness was sought and given, and the destructive wound was healed. Thank God for a *syzygus*!

Rejoicing Brings Stability (4:4)

13.1.2
OBJECTIVE

Identify Paul's reasons for emphasizing rejoicing.

Joy is an essential aspect of the Christian life and is a critical component of the life of a healthy congregation.

The Object and Source of Our Rejoicing—The Lord

"The Lord is good and his love endures forever" (Psalm 100:5; 136). This statement appears over and over again in the Bible. It is a core statement about the character of God. Paul in his circumstances, the church in Philippi in theirs, and all of us in our circumstances, whatever they are, should rejoice "in the Lord" (v. 4).

4 What statement from the Bible sums up why we rejoice?

The Time of Our Rejoicing—Always

Paul does not simply say, "Rejoice at church on Sunday." He does not say to rejoice when things go well. He knows things will not always go well. He does not say rejoice during daily devotions. He knows there are twenty-four hours in a day. He does not say rejoice when the sun is shining and birds are singing. He knows clouds, rain, and storms will come. His advice? Rejoice in the Lord all the time.

5 When everything seemed to be going wrong for the Philippian congregation, what did Paul repeatedly urge them to do?

The Constant Reminder to Rejoice Is—"I Will Say It Again: Rejoice!"

This congregation faced many challenges. They were worried. What was happening to Paul? What had become of Epaphroditus? False teachers were within the church and adversaries were without. Petty disagreements, grumbling, complaining, and arguments were creating division. It was so easy to lose perspective. Paul felt it was time to emphasize again, "Rejoice in the Lord always. I will say it again: Rejoice!"

Dorothy served as custodian for our church. She was a spiritually stable person, one of the best adult Sunday school teachers a pastor could have. I was delighted to be at the church when Dorothy was cleaning it. Her strong contralto voice would fill the place with victorious song. It was not that things were always going well for Dorothy; they were not. She knew pain, deep disappointments, frustration, and discouragements. But she had discovered a secret: rejoicing in the Lord.

Generosity Is Necessary in Light of the Lord's Return (4:5)

13.1.3
OBJECTIVE

Compare the response of the unbeliever to the gentleness with which Paul instructs each believer to respond to all people.

We live in a society that tells us, "Stand up for yourself. If you do not, no one will." But that is not Paul's advice to the Philippian Christians. God's will for them was vastly different.

What Attitude Do Believers Need to Have Toward Others?

6 How did Paul instruct believers to respond to all people?

Paul writes, "Let your gentleness be evident to all" (4:5).

The word *gentleness* (Greek *epieikos*) is difficult to translate because of all the aspects of meaning that goes along with understanding the word. Terms such as *gentle*, *yielding*, *kind*, *forbearing*, and *lenient* all help express the meaning of the word (Kent 1978, 151). This character trait implies a humble, patient, steadfast attitude, able and willing to submit to injustice, disgrace, mistreatment, and provocation without responding in kind (1 Peter 2:18–23). It is characterized by a loftiness of spirit enabling one to bear trouble calmly, to disdain meanness and revenge, and to make sacrifices for worthy ends. The *Webster's New Collegiate Dictionary* defines the word **magnanimity** as the quality of liberality in bestowing gifts, or being extremely liberal and generous of spirit (691). This later term probably best captures all the context of meaning of gentleness in spirit of which Paul speaks (691). It is the spirit of generosity that should be an integral element of the Christian life.

With What People Should We Be Gentle?

7   What kind of people are difficult?

Paul says we are to show gentleness "to all people" (v. 5). We are to be gentle toward everyone—those who are easy to show this quality to and those who are not. Gentleness is a character trait of our Lord (Titus 3:3–7). He shows no favoritism and neither should we. Christians, following the example of their Savior (Luke 23:34), forgive wrongs, love their enemies, pray for those who abuse them, and call down God's blessing on their persecutors (Luke 6:27–36). They do not return evil for evil, but "overcome evil with good" (Romans 12:17–21).

Why Should We Be Gentle?

8   What reason did Paul give the Philippians for being gentle to others?

The reason all believers should be gentle is that "the Lord is near" (v. 5). Two possibilities exist for the interpretation of this phrase. The first is based upon Paul's apparent quotation of Psalm 145:18 and would indicate, "the Lord is near to all who call on him." The other possibility is that Paul is appealing for godly behavior in light of Jesus' soon return, much as Jesus did in Matthew 24:42–51. We cannot respond in kind to others, where evil is concerned. We need to respond in a Christ-like way in view of the Lord's soon return.

Corrie Ten Boom and her family hid Jews in their home during World War II. Their illegal activity (according to the laws of the controlling government) was discovered, and Corrie and her sister Bessie were sent to the German death camp, Ravensbruck. There Corrie watched many die, including her sister. Years later she told this story:

> It was 1947, and I'd come from Holland to defeated Germany with the message that God forgives. It was the truth that they needed most to hear in that bitter, bombed-out land. The solemn faces stared back at me, not quite daring to believe. And that's when I saw him, working his way forward against the others. It came back with a rush. The place was Ravensbruck, and the man who was making his way forward had been a guard—one of the most cruel guards.
>
> Now he was in front of me, hand thrust out. "A fine message, Fraulein. I was a guard there. I have become a Christian. I know that God has forgiven me for the cruel things I did there, but I would like to hear it from your lips as well. Fraulein,—again the hand came out—'will you forgive me?'"
>
> And I stood there—I whose sins had again and again needed to be forgiven—and could not forgive. "Jesus, help me," I prayed silently.
>
> "I forgive you, brother," I cried, "with all my heart." For a long moment we grasped each other's hands, the former guard and the former prisoner. I had never known God's love so intensely, as I did then. But even then, I realized it was not my love. I had tried, and did not have the power. It was the power of the Holy Spirit (Ten Boom, 53–55).

The love and grace of Jesus are needed within to respond out of this kind of attitude—this kind of heart. Our culture is intoxicated with rights. We worship our rights. But Christ is our example. He laid down His rights to serve others (Philippians 2:5–11). A miracle of inner transformation is needed before we can be reconcilers, before we can rejoice in every situation, and for us to be big-hearted enough to respond to injustice as Christ did. It takes Jesus at work by His Spirit. Have you invited Him within? Is he transforming your life into His likeness?

Exhortation to Prayer and Positive Participation in Culture (4:6–9)

At the beginning of his letter to the church in Philippi Paul had said, "Whatever happens, conduct yourselves in a manner worthy of the gospel of Christ. Then, whether I come and see you or only hear about you in my absence, I will know that you stand firm" (1:27). The theme of "standing firm" appears again at the end of the letter. Paul writes, "Therefore, my brothers, you whom I love and long for, my joy and crown, that is how you should stand firm in the Lord, dear friends" (4:1). Godly stability is important to Paul. He wants these believers to stand firm in the face of the problems they are facing. To enable them to do this, he instructs them to help reconcile two disputing parties, to rejoice in the Lord, and to be gentle in their relationships. In verses 6 through 9, Paul continues the exhortation to stand firm, telling them more godly ways to deal with the challenges of living in a pagan environment: prayer, positive involvement, and obedience.

Prayer Is God's Cure for Anxiety (4:6–7)

13.2.1
OBJECTIVE
Explain God's antidote for anxiety.

Anxiety is a destructive emotion that characterizes our age. It saps our strength, affects our emotions, and eats away at our internal organs. We use all kinds of things, from strenuous physical exercise, alcohol, medication, and therapy to deal with anxiety. In these verses, Paul gives us a biblical antidote to anxiety.

The Antidote to Anxiety: Do Not Worry

Paul urges, "Do not be anxious about anything" or "stop being anxious" (v. 6). This is the same expression used in Matthew 6:25 and 28 when Jesus tells us not to worry about "your life" in terms of food and clothes and such. When we are anxious, our minds are divided. We emotionally turn back and forth. Paul is not calling for apathy or inaction, but stressing that anxious concern is not God's will for a believer (O'Brien 1991, 491).

Replacement for Worry: Prayer

9   If you personally obey Paul's exhortation not to be anxious, what will be your focus instead?

The corresponding exhortation against worry is, "In everything, by prayer and petition, with thanksgiving, present your requests to God" (v. 6). Every situation that could cause anxiety is an opportunity for prayer. In fact, it could be argued that praying about the issues of life protects us from worry. Every circumstance, every relationship, every need are all legitimate objects of prayer. A casual reading of the Book of Acts reveals that early Christians prayed about everything.

Kind of Prayer: Continual and All-encompassing

10   What point is Paul making by using various terms for prayer?

Paul uses various terms for prayer: *Prayer* (*proseuche*), denoting a worshipful attitude in prayer; *petition* (*deesis*), denoting prayer as an expression of need; *requests* (*aitema*), referring to the things asked for; and thanksgiving (*eucharistias*), an expression of gratitude with which prayer should be saturated. All of the expressions point to the fact that believers should pray all the time about everything (Kent 1978, 152). Paul put it this way in Ephesians, "Pray in the Spirit on all occasions with all kinds of prayers and requests" (6:18).

The Accompaniment: Thanksgiving

Stability is not just dependent on the fact that we pray. How we pray is significant. We must learn to pray with thanks. But thanksgiving should not be viewed as an additive for prayer. It is not to be tacked on to our requests. Thanksgiving ought to be the spirit and atmosphere of our praying—the very context of prayer. This means prayer is saturated with thanksgiving.

The Promise: Peace

In place of anxiety comes prayer with thanksgiving, and Paul reminds believers, then and now, that the result will be "the peace of God, which transcends all understanding, will guard your hearts and minds in Christ Jesus" (4:7). This promised "peace of God" is beyond our comprehension. No counselor can give it, no therapist can provide it, no technique can produce it. It is not human peace; it is God's peace. When Paul says, "God's peace will guard your hearts and minds," he uses a military term that means to "stand guard" or "garrison" (Fee 1995, 411). *In Christ Jesus—w*hat a wonderful, secure place in which to be safely guarded!

Frank was dying and very agitated. His anxiety troubled his family deeply, so they called me to come pray with him. I walked into the room and Frank recognized me. I read Psalm 23 and we began to pray. He quieted like a baby and a few hours later slipped away to be with Jesus.

Brenda was five and facing a tonsillectomy. Early on Monday morning, before the surgery, I stopped to pray with her and her mom. As they wheeled her down the hall, I heard a little voice begin singing quietly, "It's so good to be in the arms of the Lord." Prayer is God's wonderful antidote for worry. You will feel better after you pray.

OBJECTIVE

Explain how Paul recommends we influence our culture rather than letting it influence us in harmful ways.

11 How can we be in the world, but not of the world as Jesus spoke of in John 17:11–19?

Positive Involvement in Culture Is Imperative for Victory (4:8)

The way we connect with our culture can be either positive and wholesome or negative and polluting to our minds, hearts, and emotions. Interestingly, the apostle Paul uses terminology in verse 8 that is not drawn from the life of the church. His language is characteristic of that used in popular moral philosophy of his day (O'Brien 1991, 502–503). It would have been familiar to the Philippians, philosophies they embraced before they followed Jesus. Paul, in effect, acknowledges that Christians cannot completely isolate themselves from culture. However, they must be discerning, dwelling upon thoughts and choosing activities characterized by moral excellence and worthy of praise (Fee 1995, 414).

Christians have always struggled with how to participate in the culture at large. Should we completely separate ourselves from the broader culture or participate fully in it? We find it difficult to know where and how to draw the line between the two extremes. How can we be in the world, but not of it (John 17:11–19)?

Choices are not always easy. On one hand we can so identify with our culture that we end up participating in its sin. On the other hand, if we totally abandon our culture, we leave it to be totally formed by evil influences. In other words, we cease to be salt and light (Matthew 5:13–16). If we are not careful, we lose our redemptive influence, fail our youth, and frustrate new Christians who are ready to reach out to their world in evangelism. We can so isolate ourselves that we fail to equip Christians to live as "ambassadors for Christ" and "citizens of heaven" within a pagan culture—two things Paul would disapprove of (cf. 2 Corinthians 5:18–20; Philippians 1:27; 3:20).

Paul's words provide wise advice. He affirms freedom for constructive engagement in culture with the instruction to fill our minds with and participate in things that are:

- true (true in character, morally upright)
- noble (honorable, lofty, majestic; not vulgar or ignoble)
- right (righteous in the broadest sense possible)
- pure (purity of thought and purpose as well as words and deeds)
- lovely (used only here in the New Testament, it has to do with those things that commend themselves by their intrinsic attractiveness; they give pleasure to all and cause distaste to none)
- admirable (what is likely to win approval and avoid offense)
- excellent (excellence of any kind; meritorious; well-done)
- praiseworthy (the kinds of thing God and humanity would approve of; O'Brien 1991, 503–506).

Attention, time, and effort given to these things will bring positive results.

I read a book, and although it was not religious in nature or theme, it was powerfully written, vivid in description, captivating in plot, and uplifting in its theme. I could not lay it down; I did not want to. I went to bed that night feeling good, in right relationship with God, clean and pure. I thought to myself, "*People need to write more stuff like that.*"

I turned on the television to watch the highly touted comedy with my family. A few minutes into the program I began to feel uncomfortable. Sexual innuendos began to surface. The characters used some filthy language and cursed a time or two. It was high time to deal with this. I got up, walked to the television, explained my problems with the program, and shut it off. It took several days to rid the garbage from my mind.

Paul was right; whatever is true, noble, right, pure, lovely, admirable, excellent, and praiseworthy, think on these things. Be a discerning Christian.

OBJECTIVE

Explain the relationship between obedience and peace.

12 What is the result of obeying Paul's teaching and example?

Obedience Is Important for Peace (4:9)

Paul's final exhortation is for believers to follow what they have learned from him, both his instructions and example. Putting into practice what we have learned brings a marvelous blessing. Not only do we receive the equivalent of the ancient Hebrew blessing "Shalom" (peace, security, well-being, abundant blessing), Paul assures us that the "God of peace" will be with us.

Eugene Peterson, translator of *The Message* has said, "The Christian life is going to God. In going to God, Christians travel the same ground that everyone else walks on, breathe the same air, drink the same water, shop in the same stores, read the same newspapers, are citizens under the same government, pay the same prices for groceries and gasoline, fear the same dangers, are subject to the same pressures, get the same distresses, are buried in the same ground. The difference is that each step we walk, each breath we breathe, we know we are preserved by God, we know we are accompanied by God, we know we are ruled by God" (Peterson 2000, 45).

Are you anxious or do you talk to Him about your concerns? Do His values govern what you do, where you go, what you read, what you watch, and what you listen to? Is following Him the purpose and passion of your life? Do you want it to be?

Thanksgiving and Final Greetings (4:10–23)

Money is a major issue in the lives of many people. Some complain, "All churches ever talk about is money." But analysis of such a statement reveals it is simply not true. What is interesting is to find that many who make such a claim are themselves preoccupied with money.

Paul kept money in perspective. He knew its place and realized its importance. He appreciated having it, but could get along without it. In fact, he learned some of life's greatest lessons when he had no money. He realized people and God's will were vastly superior to money.

Paul had already expressed his appreciation for the Philippians' long-term partnership with him in spreading the gospel (1:5). Now, at the close of this letter of friendship, he pauses to thank them specifically for sending Epaphroditus to meet his needs and bring a monetary gift. Paul's message reminds us that Christian generosity meets needs, demonstrates our priorities, insures God's promised provision, and prompts praise.

13.3.1
OBJECTIVE

Describe how giving can impact people in need.

Giving Prompts Praise (4:10, 18–20)

The church in Philippi had been faithful in remembering Paul in the past. But for a long period of time, he had not heard from them. No envelopes had come with a little something extra tucked inside. What rejoicing it brought when their gift arrived with Epaphroditus. It did much more than meet a financial need. Epaphroditus' presence and the money communicated their loving concern. The word Paul used here translated "renewed" is graphic. It is the language of the flower garden and literally means "to bloom again" (Martin 1959, 174) Paul said he realized that they had been concerned for him all along but they just had not been able to express it for various reasons.

13　How has someone's giving blessed you?

We have no idea how much letters and financial support mean to those involved in missionary work around the world. Testimonies abound about the sense of connection and loving concern such gifts communicate. They produce great rejoicing and a deep sense of partnership with those who send them.

My wife and I had gone forward for the prayer time. We were in need. It is tough having a family of six, attending seminary, and trying to make ends meet. We were about one hundred dollars short for the month. Bernard Johnson was the evening speaker at Central Assembly. He gave a word, saying that the need of someone who had come forward that evening was already met. For some reason, we made no connection between his statement and our situation. The next day, I returned from class to be met at the door by my young daughter. "Daddy, did you and Mom go forward at church last night because you needed money?" she asked. I answered, "Yes, Hon, that is why we went forward." She said, "Dad you need to go look on the kitchen table." I did and there was a check for one hundred dollars. A note read, "God told us to send this to you." It had been mailed four days before our Sunday services. What rejoicing. Giving prompts praise.

Describe Paul's attitude toward money and possessions.

Giving Helps Put Things in Perspective (4:11–13)

Paul testifies about a lesson he learned when facing a shortage of funds in prison. He wants the believers to know his comments are not prompted by need or motivated by a desire for more. Paul's language indicates he went through a painful and frustrating time when there was a lack of money and no communication from his friends. In fact, he uses the aorist tense, pointing to a particular time in the past, when in a moment, he suddenly became aware of a wonderful truth. He had learned to be "content whatever the circumstances" (v. 11). The word content used here was a favorite of Stoics. They systematically deprived themselves to prove their self-sufficiency (Keener 1993, 566). Mystery religions searched for techniques that would reveal the secret of the universe (Hawthorne 1983, 200). Paul said he learned a much better secret. He learned he could handle whatever life brought— lack or plenty, a full cupboard or an empty one, riches or poverty—through Christ who empowered him. Christ was his sufficiency, his satisfaction, and his security.

14   How could Paul's attitude toward money help you?

What a lesson. What a secret. Not many people can make that claim truthfully. Paul truly believed that God enabled him to deal with whatever circumstances life brought with contentment and rejoicing. We grumble and complain when we run short and become preoccupied with money and possessions when things go well. Our security, our satisfaction, and our joy are all too often tied to things. What have your circumstances taught you?

Explain how giving is partnering with others in ministry.

Giving Demonstrates Partnership in Ministry (4:14–16)

Giving is a good way to partner with someone in ministry. The Bible teaches: "Where your treasure is, there will your heart be also" (Matthew 6:21). The church in Philippi had a long-standing pattern of contributing to Paul's ministry. They were, in fact, the only church that had contributed in this way. They had been in partnership with Paul all the way, and he was grateful.

Have you demonstrated your partnership with your church in tithes and offerings? Have you partnered with a missionary or ministry to reach the lost and disciple them in obedience to the Great Commission? More than that, are you in partnership with God? Do you have a pattern of faithfulness like that of the believers in Philippi?

Explain how giving can be both a sacrifice and an investment.

Giving Is a Heavenly Investment and Pleasing Sacrifice (4:17–18)

At this point, Paul openly adopted the language of business and finance to make his point. He speaks of the gift the church in Philippi sent as being "credited to their account" (v. 17). He refers to "receiving full payment and more" (v. 18). Paul was not looking for anything personally. He was concerned about their heavenly account. He says that in a very real sense these believers have entered into a financial transaction with God. They have made deposits in heaven's bank. Have you invested where market fluctuations have no impact, where thieves cannot steal, where depreciation cannot eat away value, where disasters cannot destroy (cf. Matthew 6:19–20)? Have you entered into a financial transaction with God?

15   How is giving to the Lord's work an investment?

But Paul moves beyond financial terminology. He claims their giving is an act of worship. We may give money—what some have called filthy lucre—but giving to the Lord's work lifts our giving to a new level (Kent 1978, 156–157). It becomes "a fragrant offering, an acceptable sacrifice, pleasing to God" (v. 18).

16   In what sense is giving worship?

How thrilling to receive letters from missionaries working in difficult fields, reporting how people have been reached for Christ. They tell stories of bodies healed, miracles performed, and spiritual victories won. How gratifying to know that resources you sent helped plant churches and extend the Kingdom. In a very real sense, givers share in these victories. They are the return on a heavenly investment.

13.3.5
OBJECTIVE

Explain how Philippians 4:19 has been improperly applied and how it can be properly applied.

Giving Results in a Wonderful Promise of Provision (4:19)

Of all the verses in the Bible that have suffered indiscriminate application, this is probably one of the greatest. Many want to see this as a promise that says if they give, God will give them everything they want.

In context, this promise is a personal assurance, given under the inspiration of the Holy Spirit, to people who have given faithfully and sacrificially to the cause of Christ. Paul, the prisoner, tells the Philippian believers that God will do what he, Paul, cannot do. God will fully meet every need they have. And God will do it, Paul says, in keeping with His glorious riches provided for in Christ Jesus. Their sacrificial generosity toward him will be exceeded by the lavish "wealth" poured out on them by the eternal God, creator of heaven and earth.

17 How has Philippians 4:19 been improperly applied in the past and how can it be legitimately applied?

Gordon Fee captures the inspiring power of this promise:

These kinds of exquisite moments call for worship because all of our analogies and metaphors are too impoverished to try to catch the sense. One thinks of Annie Johnson Flint's words:

"His love has no limit

His grace has no measure,

His power has no boundary known unto men,

For out of His infinite riches in Jesus,

He giveth, and giveth, and giveth again."

Wrap up all the personal moments of 'riches' into one (the small boy given full rein in the ice cream shoppe; landing on a patch of wild blackberries so full that one could not pick them all in a day; finding pool upon pool of 18- to 24-inch trout in an unfished stream in the Sierra Nevada Mountains; and many such experiences) and one can only catch a faint glimmer of what Paul is here recognizing of God's wealth and lavish love for His people—expressed to the full in Christ Jesus." (Fee 1995, 453)

This reality prompts Paul to explode in a doxology: "To our God and Father be glory for ever and ever. Amen" (4:20).

Paul closes this letter by sending greetings from Rome and the believers there. His final greeting is to every saint "in Christ Jesus." These churches are linked, along with all others, across cultural, economic, racial, and social barriers. His final greeting comes from his ministry associates and all the saints in Rome. Verse 22 is especially noteworthy because of its mention of Caesar's household. It points back to the beginning of this letter where Paul describes how God has used Paul's imprisonment to open a door to Caesar's household through the "whole palace guard" (cf. 1:12–13). How marvelous are God's ways. Paul started the letter by greeting them with the words "grace and peace to you." He ends by saying, "The grace of the Lord Jesus Christ be with your spirit. Amen" (v. 23). The apostle Paul understood the Christian life as grace—beginning to end.

Test Yourself

Circle the letter of the *best* answer.

1. Who were two key church leaders who had worked alongside Paul, but were now in sharp disagreement?
a) Clement and Euodia
b) Euodia and Syntyche
c) Tychicus and Euodia
d) Clement and Syntyche

2. According to Philippians 4:4, how often are believers instructed to rejoice in the Lord?
a) Often
b) Daily
c) Always
d) When the need arises

3. The believers at Philippi were losing perspective due to
a) severe persecution and hardship.
b) wealth and prosperity.
c) in fighting, outward attacks, and petty disagreements.
d) false teaching concerning the second coming of Christ.

4. How is the Greek word *epieikos* translated in English?
a) "Gentleness"
b) "Affectionate"
c) "Loving"
d) "Self-controlled"

5. Words that Paul uses in connection with prayer in Philippians include all of the following EXCEPT
a) petition.
b) confession.
c) requests.
d) thanksgiving.

6. What is Paul's cure for anxiety based upon Philippians 4:6?
a) Trust in the Lord.
b) Stay busy doing the Lord's work.
c) Practice positive thinking techniques.
d) Pray to God with thanksgiving.

7. Based upon Philippians 4:7, what will God's peace guard?
a) Heart
b) Emotions
c) Mind
d) Heart and mind

8. What eight things are believers to think about? Things that are
a) holy, honest, noble, pleasant, admirable, excellent, praiseworthy, and right.
b) true, noble, right, pure, lovely, admirable, excellent, and praiseworthy.
c) admirable, excellent, praiseworthy, honest, pleasant, right, and lovely.
d) true, admirable, noble, pleasant, honest, lovely, right, and praiseworthy.

9. In Philippians 4:10, Paul greatly rejoiced
a) in the salvation of the Philippian believers.
b) that Christ was being preached throughout the palace guard.
c) that the church in Philippi renewed concern for him.
d) in his trials and imprisonment.

10. The key to contentment is
a) being well-fed.
b) financial security.
c) Christ, who provides security and satisfaction for the believer.
d) ideal circumstances.

Responses to Interactive Questions

Chapter 13

Some of these responses may include information that is supplemental to the IST. These questions are intended to produce reflective thinking beyond the course content and your responses may vary from these examples.

1 How does conflict between believers affect the church?

A high level of conflict within a church will generate instability in the personal lives of members of the congregation.

2 What suggestions did Paul recommend for ending the conflict between Euodia and Syntyche?

The two ladies needed to be reconciled to each other. Paul first appeals to their mutual relationship to Christ. Then he asks a third, well-known and mutually respected, person in the church to serve as peacemaker to help bring them together.

3 What principles can be drawn from this passage for solving interpersonal problems within a church?

Several important principles can be used to solve interpersonal problems within the local church:

- Appeal directly to the parties involved.
- Do not be afraid to reveal your deep feelings about the situation.
- Never take sides.
- Realize the parties involved probably cannot resolve the issue without help.
- A spiritual person whom both parties respect needs to help them (i.e., be a *Syzygus* to them).
- Try to reconcile them within the redemptive atmosphere of the Body.

4 What statement from the Bible sums up why we rejoice?

"The Lord is good and his love endures forever" (Psalm 100:5; 136). This statement appears over and over again in the Bible. It is a core statement about the character of God.

5 When everything seemed to be going wrong for the Philippian congregation, what did Paul repeatedly urge them to do?

Paul emphasized: "Rejoice in the Lord always. I will say it again: Rejoice!"

6 How did Paul instruct believers to respond to all people?

Paul wrote, "Let your gentleness be evident to all" (4:5). This character trait implies a humble, patient, steadfast attitude, able to submit to injustice, disgrace, mistreatment, and provocation without responding in kind. It is characterized by a loftiness of spirit enabling one to bear trouble calmly, to disdain meanness and revenge, and to make sacrifices for worthy ends.

7 What kind of people are difficult?

Answers will vary.

8 What reason did Paul give the Philippians for being gentle to others?

The answer Paul gives is this: because "the Lord is near." Two possibilities exist for the interpretation of this phrase. The first is based on Paul's apparent quotation of Psalm 145:18 and would indicate that "the Lord is near to all who call on him." The other possibility is that Paul is appealing for godly behavior in light of Jesus' soon return.

9 If you personally obey Paul's exhortation not to be anxious, what will be your focus instead?

Answers will vary.

10 What point is Paul making by using various terms for prayer?

Paul uses various terms for prayer due to the fact that believers should pray all the time about everything.

11 How can we be in the world, but not of the world as Jesus spoke of in John 17:11–19?

Paul provides wise advice. He says we can stay pure and interact with our culture by filling our minds with things that are true (true in character, morally upright), noble (honorable, lofty, majestic; not vulgar or ignoble), right (righteous in the broadest sense possible), pure (purity of thought and purpose as well as words and deeds), lovely (things that give pleasure to all and cause distaste to none), admirable (likely to win approval and avoid offense), excellent (excellence of any kind; meritorious; well–done), and praiseworthy (the kinds of things God and people would approve).

12 What is the result of obeying Paul's teaching and example?

Putting into practice what we have learned brings a marvelous blessing. Not only do we receive the equivalent of the ancient Hebrew blessing Shalom (peace, security, well-being, abundant blessing), Paul assures us that the God of peace will be with us.

13 How has someone's giving blessed you?

Answers will vary.

14 How could Paul's attitude toward money help you?

Answers will vary.

15 How is giving to the Lord's work an investment?

Paul speaks of the gift the church in Philippi sent as being "credited to their account."

These believers have entered into a financial transaction with God. They have made deposits in heaven's bank.

16 In what sense is giving worship?

Giving to the Lord's work lifts our giving to a new level. It becomes "a fragrant offering, an acceptable sacrifice, pleasing to God."

17 How has Philippians 4:19 been improperly applied in the past and how can it be legitimately applied?

Many want to see this verse as a promise that if they give, God will give them everything they want. In context, this promise is a personal assurance, given under the inspiration of the Holy Spirit, to people who have given faithfully and sacrificially to the cause of Christ. Paul, the prisoner, tells the Philippian believers that God will do what he, Paul, cannot do. God will fully meet every need they have.

UNIT PROGRESS EVALUATION 3 AND FINAL EXAMINATION

You have now concluded all of the work in this independent-study textbook. Review the lessons in this unit carefully, and then answer the questions in the last unit progress evaluation (UPE). When you have completed the UPE, check your answers with the answer key provided in Essential Course Materials at the back of this IST. Review any items you may have answered incorrectly. Review for the final examination by studying the course objectives, lesson objectives, self-tests, and UPEs. Review any lesson content necessary to refresh your memory. If you review carefully and are able to fulfill the objectives, you should have no difficulty passing the closed-book final examination.

Glossary

Chapter

atone	— to give satisfaction for wrongdoing; to make amends	2
corporate	— relating to a unified body of individuals	1
eschatological	— having to do with the end times	5
esoteric knowledge	— knowledge that is designed for or understood by the specially initiated alone	1
imperative	— the mood of a verb in giving commands; in the sentence *Go home*, the word *go* is in the imperative mood	5
indicative	— the mood of a verb in stating a fact; in the sentence *He went to school*, the word *went* is in the indicative mood	5
koinonia	— a Greek term that means "true fellowship and sharing"	4
legalism	— excessive conformity to a rigid set of rules and regulations	1
magnanimity	— liberality in bestowing gifts; extremely liberal and generous of spirit	13
mood	— the form of a verb that often shows whether it is expressing a fact (indicative); a command (imperative) or a potential action (subjunctive)	5
motif	— a theme or an idea that is developed or repeated in literature, art, or music	5
philosophy	— the study of human thought about the meaning of life, issues of right and wrong, the relationship of mind to matter, etc.; a theory or analysis of the principles that result in attitudes, beliefs, values, or view of reality.	2
reconcile	— to change from enmity to friendship, to be friendly again, to bring back to harmony; in an individual's life, the removing of the barrier of sin so that one can be united with his or her Creator.	2
reconciliation	— the change from enmity to friendship, that restores harmony.	2
restoration	— the return to a former condition; to give back; to mend.	4
submission	— yielding voluntarily to another; not demanding one's own way; can also mean identifying with or attaching to (Grady 2000, 177–79).	1
sufficiency	— all that is needed; enough.	1
supremacy	— the quality of being highest in rank, power, or authority.	1
syncretism	— the combining of ideas and beliefs of various religions resulting in a new belief system.	1
trinitarian	— having to do with the Trinity: One God existing in three Persons—the Father, the Son, and the Holy Spirit.	5

Reference List

Arnold, C. E. 1993. Ephesus. *Dictionary of Paul and His Letters*. eds. Gerald F. Hawthorne and Ralph P. Martin. Downers Grove, IL: InterVarsity Press. 249–253.

Barth, Marcus. 1974. *Ephesians: Introduction, Translation, and Commentary,* vol. 1. Garden City, NY: Doubleday.

Barton, Bruce B., et al. 1995. *Philippians, Colossians, Philemon*. Life Application Bible Commentary, eds. Grant Osborne and Philip Comfort. Wheaton, IL: Tyndale House Publishers.

Bascom, Tim. 1993. *The Comfort Trap: Spiritual Dangers in the Convenience Culture*. Downers Grove, IL: Intervarsity.

Borthwick, Christie, and Paul Borthwick. 2001. Don't Give Up on Your Family. *Discipleship Journal*. http://www.navpress.com/EPubs/Display/Article/1/1.126.9.html.

Brauch, Manfred T. 2009. *Abusing Scripture.* Downers Grove, IL: IVP Academic.

Bruce, F. F. 1984. *The Epistles to the Colossians, to Philemon, and to the Ephesians.* The New International Commentary on the New Testament. Grand Rapids, MI: Eerdmans.

Colson, Charles, and Ellen Vaughn. 2003. Being the Body. Nashville, TN: W Publishing.

Dunn, James D. G. 1998. *The Theology of Paul the Apostle*. Grand Rapids, MI: Eerdmans.

Einstein, Albert. n.d. Quoted in Citater Fra, http://www.fys.ku.dk/`raben/einstein. (accessed July 15, 2005).

Elliot, Elisabeth. 1958. *Shadow of the Almighty*. San Francisco: Harper and Row.

Erickson, Millard J. 1986. *Concise Dictionary of Christian Theology*. Grand Rapids, MI: Baker Book House.

Fee, Gordon D. 1994. *God's Empowering Presence: The Holy Spirit in the Letters of Paul*. Peabody, MA: Hendrickson.

———. 1995. *Paul's Letter to the Philippians*. The New International Commentary on the New Testament. Grand Rapids, MI: Eerdmans.

———. 2002. "The Cultural Context of Ephesians." *Priscilla Papers* 16, no. 1 (winter): 4, 6.

Fee, Gordon, and Douglas Stuart. 1993. *How to Read the Bible for All Its Worth*. 2nd ed. Grand Rapids, MI: Zondervan.

Fenelon, Francois. *The Seeking Heart*. Christian Books Publishing, 1992.

Foulkes, Francis. 1979. *The Epistle of Paul to the Ephesians*. Tyndale New Testament Commentaries, ed. R. V. G. Tasker. Grand Rapids, MI; Eerdmans.

Frazee, Randy. 2001. Uncommon Confessions. Unpublished sermon. Pantego Bible Church. Arlington, TX.

Gill, Deborah M., and Barbara Cavaness. 2004. *God's Women Then and Now*. Springfield, MO: Grace & Truth.

Gingrich, Wilbur F. 1983. *Shorter Lexicon of the Greek New Testament*, 2nd ed., rev. Frederick W. Danker. Chicago, IL: University of Chicago Press.

Grady, J. Lee. 2000. 10 *Lies the Church Tells Women*. Lake Mary, FL: Charisma House.

Grant, David. 2004. Unpublished sermon, October 3, Cedar Hill, TX: Trinity Church.

Gundry, Patricia. 1980. *Heirs Together*. Grand Rapids, MI: Zondervan.

Gundry, Robert H. 1994. *A Survey of the New Testament*. 3d ed. Grand Rapids, MI: Zondervan.

Gupton, Kay Lawing. 1998. Finding Forgiveness. *Today's Christian Woman*. September/October: 70.

Guthrie, Donald. 1990. *New Testament Introduction*. rev. Downers Grove, IL: InterVarsity Press.

Hawthorne, Gerald F. 1983. *Philippians*. Vol. 43 of Word Biblical Commentary. Waco, TX: Word Books, 1983.

Hull, Gretchen Gaebelein. 1987. *Equal to Serve*. Grand Rapids, MI: Baker Books.

Keener, Craig S. 1993. *The IVP Bible Background Commentary: New Testament*. Downers Grove, IL: InterVarsity Press.

Kent, Homer A. Jr. 1978. *Philippians*. Vol. 11 of The Expositor's Bible Commentary. ed. Frank E. Gaebelein. Grand Rapids, MI: Zondervan. 93–159.

King, Martin Luther, Jr., 1998. *A Knock at Midnight*: *Inspiration from the Great Sermons of Reverend Martin Luther King, Jr.* Edited by Clayborne Carson and Peter Holloran. New York: Warner Books.

Kittel, Gerhard and Gerhard Friedrich, eds. 1985. *Theological Dictionary of the New Testament*, abridged. Trans. Geoffrey W. Bromiley. Grand Rapids, MI: Eerdmans.

Kruger, J., and Dunning, D. 1999. Unskilled and Unaware of It: How Difficulties in Recognizing One's Own Incompetence Lead to Inflated Self-Assessments. *Journal of Personality and Social Psychology* 77: 1121–1134.

Ladd, George Eldon. 1974. *A Theology of the New Testament*. Grand Rapids, MI: Eerdmans.

Lehman, F. M. 1976. *Hymns for the Family of God*. ed. Fred Bock. Nashville: Paragon Associates.

Lightfoot, J. B. 1876. *St. Paul's Epistles to the Colossians and to Philemon*. London: Macmillan.

Marshall, I. Howard. 2005. Mutual Love and Submission in Marriage in *Discovering Biblical Equality: Complimentary without Hierarchy*, edited by Ronald W. Pierce, Rebecca Merrill Groothuis, and Gordon D. Fee, 186–204. Downers Grove, IL: InterVarsity Press.

Martin, Ralph P. 1959. *The Epistle of Paul to the Philippians*. Tyndale New Testament Commentaries. Grand Rapids, MI: Eerdmans.

Muller, Jac. J. 1955. *The Epistles of Paul to the Philippians and to Philemon*. The New International Commentary on the New Testament. Grand Rapids, MI: Eerdmans.

Neven, Tom. 2000. A Doer of the Word. *Focus on the Family Magazine*, September. http://www.family.org/fofmag/Pf/a0026162.cfm (accessed July 13, 2005).

Noonan, Peggy. 2004. Keeping the Faith: An Interview with Mel Gibson. Interview by Peggy Nonnan. *Reader's Digest* (March 2004): 89–91.

Oates, Stephen B. 1977. *With Malice Toward None: A life of Abraham Lincoln*. New York: Harper & Row.

O'Brien, Peter T. 1982. *Colossians, Philemon*. Word Biblical Commentary. Vol. 44, ed. David A. Hubbard and Glenn W. Barker. Waco, TX: Word Books.

———. 1991. *The Epistle to the Philippians*. The New International Greek Testament Commentary, eds. I. Howard Marshall and W. Ward Gasque. Grand Rapids, MI: Eerdmans.

———. 1993. Mystery. In *Dictionary of Paul and His Letters*. ed. Gerald F. Hawthorne and Ralph P. Martin. Downers Grove, IL: InterVarsity Press. 621–623.

———. 1993. The Letter to the Colossians. In *Dictionary of Paul and His Letters*, ed. Gerald F. Hawthorne, Ralph P. Martin, and Daniel G. Reid. Downers Grove, IL: InterVarsity Press.

Opperwall, N. J. 1988. Subject. In *The International Standard Bible Encyclopedia*, Vol. 4. ed. Geoffrey W. Bromiley. Grand Rapids, MI: Eerdmans. 643–644.

Patzia, Arthur, G. 1993. Philemon. In *Dictionary of Paul and His Letters*, ed. Gerald F. Hawthorne and Ralph P. Martin. Downers Grove, IL: InterVarsity Press. 703–707.

Peterson, Eugene. 1980. *A Long Obedience in the Same Direction:Discipleship in an Instant Society*. Downers Grove, IL: InterVarsity Press.

————. 2000. *A Long Obedience in the Same Direction*. Downers Grove, IL: InterVarsity Press.

Price, Alan. n.d. Letter from Slain Missionary. As adapted in PreachingToday.com/Christianity Today International. http://www.preachingtoday.com/index.taf?_UserReference=5926A24E7E8531464113939F (accessed August 8, 2004).

Rees, Thomas. 1979. Adoption. In *The International Standard Bible Encyclopedia*, Vol. 1, ed. Geoffrey W. Bromiley. Grand Rapids, MI: Eerdmans. 53–55.

Rienecker, Fritz. 1980. *A Linguistic Key to the Greek New Testament*, ed. Cleon Rogers, Jr., Grand Rapids, MI: Zondervan.

Robertson, A. T. 1931. *Word Pictures in the New Testament*. Vol. 4. Nashville, TN: Broadman Press.

Rossier, Bernard. 1989. The Epistle of Paul to the Ephesians. Vol. 8. In *Complete Biblical Library: New Testament Study Bible,* Vol. 8, eds. Ralph W. Harris and Stanley M. Horton. Springfield, MO: World Library Press, 95–177.

Rupprecht, Arthur A. 1978. *Philemon*. In *The Expositor's Bible Commentary*, Vol. 11. ed. Frank E. Gaebelein. Grand Rapids, MI: Zondervan. 451–464.

Salmond, S. D. F. 1956. The Epistle to the Ephesians. In *The Expositors Greek Testament*, Vol. 3. ed. Grand Rapids, MI: Eerdmans.

Sheridan, Chris. 2009. Tales of the Admirable Admiral. ESPN NBA. http://sports.espn.go.com/nba/halloffame09/columns/story?page=090910robinsonHOF (Accessed December 4, 2014).

Strobel, Lee and Jane Vogel. 2001. The Case for Christ: A Journalist's Personal Investigation of the Evidence for Jesus. Grand Rapids, MI: Zondervan.

Ten Boom, Corrie. 1978. Tramp for the Lord. As Adapted in PreachingToday.com/Christianity Today International. http://www.preachingtoday.com/index.taf?.

Vajnar, Jane. 2004. Kids of the Kingdom. Christian Reader. As adapted in PreachingToday.com/Christianity Today International. http://www.preachingtoday.com/index.taf?.

Vaughan, Curtis. 1978. Colossians. In *The Expositor's Bible Commentary*, Vol. 11, ed. Frank E. Gaebelein. Grand Rapids, MI: Zondervan. 161–226.

Vine's Expository Dictionary of New Testament Word, in PCStudy Bible CD-ROM. 1985. Advanced Reference Library TM Version 4. Biblesoft, Inc. Seattle, WA: Thomas Nelson Publishers.

Watson, Karen. 2004. Quoted in Curry, Erin, Keep Sending Missionaries, BP News. http://www.bpnews.net/PrinterFriendlyArticle.asp?ID=17918.

Wilson, Grady. 1984. *Count It All Joy*. Nashville: Broadman & Holman Publishers.

Wood, A. Skevington. 1978. Ephesians. In *The Expositor's Bible Commentary*, vol. 11., ed. Frank E. Gaebelein. Grand Rapids, MI: Zondervan, 1–92.

Yancey, Phillip. 1997. *What's So Amazing About Grace?* Grand Rapids, MI: Zondervan.

Youngblood, Ronald F. 1986. Peace. In *The International Standard Bible Encyclopedia*, Vol. 3, ed. Geoffrey W. Bromiley. Grand Rapids, MI: Eerdmans. 731–733.

 # Additional Resources

Bailey, Kenneth E. 2009. *Jesus Through Middle Eastern Eyes: Cultural Studies in the Gospels*. Downers Grove, IL: IVP Academic.

Bilezikian, Gilbert. 2006. *Beyond Sex Roles: What the Bible Says about a Woman's Place in the Church and Family*, 3rd ed. Grand Rapids, MI: Baker Academic.

Birkey, Del. 2005. *The Fall of Patriarchy: Its Broken Legacy Judged by Jesus & the Apostolic House Church Communities.* Tuscon, AZ: Fenstra Books®.

deSilva, David A. 2009. *Honor, Patronage, Kinship & Purity: Unlocking New Testament Culture*. Downers Grove, IL: IVP Academic.

Payne, Philip B. *Man and Woman, One in Christ: An Exegetical and Theological Study of Paul's Letters.* 2009. Grand Rapids, MI: Zondervan.

Essential Course Materials

CONTENTS

CHECKLIST OF MATERIALS TO BE SUBMITTED TO BEREAN SCHOOL OF THE BIBLE

at Global University; 1211 South Glenstone Avenue; Springfield, Missouri, 65804; USA:

❑ Service Learning Requirement Report (required)
❑ Round-Tripper Forms (as needed)
❑ Request for a Printed Final Examination (if needed)

Service Learning Requirement Assignment

BEREAN SCHOOL OF THE BIBLE
SLR INSTRUCTIONS

This Service Learning Requirement (SLR) assignment requires you to apply something you have learned from this course in a ministry activity. Although this assignment does not receive a grade, it is required. You will not receive credit for this course until you submit the satisfactorily completed SLR Report Form. This form will not be returned to you.

Seriously consider how you can design and complete a meaningful ministry* activity as an investment in preparing to fulfill God's calling on your life. If you are already involved in active ministry, plan how you can incorporate and apply something from this course in your ongoing ministry activity. Whether or not full-time ministry is your goal, this assignment is required and designed to bring personal enrichment to all students. Ask the Holy Spirit to guide your planning and completion of this ministry exercise.

> *   Meaningful ministry is defined as an act whereby you give of yourself in such a way as to meet the needs of another or to enhance the well-being of another (or others) in a way that exalts Christ and His kingdom.

You will complete the SLR by following these instructions:

1. Complete a ministry activity of your choice that you develop according to the following criteria:
   a. Your ministry activity must occur during your enrollment in this course. Do not report on activities or experiences in which you were involved prior to enrolling in this course.
   b. Your ministry activity must apply something you learned in this course, or it must incorporate something from this course's content in some way. Provide chapter, lesson, or page number(s) from the independent-study textbook on which the activity is based.
   c. Your ministry activity must include interacting with at least one other person. You may choose to interact with an individual or a group.
   d. The activity you complete must represent meaningful ministry*. You may develop your own ministry activity or choose from the list of suggestions provided in these instructions.
   e. Consider a ministry activity outside your comfort zone such as sharing the message of salvation with unbelievers or offering loving assistance to someone you do not know well.

2. Then fill out the SLR Report Form following these instructions OR online by accessing the online course. Students who will take the final exam online are encouraged to complete the online report form.

3. Sincere reflection is a key ingredient in valid ministry and especially in the growth and development of your ministry knowledge and effectiveness.

4. Global University faculty will evaluate your report. Although the SLR does not receive a grade, it must be completed to the faculty's satisfaction before a final grade for the course is released. The faculty may require you to resubmit an SLR Report Form for several reasons, including an incomplete form, apparent insincerity, failing to interact with others, and failure to incorporate course content.

Do NOT submit your SLR notes, essays, or other documents; only submit your completed SLR Report Form. No prior approval is needed as long as the activity fulfills the criteria from number one above.

Suggested SLR Ministry Activities

You may choose to engage in any valid and meaningful ministry experience that incorporates this specific course's content and interacts with other people. The following list of suggestions is provided to help you understand the possible activities that will fulfill this requirement. Choose an idea that will connect well with your course material. You may also develop a ministry activity that is not on this list or incorporate content from this course in ministry activity in which you are actively involved at this time:

* Teach a class or small group of any size.
* Preach a sermon to any size group.
* Share the gospel with non-believers; be prepared to develop new relationships to open doors to this ministry. We strongly encourage you to engage in ministry that may be outside your comfort zone.
* Lead a prayer group experience or pray with individual(s) in need, perhaps over an extended period.
* Disciple new believers in their walk with Jesus.
* Interview pastors, missionaries, or other leaders on a topic related to something in your course (do not post or publish interview content).
* Intervene to help resolve personal conflicts.
* Personally share encouragement and resources with those in need.
* Organize and/or administer a church program such as youth ministry, feeding homeless people, transporting people, visiting hospitals or shut-ins, nursing home services, etc.
* Assist with starting a new church.
* Publish an online blog or an article in a church newsletter (include a link in your report to the content of your article or blog).
* For MIN327 only: present a summary of risk management to a church board or other leadership group; interview community business people regarding their opinion of church business practices.

To review sample SLR Reports and to access an online report form, go to this Web address: library. globaluniversity.edu. Navigate to the Berean School of the Bible Students link under "Quick Link." Another helpful resource is our GlobalReach Web site: www.globalreach.org. From that site you can download materials free of charge from Global University's School for Evangelism and Discipleship. These proven evangelism tools are available in many languages.

BSB SERVICE LEARNING REQUIREMENT (SLR) REPORT

Please print or type your responses on this form, and submit the form to Berean School of the Bible. Do not submit other documents. This report will not be returned to you.

BIB117 Prison Epistles: Colossians, Philemon, Ephesians, and Philippians, Third Edition

Your Name.. **Student Number** .... **Date** ....

1. Ministry activity date .... **Description of ministry activity and its content:** Briefly describe your ministry activity in the space provided. (You are encouraged to engage in ministry such as sharing your faith with unbelievers, or other activities that may be outside your comfort zone.)

....

....

....

Identify related course content by chapter, lesson, or page number. ....

....

2. Results: What resulted from your own participation in this activity? Include descriptions of people's reactions, decisions to accept Christ, confirmed miracles, Spirit and water baptisms, life changes, etc. Describe the individuals or group who benefited from or participated in your ministry activity. Use numbers to describe results when appropriate (approximate when unsure).

....

....

....

....

Record numbers here: Unbelievers witnessed to?...................... New decisions for Jesus?......................

Holy Spirit baptisms?...................... Other?...

3. Reflection: Answer the following questions based on your experience in completing this assignment:

Did this activity satisfy an evident need in others? How so? ....

....

Were you adequately prepared to engage in this activity? Why or why not? ....

....

What positive or negative feelings were you aware of while you were completing this activity? ....

....

In what ways were you aware of the Holy Spirit's help during your ministry activity? ....

....

What would you change if you did this ministry activity again? ....

....

What strengths or weaknesses within yourself did this assignment reveal to you?.......................................

....

Did you receive feedback about this activity? If so, describe: ....

....

....

Unit Progress Evaluation Instructions

The unit progress evaluations (UPEs) are designed to indicate how well you learned the material in each unit. This may indicate how well prepared you are to take the closed-book final examination.

Taking Your Unit Progress Evaluations

1. Review the lessons of each unit before you take its unit progress evaluation (UPE). Refer to the form Checklist of Study Methods in the How to Use Berean Courses section at the front of the IST.

2. Answer the questions in each UPE without referring to your course materials, Bible, or notes.

3. Look over your answers carefully to avoid errors.

4. Check your answers with the answer keys provided in this section. Review lesson sections pertaining to questions you may have missed. Please note that the UPE scores do not count toward your course grade. They may indicate how well you are prepared to take the closed-book final examination.

5. Enter the date you completed each UPE on the Student Planner and Record form, located in the How to Use Berean Courses section in the front of this IST.

6. Request a printed final examination **if** you cannot take the final examination online. You should do this a few weeks before you take the last unit progress evaluation so that you will be able to take the final examination without delay when you complete the course.

UNIT PROGRESS EVALUATION 1

BIB117 Prison Epistles: Colossians, Philemon, Ephesians, and Philippians, Third Edition
(Unit 1—Chapter 1–4)

MULTIPLE CHOICE QUESTIONS

Select the best answer to each question.

1. Which books of the Bible are known as the prison or captivity letters?
   a) Galatians, Philippians, Ephesians, and Colossians
   b) Ephesians, Philippians, Colossians, and Philemon
   c) Galatians, Ephesians, Titus, and 2 Timothy
   d) Ephesians, Philippians, Colossians, and 2 Timothy

2. The Book of Colossians addresses many of the same issues as
   a) Philippians.
   b) Ephesians.
   c) Galatians.
   d) 2 Timothy.

3. The false teaching at Colosse was based upon
   a) human philosophy and legalistic practices.
   b) greed and selfish ambition.
   c) the undermining influence of the Judaizers.
   d) Greek mythology.

4. Paul's answer to the false teaching and error at the Colossian church was
   a) to avoid idolatry and pagan practices.
   b) forgiveness and restoration.
   c) the supremacy and sufficiency of Christ.
   d) to rejoice in the Lord at all times.

5. Based upon Paul's prayer in Colossians 1, effective intercessory prayer is
   a) loud, intense, and continual.
   b) corporate, intense, and serious.
   c) private, serious, and filled with concern for others.
   d) corporate, continual, and filled with concern for others.

6. In Colossians 1, Paul's prayer for the believers in Colosse was that they be filled with
   a) the knowledge of God's will and live a life pleasing before God.
   b) the Holy Spirit and power.
   c) love for each other.
   d) knowledge, wisdom, and joy in the Holy Spirit.

7. In Colossians 1, Paul refers to Jesus as the
   a) first and the last.
   b) author and perfecter of our faith.
   c) soon coming King.
   d) firstborn over all creation.

8. In Colossians 1, Paul wants to establish the
   a) priesthood of Christ.
   b) supremacy of Christ.
   c) humanity of Christ.
   d) divinity of Christ.

9. What was the mystery that Paul referred to in Colossians 1:26–27?
   a) Secret knowledge about God only known to Paul
   b) That God wants to make salvation known to all people, through Christ
   c) Believers are justified by faith alone
   d) That Christ was returning soon

10. According to Colossians 1:28–2:5, bringing believers to maturity includes
    a) encouraging their hearts and helping them resist deception.
    b) reaching the lost and encouraging their hearts.
    c) building relationships with the unsaved and proclaiming to them the mystery of Christ.
    d) having good programs and fellowship.

11. What is an outward sign that signifies a believer's spiritual rebirth?
    a) Circumcision
    b) Water baptism
    c) Communion
    d) Confirmation

12. A key word Paul uses in Colossians is fullness, which he uses to emphasize the
    a) humanity of Christ.
    b) love of Christ.
    c) compassion of Christ.
    d) sufficiency of Christ.

13. Mysticism is the pursuit of
   a) legalism.
   b) knowledge and academic excellence.
   c) a higher and deeper religious experience through subjective means.
   d) self-denial in attempt to reach a higher religious experience.

14. In Colossians 3, Paul uses the analogy of
   a) sowing and reaping.
   b) taking off soiled clothes, replacing them with new spiritual garments.
   c) running a race.
   d) darkness and light.

15. According to Colossians 3, what are believers instructed to do with the deeds of their earthly nature?
   a) Flee from them
   b) Avoid them
   c) Put them to death
   d) Triumph over them

16. In Colossians 3, Paul's instruction to children is to
   a) obey their parents.
   b) listen to their parents.
   c) submit to their parents.
   d) serve their parents.

17. In Colossians 3, Paul's instruction to fathers is to
   a) discipline their children.
   b) control their children.
   c) not embitter or discourage their children.
   d) love their children.

18. In Colossians 4, Paul instructs believers to devote themselves to
   a) prayer.
   b) generous giving.
   c) serving one another.
   d) loving one another.

19. Tychicus was a person with a
   a) past.
   b) sympathetic heart.
   c) strong commitment.
   d) servant's heart.

20. Philemon, the recipient of Paul's letter, is identified as
   a) a Roman citizen.
   b) the author of the Epistle to the Hebrews.
   c) a slave owner.
   d) a proselyte (convert) to Judaism.

21. Who was Epaphras?
   a) A companion of Paul on Paul's third missionary journey
   b) The pastor of the congregation at Colosse
   c) One of the seven deacons appointed by the church at Jerusalem
   d) A member of the church at Laodicea

22. Identify a major theme in the letter to Philemon.
   a) Salvation and healing
   b) Tolerance of Gentile culture and religion
   c) Forgiveness and restoration
   d) Citizenship in heaven

23. Which of the following is a clear implication of Paul's opening greetings?
   a) Paul was making an effort to recognize Gentile Romans as Christians.
   b) Greeting fellow believers is an important part of the Christian life.
   c) The rich and powerful should serve the poor and powerless.
   d) Paul was asserting his apostolic authority.

24. Which is a valid interpretation of the difficult phrasing of Philemon 6?
   a) Philemon is to overcome his disapproval of law breakers.
   b) Paul was suggesting that Philemon should receive Onesimus into the Colossian church.
   c) Paul is referring to doctrines taught in the Epistle of James.
   d) Paul wanted Philemon to express his faith in true fellowship (koinonia).

25. Identify a principle of forgiveness that is found in the letter to Philemon.
   a) We must forgive when the offender asks for forgiveness.
   b) We should take care not to be emotionally involved with the offender.
   c) We should forgive, but serious offenses should be reported to the authorities.
   d) We should take the initiative in extending forgiveness.

After answering all of the questions in this UPE, check your answers with the answer key. Review material related to questions you may have missed, and then proceed to the next unit.

UNIT PROGRESS EVALUATION 2

BIB117 Prison Epistles: Colossians, Philemon, Ephesians, and Philippians, Third Edition
(Unit 2—Chapter 5–9)

1. The theme of Ephesians is
   a) the supremacy of Christ.
   b) God has provided everything for an effective Christian life.
   c) the power of the Holy Spirit.
   d) the priesthood of the believer.

2. The most important cultural and religious center in Asia was the city of
   a) Corinth.
   b) Rome.
   c) Athens.
   d) Ephesus.

3. The course author lists eight key themes in Ephesians. Two of them are the
   a) status of believers in Christ and spiritual warfare.
   b) joy of the Lord and the second coming of Christ.
   c) justification of believers and the second coming of Christ.
   d) justification of believers and their exalted position.

4. How many spiritual blessings does Paul list in Ephesians 1?
   a) 3
   b) 6
   c) 9
   d) 12

5. In Ephesians 1, Paul prays that the Ephesians would know all of the following EXCEPT
   a) steadfast faithfulness.
   b) the hope of their calling,
   c) their glorious inheritance in the saints.
   d) God's incomparably great power to those who believe.

6. In Ephesians 2, Paul says that people without Christ are
   a) poor, blind, lost, and headed for God's judgment.
   b) out of control, dead in their sin, lost, and poor.
   c) tormented, out of control, lost, and dead in their own sin.
   d) dead in their sin, lost, out of control, and headed for God's judgment.

7. God's grace
   a) is only needed when believers are initially saved.
   b) imparts salvation, but also sustains salvation on a continual basis in the life of a believer.
   c) is unnecessary because believers are saved by faith alone.
   d) is helpful, but is not necessary to live a consistent Christian life.

8. The process of bringing together two parties that were divided is called
   a) unification.
   b) justification.
   c) restoration.
   d) reconciliation.

9. In Ephesians 2, Paul describes unbelievers as without
   a) Christ, hope, purpose, citizenship, and significance.
   b) purpose, significance, citizenship, hope, and God.
   c) Christ, citizenship, hope, covenants, and God.
   d) hope, God, purpose, Christ and a future.

10. The word mystery as used by Paul in Ephesians is truth that
    a) can never be understood.
    b) can be understood by only a select few.
    c) was hidden for a time, but is now made known to all.
    d) was never hidden; it was just a concept that was hard to grasp.

11. In Ephesians 4:1, Paul urges believers to
    a) be filled with the Holy Spirit.
    b) live a life worthy of their calling.
    c) abstain from meat offered to idols.
    d) be ready for Christ's soon return.

12. According to Ephesians 4:12, God has appointed apostles, prophets, evangelists, and pastors/teachers to
    a) do all the work in the church.
    b) prepare believers for works of service.
    c) do the professional aspects of ministry.
    d) lead the church.

13. In Ephesians 4, what five behaviors are believers instructed to put on?
   a) A good work ethic, a positive attitude, truthfulness, righteous anger, and modesty.
   b) Righteous anger, wholesome speech, modesty, truthfulness, and a good work ethic.
   c) Truthfulness, righteous anger, a good work ethic, wholesome speech, and a positive attitude.
   d) Modesty, truthfulness, wholesome speech, a good work ethic, and a positive attitude.

14. According to Ephesians 5:1, who are believers urged to imitate?
   a) Paul
   b) Church leaders
   c) God
   d) The apostles

15. According to Ephesians 5, believers who walk in darkness are walking in ways that are
   a) evil, foolish, and criminal.
   b) despairing, evil, and unwise.
   c) fruitless, unwise, and foolish.
   d) fruitless, despairing, and evil.

16. Based upon Ephesians 5:21–33, wives demonstrate the lordship of Christ in their marriages through
   a) loving their husbands.
   b) obeying their husbands.
   c) loving submission to their husbands.
   d) serving their husbands.

17. The church's submission to Christ should flow out of
   a) obedience.
   b) fear.
   c) obligation.
   d) reverence.

18. According to Ephesians 5:25–33, Christ's love for the church can be characterized as
   a) selfless, lavish, and indissoluble.
   b) sacrificial, eternal, and indissoluble.
   c) lavish, eternal, and out of obligation.
   d) indissoluble, selfless, and out of obligation.

19. According to Ephesians 6, parents are not to exasperate their children, but instead they should
   a) discipline them in a loving manner.
   b) train them and instruct them in the Lord.
   c) love them and overlook their shortcomings.
   d) respect them and love them for who they are in Christ.

20. Based upon Ephesians 6, Christian employees must have a proper perspective, a right attitude, right motives, good work habits, and a
   a) servant's heart.
   b) generous heart.
   c) joyful heart.
   d) grateful heart.

21. According to Ephesians 6, a Christian warrior must
   a) fight and not give in.
   b) be strong and stand firm.
   c) lay down his life.
   d) retreat and seek refuge in God.

22. Which piece of armor is needed to protect believers against a satanic attack by providing an inner witness that they are God's children?
   a) The shield of faith
   b) The helmet of salvation
   c) The sword of the Spirit
   d) The belt of truth

23. What piece of armor is essential for protecting a believer's heart and life from Satan's fiery darts?
   a) The belt of truth
   b) The sword of the Spirit
   c) The shield of faith
   d) The breastplate of righteousness

24. What piece of armor does Paul equate with sharing the good news?
   a) Sword
   b) Breastplate
   c) Shoes
   d) Helmet

25. In Ephesians 6, Paul instructs believers to pray
   a) in the Spirit at all times.
   b) many different prayers and requests.
   c) for all the saints.
   d) doing all of the above.

After answering all of the questions in this UPE, check your answers with the answer key. Review material related to questions you may have missed, and then proceed to the next unit.

UNIT PROGRESS EVALUATION 3

BIB117 Prison Epistles: Colossians, Philemon, Ephesians, and Philippians, Third Edition
(Unit 3—Chapter 10–13)

MULTIPLE CHOICE QUESTIONS

Select the best answer to each question.

1. In the opening sentence of Philippians, Paul identifies himself as
   a) an apostle and teacher.
   b) an apostle of Jesus Christ.
   c) a servant and apostle of Jesus Christ.
   d) a servant of Jesus Christ.

2. What was Paul's purpose in writing to the church at Philippi?
   a) To encourage, rebuke, correct, impart wisdom, and express appreciation
   b) To emphasize unity, impart wisdom, stir up their spiritual gifts, rebuke, and encourage
   c) To restore perspective, encourage, warn, emphasize unity, and express appreciation
   d) To express appreciation, restore perspective, emphasize unity, impart wisdom, and correct

3. What are the two major themes of Philippians?
   a) The joy of the Lord and the advancement of the gospel
   b) The centrality of Christ and the joy of the Lord
   c) The supremacy of Christ and the advancement of the gospel
   d) The second coming of Christ and the joy of the Lord

4. In Philippians 1:8, the Greek word *splagchnon* is translated as
   a) knowledge.
   b) partnership.
   c) affection.
   d) thanksgiving.

5. Which is NOT one of the four outcomes Paul sought in prayer for the Philippian believers?
   a) Steadfastness in suffering
   b) Discern what is best
   c) Everything for God's glory and praise
   d) Prepare for Christ's coming

6. A key verse in Philippians that emphasizes that God completes what He has started is
   a) 1:6.
   b) 1:10.
   c) 1:12.
   d) 1:21.

7. What was Paul's attitude towards his imprisonment?
   a) He was regretful of this experience.
   b) He saw it as an opportunity to further and defend the gospel.
   c) He saw it as an opportunity to get sympathy from his enemies.
   d) He was resentful towards God and the church.

8. There are five anchors that sustained Paul in the face of an uncertain future and they are a confidence in
   a) the Roman judicial system, the prayers of God's people, the help of the Holy Spirit, God's plans and purposes, and that he would not be put to shame.
   b) the goodness of the Caesar, the Roman judicial system, the prayers of God's people, the help of the Holy Spirit, and God's plans and purposes.
   c) God's faithfulness, the prayers of God's people, the help of the Holy Spirit, God's plans and purposes, and that he would not be put to shame.
   d) the prayers of God's people, the help of the Holy Spirit, God's plans and purposes, the goodness of the Caesar, and that he would not be put to shame.

9. In the face of opposition, Paul challenges (Philippians 1:27) the church in Philippi to
   a) live in harmony with other believers.
   b) be orderly and kind to one another.
   c) take responsibility for their actions.
   d) to live their lives in a manner worthy of the gospel.

10. Paul assures the congregation in Philippi that Satan is defeated through the qualities of
   a) unity, cooperation, and resolve.
   b) unity, peace, and honesty.
   c) harmony, peace, and resolve.
   d) honesty, resolve, and hospitality.

11. Paul saw suffering for Christ as a
   a) curse.
   b) privilege.
   c) a sign of sin.
   d) difficulty to be overcome.

12. While living in a crooked and depraved generation, believers at Philippi are instructed to do everything
   a) with diligence and grace.
   b) with joy and kindness.
   c) without murmuring or complaining.
   d) without envy or deceit.

13. Whom was Paul sending to Philippi that had a genuine interest in their welfare and who put the interests of Christ above his own?
   a) Timothy
   b) Epaphras
   c) Tychicus
   d) Epaphroditus

14. In Philippians, whom does Paul call my brother, a fellow worker, and a fellow soldier?
   a) Epaphroditus
   b) Epaphras
   c) Tychicus
   d) Timothy

15. Whom does Paul instruct the church in Philippi to welcome with great joy and honor?
   a) Epaphras
   b) Tychicus
   c) Timothy
   d) Epaphroditus

16. Legalism is dangerous because it
   a) sets people up for failure.
   b) adds requirements to salvation, making Christ's sacrifice meaningless.
   c) encourages people to seek out other religions.
   d) destroys a believer's joy in the Lord.

17. For those living in a state of lawlessness, their
   a) destiny is sure, their god is their pride, their glory is their shame, and their mind is on evil things.
   b) destiny is destruction, their god is their stomach, their glory is their shame, and their mind is on earthly things.
   c) destiny is sure, their god is their stomach, their glory is their shame, and their mind is on heavenly things.
   d) destiny is destruction, their god is their sinful desires, their glory is their fame, and their mind is on earthly things.

18. What was most important to Paul?
   a) His national and religious heritage
   b) His accomplishments and achievements
   c) Knowing Christ
   d) Knowledge and prestige

19. According to the IST, if believers want to walk in victory they must focus on the prize, forget the past, forge ahead, forgo comparisons, and face their
   a) future.
   b) deficiencies.
   c) enemies.
   d) fears.

20. Who did Paul instruct to help with the reconciliation process between Euodia and Syntyche?
   a) Clement
   b) Loyal yokefellow or Syzygus
   c) Aristarchus
   d) Epaphroditus

21. According to Philippians 4:5, what trait should believers possess in light of the Lord's soon return?
   a) Determination
   b) Gentleness
   c) Zeal
   d) Peacefulness

22. A believer's prayers and petitions should be accompanied with
   a) joy.
   b) zeal.
   c) thanksgiving.
   d) patience.

23. In the place of anxiety, God gives believers
   a) peace.
   b) love.
   c) patience.
   d) grace.

24. What eight things are believers to think about? Things that are
   a) holy, honest, noble, pleasant, admirable, excellent, praiseworthy, and right.
   b) admirable, excellent, praiseworthy, honest, pleasant, right, and lovely.
   c) true, admirable, noble, pleasant, honest, lovely, right, and praiseworthy.
   d) true, noble, right, pure, lovely, admirable, excellent, and praiseworthy.

25. What was Paul's source of contentment?

    a) Food
    b) Clothes
    c) Christ
    d) Finances

After answering all of the questions in this UPE, check your answers with the answer key. Review material related to questions you may have missed. Review all materials in preparation for the final exam. Complete and submit your SLR assignment and take the closed-book final examination.

Taking the Final Examination

1. **All final exams must be taken closed book**. You are not allowed to use any materials or outside help while taking a final exam. You will take the final examination online at www.globaluniversity.edu. If the online option is not available to you, you may request a printed final exam. If you did not request a printed final exam when you ordered your course, you must submit this request a few weeks before you are ready to take the exam. The Request for a Printed Final Examination is in the Forms section of Essential Course Materials at the back of this IST.

2. Review for the final examination in the same manner in which you prepared for the UPEs. Refer to the form Checklist of Study Methods in the front part of the IST for further helpful review hints.

3. After you complete and submit the online final examination, the results will be immediately available to you. Your final course grade report will be e-mailed to your Global University student e-mail account after your Service Learning Requirement (SLR) report has been processed.

4. If you complete the exam in printed form, you will send your final examination, your answer sheets, and your SLR report to Berean School of the Bible for grading. Your final course grade report will be sent to your GU student e-mail account. If you do not have access to the Internet, your grade will be sent to your mailing address.

Answer Keys

- Compare your answers to the Test Yourself quizzes against those given in this section.

- Compare your answers to the UPE questions against the answer keys located in this section.

- Review the course content identified by your incorrect answers.

TEST YOURSELF ANSWER KEYS

BIB117 Prison Epistles: Colossians, Philemon, Ephesians, and Philippians, Third Edition

Answers below are followed by the number of the objective being tested. For any questions you answered incorrectly, review the lesson content in preparation for your final exam.

Chapter 1			Chapter 5			Chapter 9			Chapter 13		
1.	D	1.1.1	1.	D	5.1.1	1.	C	9.1.1	1.	B	13.1.1
2.	A	1.1.2	2.	A	5.1.1	2.	A	9.1.2	2.	C	13.1.2
3.	B	1.1.2	3.	A	5.1.2	3.	C	9.1.2	3.	C	13.1.2
4.	B	1.1.2	4.	B	5.1.2	4.	D	9.1.3	4.	A	13.1.3
5.	B	1.1.4	5.	D	5.1.5	5.	A	9.1.3	5.	B	13.2.1
6.	A	1.2.2	6.	C	5.2.2	6.	A	9.1.3	6.	D	13.2.1
7.	A	1.2.3	7.	B	5.2.3	7.	D	9.1.3	7.	D	13.2.1
8.	D	1.2.5	8.	B	5.2.7	8.	B	9.1.3	8.	B	13.2.2
9.	B	1.3.1	9.	C	5.3.2	9.	C	9.1.3	9.	C	13.3.1
10.	D	1.3.3	10.	B	5.3.3	10.	D	9.2.1	10.	C	13.3.2

Chapter 2			Chapter 6			Chapter 10		
1.	D	2.1.2	1.	B	6.1.1	1.	C	10.1.1
2.	C	2.1.2	2.	A	6.1.3	2.	B	10.1.2
3.	B	2.1.4	3.	B	6.2.2	3.	B	10.1.2
4.	C	2.2.1	4.	D	6.2.3	4.	A	10.1.3
5.	C	2.2.2	5.	D	6.2.4	5.	D	10.1.4
6.	B	2.2.3	6.	C	6.3.1	6.	B	10.2.2
7.	A	2.3.1	7.	B	6.3.2	7.	C	10.2.2
8.	C	2.3.2	8.	A	6.3.3	8.	C	10.2.5
9.	C	2.3.3	9.	C	6.3.3	9.	A	10.2.4
10.	A	2.3.4	10.	B	6.4.2	10.	A	10.2.5

Chapter 3			Chapter 7			Chapter 11		
1.	C	3.1.1	1.	C	7.1.1	1.	C	11.1.1
2.	C	3.1.2	2.	D	7.1.3	2.	A	11.1.3
3.	C	3.1.2	3.	A	7.1.4	3.	D	11.1.2
4.	A	3.1.3	4.	D	7.2.1	4.	B	11.2.1
5.	B	3.2.1	5.	A	7.3.2	5.	B	11.2.2
6.	B	3.2.2	6.	C	7.3.3	6.	D	11.3.1
7.	D	3.2.2	7.	D	7.4.1	7.	A	11.3.2
8.	B	3.2.6	8.	B	7.4.2	8.	A	11.3.3
9.	C	3.3.4	9.	D	7.4.3	9.	B	11.4.1
10.	B	3.3.4	10.	A	7.4.3	10.	D	11.4.3

Chapter 4			Chapter 8			Chapter 12		
1.	D	4.1.1	1.	A	8.1.1	1.	D	12.1.1
2.	C	4.1.2	2.	C	8.1.1	2.	C	12.1.1
3.	A	4.1.2	3.	B	8.1.2	3.	B	12.1.1
4.	B	4.1.3	4.	C	8.1.3	4.	C	12.1.2
5.	A	4.2.1	5.	A	8.1.3	5.	B	12.2.1
6.	A	4.2.2	6.	D	8.1.4	6.	A	12.2.2
7.	A	4.2.3	7.	D	8.2.2	7.	C	12.2.3
8.	B	4.3.1	8.	D	8.2.3	8.	B	12.3.1
9.	D	4.3.1	9.	A	8.3.2	9.	C	12.3.2
10.	C	4.3.1	10.	C	8.3.3	10.	A	12.3.3

UNIT PROGRESS EVALUATION ANSWER KEYS

BIB117 Prison Epistles: Colossians, Philemon, Ephesians, and Philippians, Third Edition

Answers below are followed by the number of the objective being tested. For any questions you answered incorrectly, review the lesson content in preparation for your final exam.

UNIT PROGRESS EVALUATION 1

1.	B	1.1.1	14.	B	3.1.2
2.	B	1.1.3	15.	C	3.1.2
3.	A	1.1.4	16.	A	3.2.4
4.	C	1.1.5	17.	C	3.2.5
5.	D	1.3.1	18.	A	3.3.1
6.	A	1.3.2	19.	D	3.3.4
7.	D	2.1.2	20.	C	4.1.1
8.	B	2.1.3	21.	B	4.1.1
9.	B	2.2.2	22.	C	4.1.3
10.	A	2.2.3	23.	B	4.2.1
11.	B	2.3.3	24.	D	4.2.3
12.	D	2.3.3	25.	D	4.3.1
13.	C	2.3.4			

UNIT PROGRESS EVALUATION 2

1.	B	5.1.1	14.	C	7.3.1
2.	D	5.1.2	15.	C	7.4.2
3.	A	5.1.5	16.	C	8.1.1
4.	B	5.2.1	17.	D	8.1.2
5.	A	5.3.3	18.	B	8.1.4
6.	D	6.1.1	19.	B	8.2.3
7.	B	6.1.2	20.	A	8.3.3
8.	D	6.2.1	21.	B	9.1.2
9.	C	6.2.2	22.	B	9.1.3
10.	C	6.3.1	23.	C	9.1.3
11.	B	7.1.1	24.	C	9.1.3
12.	B	7.1.3	25.	D	9.2.1
13.	C	7.2.2			

UNIT PROGRESS EVALUATION 3

1.	D	10.2.1	14.	A	12.1.2
2.	C	10.1.3	15.	D	12.1.2
3.	A	10.1.4	16.	B	12.2.2
4.	C	10.2.4	17.	B	12.2.3
5.	A	10.2.5	18.	C	12.3.1
6.	A	10.2.3	19.	B	12.3.2
7.	B	11.1.2	20.	B	13.1.1
8.	C	11.1.3	21.	B	13.1.3
9.	D	11.2.2	22.	C	13.2.1
10.	A	11.2.3	23.	A	13.2.1
11.	B	11.2.4	24.	D	13.2.2
12.	C	11.4.2	25.	C	13.3.2
13.	A	12.1.1			

Forms

The following pages contain two course forms: the Round-Tripper and the Request for a Printed Final Examination.

1. For students who do not have access to e-mail, we are including one **Round-Tripper** for your use if you have a question or comment related to your studies. If you do not have access to the Internet, you will want to make several photocopies of the Round-Tripper before you write on it. Retain the copies for submitting additional questions as needed. Students who have access to e-mail can submit questions at any time to bsbcontent@globaluniversity.edu.

2. Students who do not have access to the Internet-based tests may request a printed final examination. For faster service, please call Enrollment Services at 1-800-443-1083 or fax your **Request for a Printed Final Examination** to 417-862-0863.

ROUND-TRIPPER

BIB117 Prison Epistles: Colossians, Philemon, Ephesians, and Philippians, Third Edition

Date ....

Your Name .... Your Student Number ....

Send questions and comments by e-mail to bsbcontent@globaluniversity.edu. If you do not have access to e-mail, use this form to write to Berean School of the Bible with questions or comments related to your studies. Write your question in the space provided. Send this form to Berean School of the Bible. The form will make its return, or round-trip, as Berean School of the Bible responds.

YOUR QUESTION:

FOR BEREAN SCHOOL OF THE BIBLE'S RESPONSE:

GLOBAL UNIVERSITY

1211 South Glenstone Springfield, MO 65804
1-800-443-1083 * Fax 1-417-862-0863
www.globaluniversity.edu

BEREAN SCHOOL OF THE BIBLE REQUEST FOR A PRINTED FINAL EXAMINATION

NOTE: All final exams are to be taken closed-book.

Final examinations are available online at www.globaluniversity.edu.

Taking the test online gives immediate results and feedback. You will know your test grade and which learning objectives you may have missed.

Students who do not have access to the Internet-based tests may request a printed final examination. For faster service, please call Enrollment Services at **1-800-443-1083** or fax this form to **417-862-0863**.

If preferred, mail this form to:
    Berean School of the Bible, Global University
    Attn: Enrollment Services
    1211 South Glenstone
    Springfield, MO 65804

Please allow 7–10 business days for delivery of your final examination. **You may only request an exam for the course or courses in which you are currently enrolled.**

_____
Student Number

_____
Name

_____
Address

_____

_____
City, State, Zip Code

_____
Phone

_____
E-mail

Certified Minister	Licensed Minister	Ordained Minister
☐ BIB114 Christ in the Synoptic Gospels	☐ BIB212 New Testament Survey	☐ BIB313 Corinthian Correspondence
☐ BIB115 Acts: The Holy Spirit at Work in Believers	☐ BIB214 Old Testament Survey	☐ BIB318 Pentateuch
☐ BIB117 Prison Epistles: Colossians, Philemon, Ephesians, and Philippians	☐ BIB215 Romans: Justification by Faith	☐ BIB322 Poetic Books
	☐ THE211 Introduction to Theology: A Pentecostal Perspective	☐ THE311 Prayer and Worship
☐ BIB121 Introduction to Hermeneutics: How to Interpret the Bible	☐ THE245 Eschatology: A Study of Things to Come	☐ MIN325 Preaching in the Contemporary World
☐ THE114 Introduction to Pentecostal Doctrine	☐ MIN223 Introduction to Homiletics	☐ MIN327 Church Administration, Finance, and Law
☐ THE142 Assemblies of God History, Missions, and Governance	☐ MIN251 Effective Leadership	☐ MIN381 Pastoral Ministry
	☐ MIN261 Introduction to Assemblies of God Missions	☐ MIN391 Advanced Ministerial Internship
☐ MIN123 The Local Church in Evangelism	☐ MIN281 Conflict Management for Church Leaders	
☐ MIN171 A Spirit-Empowered Church	☐ MIN291 Intermediate Ministerial Internship	
☐ MIN181 Relationships and Ethics in Ministry		
☐ MIN191 Beginning Ministerial Internship		

Signature _____   Date _____